A New History of "Made in Italy"

A New History of "Made in Italy"

Fashion and Textiles in Post-War Italy

Lucia Savi

BLOOMSBURY VISUAL ARTS
LONDON • NEW YORK • OXFORD • NEW DELHI • SYDNEY

BLOOMSBURY VISUAL ARTS
Bloomsbury Publishing Plc
50 Bedford Square, London, WC1B 3DP, UK
1385 Broadway, New York, NY 10018, USA
29 Earlsfort Terrace, Dublin 2, Ireland

BLOOMSBURY, BLOOMSBURY VISUAL ARTS and the Diana logo are trademarks of
Bloomsbury Publishing Plc

First published in Great Britain 2023
This edition published 2024

Copyright © Lucia Savi, 2023

Lucia Savi has asserted her right under the Copyright, Designs and Patents Act,
1988, to be identified as Author of this work.

For legal purposes the Acknowledgments on p. x constitute an extension of this
copyright page.

Cover design by Holly Capper
Cover image by Henry Clarke, Vogue UK © Condé Nast

All rights reserved. No part of this publication may be reproduced or transmitted
in any form or by any means, electronic or mechanical, including photocopying,
recording, or any information storage or retrieval system, without prior
permission in writing from the publishers.

Bloomsbury Publishing Plc does not have any control over, or responsibility
for, any third-party websites referred to or in this book. All internet addresses given
in this book were correct at the time of going to press. The author and publisher
regret any inconvenience caused if addresses have changed or sites have ceased
to exist, but can accept no responsibility for any such changes.

A catalogue record for this book is available from the British Library.

A catalog record for this book is available from the Library of Congress.

ISBN: HB: 978-1-3502-4775-8
       PB: 978-1-3502-4779-6
       ePDF: 978-1-3502-4776-5
       eBook: 978-1-3502-4777-2

Typeset by RefineCatch Limited, Bungay, Suffolk
Printed and bound in Great Britain

To find out more about our authors and books visit www.bloomsbury.com
and sign up for our newsletters.

To Leonardo and Thalia

Contents

Illustrations

Plates

Figures

Acknowledgments

The seed for this book was planted a decade ago when I joined the Victoria and Albert Museum to work on the *Glamour of Italian Fashion* exhibition. The research for this publication and my PhD research owns a lot to the work done on the occasion of that exhibition and I cannot thank Sonnet Stanfill enough for giving me the opportunity to work on such an exciting project.

This publication is the result of my PhD research and I would like to thank my supervisors, Catharine Rossi and Penny Sparke, for their continuing mentorship that extended well beyond my time at Kingston University.

I am indebted to Frances Arnold and Rebecca Hamilton at Bloomsbury for believing in this idea and for their support and advice on how to transform my PhD research into an engaging book.

I am grateful to interviewees Rita Airaghi, Brenda Azario, Cleonice Capece, Franco De Felice, and Roberto Sarti for their time and enthusiasm in sharing with me their personal and professional memories and specialist knowledge of the Italian fashion and textile system.

This book lays its foundations on the extensive research undertaken in many archives in Italy, the UK, and the USA. Archivists, curators, and librarians have kindly opened their doors to me, and they have been extremely supportive along the way. Heartfelt thanks goes to Andrea Lovati, Archivio Storico Fondazione Fiera Milano; Federica Centulani, Biblioteca del Centro Studi di Storia del Tessuto e del Costume di Palazzo Mocenigo; Tiziana Dassi and Elisabetta Merlo, Bocconi University; Luigia Borgonovo, Clerici Tessuto; the staff at Brooklyn Museum Archives; Paola Pagliari, CSCA Parma; April Calahan, FIT Archive; Elizabeth Way, FIT Museum; Margherita Rosina, Francina Chiara, and Maddalena Terragni, Fondazione Antonio Ratti, Como; the staff at the Fondazione Gianfranco Ferré; Roberto Fuda, Florence State Archive; Sebastian Wormell at Harrods Archive; Federica Fornaciari at Max Mara Archive; Caterina Chiarelli and Katia Sanchioni at Museum of Costume and Fashion at Pitti Palace; Cristina Azario, Nattier Archive; Dilys Blum at Philadelphia Museum of Art; Clare Sauro at Robert and Penny Fox Historic Costume Collection.

I am grateful to the Pasold Research Fund and the Design History Society for their invaluable financial support to fund the images in this book and for the archives and institutions that granted permission to use their images free of charge.

I am indebted to several colleagues for their support and advice. A special thanks to Susan North, Alexis Romano and Ellen Sampson for their tips on how to put together a book proposal and Matteo Augello for being with me along the long way of publishing research. And to Alessandra D'Innella for the expert photography and to my friends and family in Italy and London for always believing I would make it at the end.

Last, but not least, I would like to thank Ioannis Bakolis for always being there and providing me with much-needed encouragement along the way. Finally, to our children, Leonardo and Thalia, who have so patiently accompanied me during research trips, lectures, writing and editing, for being so understanding when this book and this research took me away from them.

All the translations of Italian quotes are my own and only the translated version is given throughout the text.

Every effort has been made to trace copyright holders and to obtain their permission for the use of copyright material. However, if any have been inadvertently overlooked, the publishers will be pleased, if notified of any omissions, to make the necessary arrangement at the first opportunity.

Glossary

alta moda, high fashion or couture.

alta moda pronta, literally ready-made couture. These are cheaper and readily available garments, often simplified versions of couture pieces by the same atelier. Items are available off the rack and they are made in automated factories rather than in ateliers.

anni di piombo, literally years of lead. The expression indicates the period in Italy between the end of the 1960s and the beginning of the 1980s, characterized by extremization of politics that translated into violent demonstrations, armed fights and terrorism.

carnettisti, a type of textile wholesalers active mainly between the 1950s and late 1960s. They acted as intermediaries, as bridges between the many textile producers and couturiers and dressmakers scattered around Italy and beyond. They used their technical knowledge of production as well as their understanding of the fashion market. Their main function was to choose fabrics from many manufacturers. The result of their selection was a *carnet* signed with their name. They attempted to sell these textiles to couturiers.

confezione, clothing mass manufacturer.

croquis, a French word which refers to a sketch, but in this publication I refer to Bianchino's definition given at p. 107.

distretti industriali, industrial districts. An innovative structure based on clusters of small independent companies dispersed in the territory, each producing only a small phase of the final product, all specializing in the same sector, and together constituting almost a virtual factory.

figurinista, the person responsible for visualizing garments for the clients to choose from.

libro tecnico, technical book.

marca di garanzia, mark of guarantee, a label aimed to incentivize the production of purely Italian creations and guarantee that the producer adhered to wartime restrictions. The first marks of guarantee were awarded in 1936.

moda boutique, boutique fashion. It can be defined as the Italian equivalent of American sportswear and it combined high-volume production with the allure of known couturiers' names.

modellista, a term with two different meanings. In the 1950s it indicated a professional whose role was to go to Paris and acquire the exclusive rights to reproduce in Italy certain couture garments, and to sell the toile (*tele*) to more than one dressmaker. Later, in mass-manufactured fashion, mainly of ready-to-wear items, the term came to indicate a factory worker who is in charge of translating the drawing and view of the *stilista* into a garment that can be mass produced.

Prêt-à-porter, a term indicating high-end ready-to-wear fashion.

sarta, dressmaker.

scheda colori, a group of swatches of textile and/or yarns in a number of colors used in a collection of clothing, knitwear, textile, or yarns that will be produced.

stilista, a term for which the usual English equivalent of "designer" or "stylist" does not have the same connotation. A *stilista* is someone active in Italy after the 1970s and who mediated between the ready-to-wear industry, the requirements of the retailers and press, and the needs of the public, by creating a unified style.

tirella, textile swatch

ventennio fascista, literally Fascist twenty years, the period between October 31, 1922 when Mussolini ascended to power to the end of his regime, formally on July 25, 1943.

Introduction

When historians return to the past with new questions inspired by current developments, they often (re)discover important phenomena which were well known to contemporaries, but forgotten or obscured by succeeding generations.[1]

My interest in the subject of Italian textiles and fashion emerged when working as a research assistant on *The Glamour of Italian Fashion 1945–2014*, an exhibition at London's Victoria and Albert Museum (April 5–July 27, 2014). During this period, a considerable amount of time, especially in the first year of the project, was spent traveling around Italy visiting little-known state archives, company collections, and textile manufacturing plants. While all the activities involved in the preparation of the exhibition exposed me to the country's creativity, production skills, and history, these visits were a particularly eye-opening experience. I knew *what* Italy was producing in terms of textiles, but I did not know *how*. Visiting a wool manufacturing company in Prato and then a silk one in Como became the starting point of my PhD project on which this book is based. Since then, I have become fascinated with the production journey of highly desirable objects, such as textiles and fashion items.

Textile and clothing production constitute a principal sector of Italian industry. However, such a strong performance on the international market during the last few years is not the result of a long history of fashion production. Italian fashion developed later than in the USA and other European countries and was and is structurally different. As Nicola White explains, large-scale ready-to-wear women's wear emerged in the USA and UK in the mid-to-late nineteenth century, while in Italy, even after the Second World War, there was no fashionable industrial-scale production of women's ready-to-wear.[2] By the 1980s, however, Italy's fashion industry was "heralded by the international fashion press as one of the top three players on the international fashion stage."[3]

The Italian ready-to-wear phenomenon has often been analyzed in its more commercial outputs, with most studies placing fashion designers and couturiers at the forefront of the investigation.[4] Inevitably, this has produced a sort of mythologization of such figures.

This book seeks to understand how the country transformed from the 1940s to the 1980s, starting when there was practically no international Italian fashion industry of any real economic importance, to achieving international prominence. It specifically explores the role that textile manufacturing played in the rapid transformation of Italy in terms of fashion from a country of dressmakers and couturiers to a producer of ready-to-wear at the forefront of the international scene.

With this book I intend to return to the past, as historian Jonathan Zeitlin suggests in the quotation that opens this Introduction, in order to bring to light phenomena and mechanisms that were well known to contemporaries, and fundamental in devising the Italian textile–fashion system, but that have since been obliterated by the passing of time.

The aim of this book is to assess the relationship between Italian textile and fashion production and the development of the Italian fashion system between 1945 and 1985. This research connects production and commerce with aesthetics, and situates national change within global contexts. It fuses textile history, fashion history, and design history in a multidisciplinary approach in order to examine Italian textile specialisms within the wider context of fashion production.

In addition, this book seeks to determine the role played by the materials and production of both textile and fashion in the development of a mature fashion system in Italy. In doing so, this project aims to answer the question of why and how Italian fashion and textile production worked together and influenced each other in developing an integrated fashion system between 1945 and 1985. As such, my research addresses a key absence in the history of Italian textiles, design, and fashion. Extensive scholarship has focused on defining Italian style, on the study of the Italian fashion industry's relationship with the United States of America, on the history of the country's most prolific couturiers, dressmakers, tailors, and designers, and in the last two decades also on the business of fashion.[5] However, existing literature has so far not made a direct link between Italy's textile and fashion manufacturing and the country's rapid evolution into a producer of "iconic" and high-quality ready-to-wear fashion garments.[6] The importance of the quality of materials employed in Italian fashion has often been quoted as a very important characteristic of the country's style, but its impact has not yet been critically assessed.[7] Furthermore, as Italian economic historian Ivan Paris highlights in the introduction to his study *Oggetti Cuciti*, Italian scholarship so far has not focused on the fashion industry and its rapid development.[8] The lack of studies on textiles and their role in fashion is, however, not a peculiarity only of the Italian landscape: English design historian Christine Boydell has also pointed out the dearth of information about fashion fabrics in British fashion literature.[9]

This book is the first to critically assess the role that materials within Italy's textile and fashion industries played in the shift from the production of hand-made garments, such as couture and high fashion (*alta moda*), to designer mass-produced garments (*prêt-à-porter*). This book observes the post-war Italian fashion system through a new lens, focusing on textiles, their fibers, and the way in which they are manufactured, commercialized, and employed by couturiers and designers. This research examines the intrinsic materials of fashion in terms of their quality, innovation in design, their composition (natural, artificial, man-made fibers), production techniques, commerce, and their impact on the country's overall fashion system.

Locating Italian Fashion

Fashion history is a relatively young discipline. In the last thirty years the field has been preoccupied with studying fashion from different angles as well as defining its boundaries, methodologies, and objectives.[10] The relative newness of the field, and its struggle to define its borders, have led to certain aspects of fashion being overlooked or only marginally considered in the literature. The relationship between fashion and textile production, and the analysis of fashion production in itself, are both examples of such understudied subjects. In 1992 Ellen Leopold stated that there was an absence in the literature of any "consideration of the determining role that might be played by clothing production and its history."[11] As Elizabeth Wilson points out, "the serious study of fashion has traditionally been a branch of art history" and has used art-historical methods of stylistic analysis.[12] In the late 1970s the field expanded to include consideration of wider contexts and drew on approaches such as "Marxism, feminism, psychoanalysis and structuralism."[13] In 1985 Wilson's seminal book *Adorned in Dreams* expanded the field of research to include a method that attempted to "view fashion through several different pairs of spectacles simultaneously."[14] One of these was fashion production. In this chapter of the book she chronicled the development of "economics of the fashion industry," mainly looking at how it exploits developing countries and women.

Christopher Breward's 1995 book *The Culture of Fashion* "aimed to incorporate elements of art historical, design historical and cultural studies approach in an attempt to offer a coherent introduction to the history and interpretation of fashionable dress."[15] However, he explicitly excluded from his study the description of the construction and production of dress and textiles.[16]

Writing in 1997, curator and fashion historian Alexandra Palmer pointed out how some of the fashion studies of the late 1990s, focusing on French couture and its production, contained aspects that destabilize the idea of the couturier as a lonely great artist, instead situating her/him as part of a wider mechanism. Among these publications was Dominique Veillon's study of Parisian fashion during the years of the German occupation from 1940 to 1944, which connects fashion with politics, economy, and the social and cultural realms of Paris. It explains the role French fashion played in the domestic and foreign economy and how the political situation influenced design, production, the type of raw materials used, and the style of what people could and wanted to wear.[17]

In 1997 historian Nancy L. Green published *Ready-to-Wear and Ready-to-Work*, a study of the fashion industry and its relationship with the labor force and immigration. In the book's first half she problematizes and analyzes the fashion industry in the cities of New York and Paris in the nineteenth century. Her point of view on production and labor and immigration offers an innovative take on the fashion industry but does not take into consideration the final garments.[18]

In 2005 Yuniya Kawamura, with her book *Fashion-ology*, defined how the field of the "sociological investigation of fashion" is concerned with the "social nature of fashion in its production, distribution, diffusion, reception, adoption and consumption."[19] Kawamura differentiates between fashion and clothing and her approach looks exclusively at processes rather than analyzing any visual material. A point of contact with this study is how *Fashion-ology* "debunks the myth that the creative designer is a genius" and instead presents fashion as a collective activity. However, Kawamura's study is mainly interested in the social process of fashion: the production of clothing does not fit its remit.[20]

More recently, in 2008 Jonathan Faiers with his monograph on *Tartan* aimed to reaffirm "textiles studies as an independent field of enquiry rather than, as has often been the case, an occasional adjunct to fashion theory, art history, or cultural studies."[21] His book on the Scottish textile was the first of the series "Textiles that Changed the World," edited by fashion historian Linda Welters, which intends to investigate "the cultural life of individual textiles."[22] These kinds of studies with their focus on one textile or technique start to correct the unbalanced weight of fashion over textiles studies.

This book aims to bring together the studies of textiles and their fibers as a way of analyzing fashion's materiality as well as its production. This research is further characterized by the use of objects as a primary source. It subscribes to fashion historian and curator Valerie Steele's statement that "of all the methodologies used to study fashion history, one of the most valuable is the interpretation of objects," and to dress historian Lou Taylor's opinion that "object-based research focuses necessarily and unapologetically on examination of the details of clothing and fabric."[23]

This research, however, seeks to understand the role that textile manufacturing played in the rapid development of Italian fashion from a country of dressmakers and couturiers to a producer of ready-to-wear at the forefront of the international scene. The isolated study of textiles, fibers, and labels, though key, is not enough to answer to this. Object-based research needs to be embedded in cultural and historical settings. As explained by anthropologist Kaori O'Connor in relation to production: "The new material culture is not concerned primarily with the mechanics of technology or the aesthetics of style, but with production in a larger, cultural sense, in which production is seen as a cultural process and mass-produced goods constitute social values in material form."[24] In line with this, I analyze the full spectrum of fashion production, from fiber manufacturing to textile design, production and commercialization, and from the designers and couturiers' inventiveness to its translation into mass production, or unique couture pieces.

Made in Italy

The literature in this field commonly places the starting point of Italian fashion's history in the twentieth century with the patriotic attempts of activist and designer Rosa Genoni in 1906. As fashion historians such as Sofia Gnoli have recounted, at the *Esposizione Internazionale di Milano* (Milan International Expo) of that year, Genoni promoted an Italian fashion that was decisively not influenced by France, then the dominant force in European fashion, but presented a collection of dresses made only with Italian textiles and inspired by the Italian Renaissance.[25] The state of Italian fashion during the interwar period has more recently been covered by a body of work, written in both Italian and English by Gnoli and Eugenia Paulicelli.[26] Gnoli's *La Donna, L'Eleganza, Il Fascismo: La Moda Italiana Dalle Origini all'Ente Nazionale della Moda* reconstructs historically, through in-depth archival research, the Fascist fashion system and its rules, regulations and promotion.[27] Paulicelli's *Beyond the Black Shirt* focuses on the construction of national identity and *Italianità* during the Fascist period by analyzing a variety of sources such as novels, magazines, and films. However, in both these publications, garments and accessories are mainly used as illustrations of historical facts rather than engaged from a production and critical point of view.

These publications build on the earlier contributions about this period by fashion historians and curators such as Grazietta Butazzi and Caterina Chiarelli.[28] Similarly to my approach, these scholars notably use surviving objects, among other sources, to investigate the interwar period and to scrutinize the effectiveness of the style imposed by the Fascist regime.

The 1970s generation of Italian fashion historians, including Grazietta Butazzi, Gloria Bianchino, Alessandra Mottola Molfino, and Bonizza Giordani Aragno, used art history as their main methodology and laid the groundwork, with their seminal contributions, for the wider scholarly interest in the study of Italian fashion in the last thirty years.[29] Their work culminated with the publication in 1985 of two volumes of *La Moda Italiana* (later translated into English), an extensive compendium of essays encapsulating "the attempt to reflect the complexity of problems that the Italian fashion system had to deal with," as Butazzi explains in her introduction to the first volume.[30] The publication of these two volumes fulfilled a double aim, on the one hand the presentation of a historic text and on the other the promotion of a museological idea. There was no museum of contemporary fashion in Italy at the time, and the tomes prompted a drive to collect, catalog, and investigate fashion objects to facilitate the opening of such an institution. Unfortunately, these hopes remain unrealized, and no such museum has ever opened. Thirty years on, this diverse collection of researches on Italian fashion remains a key point of reference for the study of this subject. Among its many contributions, it pioneered the study of contemporary 1980s fashion with the rigor and scholarly interest previously reserved for past historical periods, and made use of objects as a valuable primary source.

These efforts motivated in part the 1989 pioneering exhibition and catalog *Gianni Versace: L'abito per pensare*. This project, especially in the catalog edited by fashion historian Nicoletta Bocca and textile historian Chiara Buss, provides an in-depth analysis of the contemporary production of Gianni Versace through a rigorous study of its influences, mode of work and materials. The press at the time reported on this innovative approach with admiration:

> The exhibition dedicated to Gianni Versace is ambitious. It has as its objective not only to reconstruct the creative itinerary of an international fashion designer, but to precisely analyze it as if it is was a retrospective on a figurative artist. In order to analyze the development of a fashion creator, the curators of the exhibition have done something very innovative: they have studied in depth the

way in which Gianni Versace works to invent a fashion grammar and were able to describe the dresses in an objective manner.[31]

The Gianni Versace experiment remains an isolated event. Although increasingly more studies have been conducted since the late 1990s and the early 2000s, this field in Italy is still in its infancy in comparison to the development in Anglo-Saxon countries, as anthropologist Simona Segre Reinach laments.[32]

Despite the lack of a centralized fashion museum collection and institution, fashion curation has in some way bridged the gap. For example, critic and fashion curator Maria Luisa Frisa has mainly devoted her work to fashion curation and has contributed several monographs and exhibition catalogs to various aspects of Italian fashion. Her contribution has benefited Italian fashion curation practice and, with one of her latest exhibitions *Bellissima* and *Italiana*, she has brought Italian fashion to the contemporary art museum MAXXI and to the Palazzo Reale in Milan. In so doing she has opened the subject by showcasing fashion production as part of the country's cultural and artistic scene and presenting to a larger number of visitors than ever previously connected to fashion exhibitions.[33]

Fashion historian Enrica Morini has contributed to significant projects, such as the study on Max Mara's coats archive, and has written Italian fashion history that provides a solid reference point to any study on the field.[34] Anthropologist Simona Segre Reinach's research focuses mainly on the city of Milan and its ready-to-wear industry, and on the relationship between Italian and Chinese manufacturing and fashion.[35] In the field of textile history, Chiara Buss stands out with her breadth of publications on historical textiles, such as silks and velvets, but also through her contribution to the literature on Italian fashion with her volumes on Gianni Versace, which examine the designer's use of materials. Textile historian Margherita Rosina paves the way to challenging the dichotomy between fashion and textiles in her important publications that use in-depth archival and object-based research to demonstrate the fundamental connection between these two worlds.

The neighboring field of economic history has also recently taken an interest in the subject of fashion. Economic historians such as Elisabetta Merlo have contributed important studies of the economic history of Italian fashion over the last decade.[36] Similarly, economist Ivan Paris's work on ready-to-wear has offered Italian fashion history a solid grounding in economic theory and data. His work is particularly significant for its definition of the characteristics of the different "levels," as he calls them, of Italian fashion (*alta moda* or couture, *prêt-à-porter* or ready-to-wear, mass production or *confezione*). His study, however, uses an economic perspective and therefore lacks an analysis of the stylistic contribution of Italian fashion to the international arena in relation to these "levels." As Segre Reinach states in her review of his book, Paris's analysis tends to lean toward the financial side, favoring a focus on quantitative factors over an assessment of cultural implications.[37] Clothing manufacturing has been mainly explored by business history, and studies in this field are very significant for their investigation of company archives, which are often left unexplored by fashion historians (mainly because of the nature of the documents preserved, such as legal papers, data, etc.). However, these studies focus for the most part on the business operations of clothing and textile companies and do not draw from the analysis of primary sources such as garments and textiles.[38]

Italian historian of culture and consumerism Emanuela Scarpellini has recently published a historical and cultural study of Italian fashion from 1945 to today. Rather than analyzing fashion mediation in the form of fashion display, its styles changing every season or its promotion on social media, as many Italian studies have done before, her research focuses on the cultural dimension of fashion and the influence of economic and technological factors on its development. Her work is also noteworthy for its consideration of the consumption of clothing by different sectors of the population, including factory workers, the middle classes, and young students taking part in the revolution of 1968.[39]

In addition, monographs on individual fashion designers and fashion houses are increasingly commissioned by designers' archives, brand museums, or in relation to specific exhibitions.[40] These often self-referential publications are, however, limited by their aim to commemorate and celebrate, and rarely offer any critical assessment of the role of the brand or designer in terms of the wider history or fashion system.[41]

The literature on Italian fashion history has been traditionally written by Italians in Italian, consequently limiting the debate outside of the country. An important exception is the seminal work by Nicola White, whose 1997 MPhil thesis and subsequent publication *Reconstructing Italian Fashion* started a trend of non-Italians writing on Italian fashion, highlighting the topic's appeal in the last few decades for British and American academics and museum curators.[42] White's research was based on the premise that the years between 1945 and 1965 were the "unrecognized foundation of the post-1980 success" of Italian fashion.[43] She went on to examine the fundamental role that the USA had in the evolution of Italian fashion and she attempted to define what the characteristics of Italian style were. Reading her book in the summer of 2012 encouraged me to look at this field and inspired me to continue building on the grounds that she started. This book is indebted to White's work but starts with a different perspective as it aims to look at both Italian fashion and textile production and at the intersection between the two systems. It examines a larger chronology and is not focused on defining Italian style, but investigates the role of materials in the development of Italian fashion production. This new perspective, together with research gathered from archives previously not available to White, adds to the originality of this research.

Lastly, one phenomenon that has helped expand writing on Italy's fashion affairs beyond Italians came with the development of fashion exhibitions in foreign museums over the last three decades. The initial tendency with these fashion exhibitions was to present monographic shows devoted to an important fashion personality. Examples of these include the Victoria and Albert Museum's exhibitions on Salvatore Ferragamo in 1987, Gianni Versace in 2002, and journalist Anna Piaggi in 2006 in London.[44] American museums have also contributed to this trend with Gianni Versace in 1997 and *Schiaparelli and Prada: Impossible Conversations* in 2012 at the Metropolitan Museum of Art in New York.[45] Also in America, the work of Giorgio Armani was chronicled in a retrospective at the Guggenheim New York in 2000 and Roberto Capucci at the Philadelphia Museum of Art in 2011.[46]

A more recent trend has seen the subject of Italian fashion addressed through wider survey exhibitions. Major examples include the Fashion Institute of Technology's *Italian Style* curated by Valerie Steele in 2003 in New York; the Hasselt Fashion Museum's *La Moda—Made in Italy* in 2013; and the Victoria and Albert Museum's *The Glamour of Italian Fashion 1945–2015* in 2014 in London.[47] These survey exhibitions have presented historical overviews of Italy's fashion output and contextualized Italian fashion culturally, socially, and economically.

Researching "Made in Italy"

When speaking of Italian fashion, it is almost impossible to separate the subject from a debate about "Made in Italy." The expression has been unpacked, analyzed, critiqued, and historicized.[48] Design historian Grace Lees-Maffei highlights an emphasis on production in research of the subject due to the use of the term "made."[49] While this might be the case in design history, the opposite may be argued about critical studies of Italian fashion, which focus most prominently on the style and quality associated with the tag at the expense of any in-depth study of the production of these goods. This is one of the main reasons that led me to go back to the literal meaning of "Made in Italy." As Paris argues, it is necessary to recognize that the success of the Italian fashion system was based on three main players: textile manufactures, designers, and the clothing industry. Literature on the topic, both in Italy and abroad, has historically devoted most attention to the role played by individual creators, such as designers and couturiers, while more recent business history studies, especially in the last twenty years, have shed light on the role of the clothing industry in developing the Italian fashion system.[50]

In response to the research landscape described above, this book is positioned at the intersection between the object-based approach typical of curatorial museum practice and the sensibility of business history that privileges the investigation into production processes. This research focuses on the mechanisms and actors within textile and fashion manufacturing and investigates the relationships that linked textile and clothing productions. This approach, by reversing the usual accent placed on the role of the designers, unravels often complicated structures and systems operating behind the scenes of fashion and textile making. By looking at how things are made, by whom, and where, in a spectrum that encompasses the full range of players involved—from the fiber manufacturers in Chapters 1 and 2, through the textile intermediaries in Chapters 3 and 4, to the places of design, ideation, and delocalized production in Chapters 5 and 6—this book seeks to unpack the "Made in Italy" label by looking into the process of making. This process is informed by extensive archival materials retrieved from a wide-range of sources and brings together the often-separated disciplines of fashion, textile, and design studies.

Primary Research Sources

The primary research undertaken for this project can be categorized into three types: archives, interviews, and mass media (magazines and newspapers). Archival research is the backbone of this book and the research has taken me to archives in cities such as Florence, Milan, and Como, but also Prato, Parma, Venice, London, Bath, New York, Philadelphia, and Wilmington. These include textile manufacturing and fiber producers' archives, museum garment collections, personal archives, exhibition archives; archives that collect fashion drawings; archives of designers and brands, department store archives; and archives documenting events and institutions.

Furthermore, this project has been shaped by extensive research in archives which have previously been little investigated, such as the *Camera Nazionale della Moda Italiana* and *Archivio Storico Fondazione Fiera Milano*. This has added new knowledge and enhanced our understanding of post-war Italian textile and fashion history.

The notion that Giovanni Battista Giorgini acted as the "father" of Italian fashion has been omnipresent in virtually every single book and article ever written on Italian fashion.[51] Because Giorgini's role had been so widely established, at the beginning of this research I was tempted not to research Giorgini. However, by undertaking primary archival research, it quickly became clear to me that other researchers had only repeatedly referred to the same sources within the Giorgini archive. The materials that constitute the Giorgini archive were deposited in the Florence State archive in 2005 and are not entirely cataloged.[52] Among the available documents that can be requested to study are fifty-eight albums dated between 1951 and 1965. These leatherbound volumes, with the initials G.B.G. embossed on the spines, contain a mixture of newspaper and magazine articles, promotional materials, photographs, and correspondence connected with the organization of the fashion events in Italy that started in 1951 in Giorgini's house.[53] These albums were the primary sources mainly used by researchers to define the role Giorgini played during the early days of Italian fashion in Florence in the 1950s. Notwithstanding the important of such materials, it is paramount to highlight that these albums were put together by Giovanni Battista Giorgini's daughter Matilda Giorgini as instructed by her father.[54] In reading and researching such material it is important to keep in mind that these documents were collected and assembled as scrapbooks and therefore the decision to include some material rather than other items would have formed a particular point of view.

I, like seemingly every other researcher, started to study this archive by reading the wealth of information included in these albums. However, instead of stopping there, I continued further by also consulting unbound, lesser-known folders together with a wealth of uncataloged material.[55] As I wanted to know other points of views different from Giorgini's, I also traveled to New York to retrieve relevant correspondence included in the *Italy at Work* archive at the Brooklyn museum. This offered the unique opportunity to reconstruct the full correspondence that is not completely represented in the Giorgini archive.

In so doing I built a complete picture and I was able, for the first time, to shed new light on what seemed to be a well-established story. Furthermore, letters found in the yet-to-be cataloged folders of the Giorgini archive have demonstrated how Giovanni Battista Giorgini's activities went beyond solely promoting Italian *alta moda*, which is what was previously believed. His enterprise branched out much wider in a very strategic way, for example in the realm of mass manufacturing. This supports the idea developed in the book that elements of Italian mass-manufactured fashion were being developed earlier than previously thought. Furthermore, as demonstrated in Chapter 2, because Giorgini and his office took seven percent commission on sales, he prioritized the promotion of items which would sell best to the most profitable foreign market, which in this case was the USA. This often meant that Giorgini not only promoted *alta moda* on its own, but also used its allure to endorse the more lucrative realm of mass production by fostering collaboration between industry and fashion. This is a very important aspect that this research has uncovered, as he was not previously known to promote this sector "officially" and visibly, but, as letters in the archive demonstrate, he was interested in developing it and getting a slice of the profits.[56] Furthermore, the archival research brought to light his involvement in the little-known fashion label "Lucrezia" set up in 1963. This venture demonstrates his far-reaching influence and explains the different types of internationalization that Italian fashion participated in. Researching new material in a known archive was at the basis of my redefinition of Giorgini's role within Italian textile and fashion promotion. By giving a more rounded portrait of Giorgini's activities it has been possible to describe other types of productions that were encouraged.

Giorgini was also one of the promoters and founders of the *Camera Nazionale della Moda Italiana* (CNMI), an organization still active today and responsible for organizing Milan Fashion Week, but whose previous history and role was still little known in the literature, where scant mentions of the CNMI suggested a lack of importance.[57] However, through researching the documents in the archive located at Milan's Bocconi University, I have shown that while the CNMI was sometimes slow and over-bureaucratic, it played a significant role in promoting a shift toward a much more integrated system of fashion and textile production in Italy.

Archival research also offered the opportunity to investigate fashion production from the point of view of fashion drawings. The very rich collection of CSAC in Parma, containing thousands of working fashion drawings by several *stilisti*, such as Giorgio Armani, Gianni Versace, Krizia, and Walter Albini, presented the unique opportunity to compare bodies of work by different hands operating in the same environment, the city of Milan. The overview of hundreds of sketches and drawings allowed me to identify common characteristics and threads in the work of different creative personalities. I have demonstrated how the inscriptions, and the multiple hands identifiable on the same sheet of paper, testify to a complex and structured system of fashion production that not only relied on the *stilista*'s creativity, but operated on a close collaboration with specialists based in textile companies, embroidery workshops, leather specialists, and so forth. This general assessment of the field of Italian fashion drawings formed the basis for the analysis of one *stilista*'s drawing production, as seen in Chapter 6 with the focus on the work of Gianfranco Ferré.

The process of researching these visual materials has been as rich and significant as the document-based analysis. I examined fashion drawings as a primary source worthy of consideration in their own right and not simply used as an illustration, as often happens in fashion history. While drawings are the principal primary source in Chapter 6, they have been vital sources throughout the book, as they are key means for better understanding the processes of ideation, copy, and commercialization. For example, my examination of the drawing of the Schuberth cerise dress in Chapter 2, together with other sources such as press photographs and existing garments, brought to light the process of adaptation that some Italian couture pieces undertook, once sold in overseas department stores. This process, although well documented for French fashion, was still little studied for Italian couturiers. Furthermore, the fashion drawings I utilize in Chapter 4 represent some of the few surviving documents to chronicle the existence and operational activities of the *modellisti* in the transnational business of copies between Italy and France, and shed new light on that operation. Archival research has deeply influenced, at different levels, the direction of this book and enriched the perspective from which to scrutinize complex structures of production.

Interviewing key protagonists from the Italian fashion and textile world has also been invaluable to understanding how certain mechanisms of making and production would have worked at the time. These encounters have allowed me to retrieve narratives that could not be found in the literature on the subject. In addition to press clipping books and articles included in personal archives, I surveyed fashion and textile magazines, economic newspapers, and trade journals. Articles, advertisements, and magazine covers provided information and images on some aspects, such as *moda boutique*, that were not addressed in depth in the secondary literature.

A focus on production drives the first four chapters of this book. Chapters 1 and 2 focus on the making of fibers and textiles in the context of *alta moda* and its cheaper and more export-focused equivalent *alta moda pronta*. Chapters 3 and 4 look at the *carnettisti*, a type of production intermediary, and investigate their role in close proximity to *alta moda* and how they were influential in defining what textile mills were making.

If production is the main lens through which the first four chapters are examined, Chapters 5 and 6 focus on both production and mediation. I achieved this by looking at the city of Milan in its role of mediator and also, through a close-up study of working fashion drawings, in its role of virtual capital of manufacturing, by examining in detail some of the mechanisms of production behind *prêt-à-porter*, the new language of Italian fashion.

The mediation aspect is mainly addressed through the analysis of fashion and textile magazines such as *Harper's Bazaar, Vogue* (Italy, UK, and USA), *American Fibers, Linea Italiana, Bellezza*, and *Novità*.[58] This survey focuses on the features, advertisements, and reports on Italian fashion that shaped the country's image and aesthetic in the eyes of both local and overseas consumers. It also offers an insight into the types of collaborations that took place between textile manufacturers, clothing producers, couturiers, and designers. Mediation also manifests in the organization of events, such as catwalk shows, textile fairs, and international partnerships. These are examined through archival research in the papers of relevant individuals, such as Giovanni Battista Giorgini, the organizer of the collective International High Fashion Show in the *Sala Bianca* in the post-war years, or institutions, such as the *Camera Nazionale della Moda* (Italian Fashion Chamber) and the *Fiera Campionaria di Milano* (Milan Trade Fair). These documents illuminate the intentions and aspirations of the Italian fashion system on a local and international levels.

To put it in the words of anthropologist Tim Ingold, this approach aims to bring forward the "creativity of the productive processes that bring the artefacts into being."[59] In that sense, consumption and mediation are here considered as end phases of production that influence each other, as Maffei highlighted, rather than distinct focal areas of investigation.[60]

The spectrum of production ranges from the hand-made tradition, embedded in historical know-how and craft, to machine-made mass production. This book spans the entire spectrum, considering the first extreme with *alta moda* and ending at the other with *prêt-à-porter*.

My research acknowledges the scholars who have considered the Renaissance as a key factor, justification, or even, as economic historian Carlo Marco Belfanti describes it, a "guarantee of provenance" for Italian fashion in the post-war style.[61] However, my aim is to look beyond this historical link and to study the development of new fabrics, machineries, and techniques that shaped the Italian fashion system, and to look at the ways in which the country's fashion production has been branded not only traditional and artisanal, but also modern, simple, and sporty—aspects that cannot be ascribed to the Renaissance paradigm.

The Inside-Out Method

This book considers Italian textile and fashion production, and therefore the "Made in Italy" label, not as a brand but as a process and a network. It goes behind the scenes to explore what the "Made in" involves. The following six chapters endeavor to get under the glossy surface and expose the many threads, knots, and connections "inside" the finished products. Similarly to what happens when one looks inside an object, this book looks also into fashion production processes, opening them up and exposing aspects previously unseen or overlooked in the literature.

This type of approach highlights how materials influence style, and processes determine final products. I interrogate and challenge histories and investigate aspects of production and mediation that otherwise would have remained hidden if were to analyze only from a stylistic angle. This had led me to uncover actors and agents that have not been looked at before. Understanding who is pushing innovations, and how, and what actors are dominating at given times, inevitably creates a patchwork rather than a linear, seamless story. This approach has a threefold aim. It first seeks to temporarily obscure from view the style, shape, and external appearance of the garments studied in order to focus instead on the types of textile, the specific fibers used (artificial or natural, domestic or imported), and the means of production, distribution, and commercialization of the garments. O'Connor explains that "focusing on fabric is a useful way to avoid the confusion induced by concentrating on constantly changing fashion styles."[62] She also advocates an approach for the analyses of contemporary society where mass production is the rule and she suggests that cloth and textiles, although an essential part of the finished garment, have received little attention relative to fashion designers.[63]

Secondly, this method endeavors to shed light on the garments' labels and makers' marks, such as "Made in Italy" and "Exclusively for."[64] Aspects of this approach are shared with fashion historian Alexandra Palmer's method. In her study on Canadian couture, Palmer uses couture objects in public and private collections as primary evidence, and extensively analyzes labels within these garments.[65] Labels, textile codes, marks in technical drawings, and captions in fashion advertisements are often overlooked in fashion history. In this book, they instead provide the starting point to explore themes connected with the mechanisms of textile and fashion manufacturing, promotion, and commerce.

Finally, by privileging the analysis of materials and production, this approach aspires to reveal aspects that would have previously passed unnoticed, such as the use of artificial and synthetic material in couture and its implications, as explored in Chapter 1. Similar preoccupations are at the core of historian Regina Lee Blaszczyk's study "Styling Synthetics," which suggests that the mass-market success of DuPont owed as much to creative marketing, styling, and performance as it did to industrial research and organizational innovation. According to Blaszczyk, the casual and comfortable American look that developed in the USA in the post-war era depended in large part on the fabrics made from novel synthetic fibers.[66]

Research Parameters

Writing in 1955, Irene Brin, Rome editor of *Harper's Bazaar* between 1950 and 1969 and perhaps the most influential Italian fashion journalist of the post-war years, asserts that, without doubt, Italian high fashion was born in 1945 when the Allies "discovered in bombed-out cities filled with starving workers the clever, fragile and heroic inventions of Carosa and Simonetta, of Fontana and Schuberth."[67] Using 1945 as the starting date of this project acknowledges the phenomenon described by Brin.

Traditional literature on the subject usually presents Giovanni Battista Giorgini's First High Fashion Show in Florence in 1951 as the event signaling the birth of Italian fashion. This show's impact on the image of Italian fashion and its export, and Giorgini's role and contribution, have been extensively studied.[68] In this project, I do refer to Giorgini and the significance of his marketing of Italian fashion, but I also prefer to focus on lesser-known initiatives promoting the country's fashion and textile productions after the war, such as *Italy at Work* and entrepreneur Franco Marinotti's Centro Internazionale delle Arti e del Costume (CIAC) examined in Chapter 1, and the *Camera Nazionale della Moda Italiana*, considered in Chapter 4.

Giorgio Armani's portrait on the cover of *Time* magazine in April 1982 heralded the emergence of the man behind the very successful label on the international scene, but also highlighted a further shift in the production of Italian fashion.[69] As the Italian fashion system was being celebrated, it had also started to change. The date of 1985 is used as the end point of this project because it marks the culmination of the system described throughout this book. It also signals the advent of a different environment characterized by increased competition from China from the late 1980s and the rise of international luxury conglomerates.

Chapter Structure

Writing about fashion and textiles over such an extended time frame inevitably requires chronological jumps and exclusions. This project does not aim to present a complete history of Italian fashion and textiles between 1945 and 1985, but instead focuses on key stories and issues informed by the primary material available. The book is organized into six loosely chronological chapters with extensive case studies that illuminate the interconnections between textiles and fashion and their production, commerce, and mediation.

The book starts with the post-war years 1945 to 1958, when *alta moda* was at the helm of the country's post-war recovery. Chapter 1 explores the significance of Italian fibers, textiles, and fashion for the country's export markets, especially North America: during this period the domestic market was of less concern as the country was still battling with the effects of the war. The production and promotion of export goods is explored in Chapter 2, which analyzes the role that textiles played in two events organized in the USA and Italy. The first one, *Italy at Work: Her Renaissance in Design Today*, was an American-organized exhibition which opened at the Brooklyn Museum in 1950, showcasing Italian designs for an American public. The second, the *Sala Bianca*, was a promotional fashion show organized in Italy for an American public of buyers and press in 1951. The chapter concludes with a case study that explores the relationship between Italian fashion made in Italy and its transatlantic commerce to the USA and how this helped Italy to develop its own distinctive productive specialization.

With the end of the 1950s, the book shifts its focus from the export market to the domestic one. From 1958, with the country's "economic boom," domestic consumption grew and became a much more important player. Chapter 3 explores how institutions such as the *Camera Nazionale della Moda Italiana* attempted to organize the domestic production of fashion and textiles in order to create a coherent system able to better compete on the international scene. Within this context, Chapter 4 analyzes the role played in the Italian fashion and textiles system of the 1960s by a little-known intermediary: the *carnettisti*.

The last two chapters explore the years between the early 1970s and 1985 in Italy. Chapter 5 considers the city of Milan and its role of mediation in raising the profile of the Italian fashion and textiles system to the level of other international players such as Paris and New York. The well-known phenomenon of the explosion of Italian *prêt-à-porter* is investigated through the lesser-known aspects of its production (*distretti industriali*) and the role of the designers (*stilisti*). Chapter 6 delves deeper and analyzes, through a close look at fashion working drawings, the way in which design and production communicated with one another.

1

Fibers and the Making of Italian Textiles in the Post-War Period

Introduction

The first part of this book considers the years after the Second World War until about 1958. This period saw numerous shifts and changes that influenced the development of a mature textiles and fashion manufacturing system in Italy. It is also characterized by a scarcity of archival material about both textile manufacturers and couturiers, and by the paucity of studies which have tried to unpick it.[1] I have approached this period by focusing on the materiality of surviving objects and by using the "inside-out" method outlined in the introduction to understand the production, mediation, and forms of consumption of Italian fashion and textiles. This approach brings to the fore aspects of production that have been unnoticed so far. For example, the extent to which artificial and synthetic yarns featured in the textiles used in Italian high fashion, an aspect which has not been fully investigated in relation to the period in question.[2]

The existing literature has so far privileged a narrative that focuses on natural fibers such as silk, wool, and cotton, leaving out the significance of the use of artificial and synthetic fibers.[3] Reversing this focus is key to unraveling "threads" and narratives which were significant at the time but that have fallen out of the spotlight.

When analyzing production, my primary concern is the study of objects such as day dresses, evening gowns, sportswear, accessories, and textiles designed and made by Italian dressmakers, tailors, and manufacturers, and conserved in private and public collections in Italy, the UK, and the USA. These objects are analyzed from within in order to bring to the surface previously unexplored aspects, specifically in relation to the realm of making. These include an identification of the means of production (hand-made, machine-made, mass-produced), issues related to the provision of raw materials, the quality of the final products and their relations to export markets. Textiles and fibers are at one end of the cycle, and they are aligned with the production of fashion. At the opposite end stands the consumption of goods in the domestic and foreign markets. The various markets targeted by Italian fashion production are considered, especially in their macro categories of domestic market versus export market. Together with the role played by materials, the demands of distinctive types of consumers also helped shape the means of production and must be considered to explain variations in and typologies of manufacturing systems.

The perspective I am using to scrutinize these early years is the significance of Italian fashion and textiles in foreign markets. I argue that, alongside the materiality of fibers, textiles, and fashion, the attempt to obtain a slice of the export market was a major factor driving Italian fashion's development of an independent style and identity. The export of luxury goods in the years immediately after the end of the Second World War was crucial for Italy's fashion industry, especially the import of raw materials. This was true for countries such as Italy and the United Kingdom, which emerged destroyed and starved by the war and which were competing to get North America's attention as a market for their luxury goods.

The central role played by materials and processes is linked to the promotion of Italian-made and designed goods. Events that took place in Italy, such as the export-focused *Sala Bianca* in Florence and *Il Centro Internazionale delle Arti e del Costume* (International Center of Arts and Costume—CIAC) in Venice, and in the USA, such as the exhibition *Italy at Work*, are highlighted to show how the focus on textiles was key in promoting and defining the image and the essence of a nascent Italian fashion, especially abroad.

The significance of textile promotion is evident in the display, commerce, and advertisement of Italian fashion during that period. Foreign press and buyers regularly commented upon Italian fibers, textiles, and their means of production. Praise for their qualities often eclipsed any appreciation of the Italian fashion style. Indeed, articles in many newspapers and fashion and textiles journals single out the importance of Italian textiles when speaking of the Italian fashion output. The *New York Times*, for example, reports in July 1951 after the fashion collective show in the Grand Hotel in Florence:

> Honors in the show were shared, however, with un-programmed fabric manufacturers whose product of rich and unusual designs and quality had the Americans stopping the mannequins continually for a closer look at the materials.[4]

The upscale American magazine *Town & Country* likewise comments upon the fabrics being displayed at the Florence show, reporting in September 1951:

> They [the designers] are grateful for what the Marshall Plan has done for them in equipping their factories with modern machinery. With this asset, they have created some of the most beautiful fabrics in the world.[5]

The trade monthly review *Italian-American Business* declared in a similar vein in 1952:

> American buyers who attended the fashion shows held in Rome and Florence were struck by the unusually beautiful fabrics, the designs of the silks, the embroidered materials and the fine laces, together with their competitive prices.[6]

The interest in the intrinsic quality of Italian textiles production and its products provided a way for Italy in the post-war period to find its own voice. The relatively untarnished textiles industries enabled the country to build its own post-war fashion industry.

This chapter considers fashion through its fibers. The interwoven coexistence of artificial, synthetic, and natural fibers in these years is explored through their use in the production of textiles in Italian mills and through their domestic promotion in fashion magazines such as *Novità*. The role of artificial and synthetic fibers is further unpicked through the analysis of the fashion festivals organized by SNIA Viscosa's CNIAC in Venice.

Italy Between Tradition and Modernity

Over a span of fifteen years, Italy went from being an agricultural economy to an industrialized one. The years following the 1945 armistice brought in rapid succession the referendum of June 2, 1946, when the country decided to abandon monarchy in favor of the Republic, and a new constitution that came into force on January 1, 1948. Such rapid transformations in the political realm, however, did not always correspond directly to social and cultural changes. As historian Paul Ginsborg explains, "in 1951 the elementary combination of electricity, drinking water and an inside lavatory could be found in only 7.4 per cent of Italian households."[7]

The period between 1945 and 1958 was characterized by many dichotomies. Italy was, on the one hand, an agricultural country that had just been destroyed by the Second World War and which was also recovering from the *Ventennio*

Fascista (the Fascist period); on the other hand, Italy was also a country modernized by the influence of Americanization and the funds offered by the Marshall aid plan.[8] The Italian Communist party was the largest in Europe at that time, while, simultaneously, the Italian population was fascinated by American film stars and Rome was re-baptized "Hollywood on the Tiber."[9] This was the country of craft and hand-made goods, while at the same time it was the cradle for manufactured goods such as Fiat.

Between Couturiers and Manufacturers

Italian fashion and textile manufacturing were also Janus-faced.[10] At one end of the spectrum there were large-scale clothing manufacturers such as Max Mara. This company, according to White and to fashion historian Enrica Morini, followed American models of production with the introduction of multilayer cutting techniques, the principle of a production line, and a generally more "efficient industrial organization."[11] Max Mara was one of the earliest fashionable ready-to-wear manufacturers in Italy and was established in 1951 in Reggio Emilia by Achille Maramotti in a period when Italian fashion was mainly tailored and took inspiration from Paris. During its history Maramotti commissioned designers such as Emmanuelle Khanh, Karl Lagerfeld, and Dolce & Gabbana to name a few to design the Max Mara style, although their names remained hidden behind the Max Mara umbrella.[12] The company still exists today, and it is still owned by the Maramotti family.

Max Mara pursued a similar path to other Italian "Fordist"- influenced companies, such as Fiat, Olivetti, and Pirelli.[13] Also belonging to this category of American-inspired companies was the Milanese department store La Rinascente. Initially inaugurated on December 7, 1918 and given its name by Italian poet Gabriele D'Annunzio, the store represented modernity; clothes shops in Italy were rare.[14] As economists Elisabetta Merlo and Francesca Polese note, La Rinascente's president Umbertio Burstio turned to America for architectural and functional inspiration when he was preparing to reconstruct his store in Milan after the war.[15] Furthermore, in 1950 La Rinascente signed an agreement with USA ready-to-wear manufacturers Donnybrook and Rosenfeld for the production in Italy of American-designed women's dresses and coats. The machines for cutting, sewing, and finishing needed for the manufacturing were provided by the American Ginsberg Machine Company. La Rinascente was promoting to its clients how, thanks to this exclusive agreement, it could finally offer to millions of women the opportunity to buy ready-made garments that were elegant, practical, and made in modern textiles and colors.[16] Both Max Mara and La Rinascente adopted different strategies to reach American standards for mechanization, series production, and distribution.

At the opposite end of the spectrum of clothing production stood the small-scale ateliers, dressmakers, and couturiers. As the Simonetta case study in Chapter 2 will demonstrate, these widespread enterprises maintained artisanal production and at the same time catered to a growing export market. The USA was one of Italy's biggest overseas markets in this period and, as revealed by White, it was therefore influencing the style of the country's fashion output.[17]

Italy in the post-war years was torn between capitalism and communism and between tradition and modernity, as a result of which it developed a fashion system that combined these various influences. As White thoroughly demonstrates, Italy borrowed and was inspired by the American system of production. However, it also integrated it with its own craft base, traditions, and small couturiers' style. Merlo highlights how the United States aimed to penetrate Italy with a "productivity" culture, which meant an improvement and modernization of existing machinery, equipment and labor organization. In fact, as Merlo reports, the Export and Import Bank (EximBank) decided to subdivide the American loans to Italy in favor of the purchase of textile machineries.[18] In 1949, the American Marshall Plan favored the Italian wool industry because it was considered the most promising sector to supply fabrics to the American clothing manufacturers.[19]

According to Merlo, Italian clothing manufacturers did not benefit directly from much American aid and were only influenced indirectly through the textile industry.[20] This is confirmed by Achille Maramotti of Max Mara, who declares he did not receive any American funds despite many of his contemporary textile producers, such as Rivetti and Marzotto, receiving Marshall aid, mainly to buy weaving machines.[21] Maramotti explains that because of this, textile and synthetic fiber manufacturers such as SNIA Viscosa "always helped with the finance, promotion and organization of ready-to-wear trade shows."[22]

From Paris to the USA's Influence

Following the end of the Second World War, Italian fashion was slowly moving away from Parisian influence toward a new, more market-driven relationship with North America. Paris had been the European capital of fashion since the late seventeenth century and Italy had been in a position of subordination to

French influence since then. This dependent relationship was not without debate, especially during the early twentieth century. At the *Esposizione Internazionale di Milano* (Milan International Expo) in 1906, dressmaker Rosa Genoni fervently promoted an Italian fashion free from French influences and presented a collection of dresses inspired by the Italian Renaissance and made exclusively with Italian textiles.[23] This was not the only attempt to build an independent Italian fashion and more examples followed, particularly in the wake of the Fascist regime, such as the establishment of the *Ente Autonomo per la Mostra Permanente Nazionale della Moda* (The Independent Body for the Permanent National Fashion Exhibition) that aimed to nationalize the full cycle of fashion production.[24] In 1931, a report on commerce published in the Fascist newspaper *Il Popolo d'Italia* showed that Italy absorbed one third of French fashion exports. This finding inflamed the Fascist press and led Mussolini to invoke the necessity of creating an Italian fashion system.[25] Many studies have been devoted to evaluating the regime's attempt to reach Italian independence in this field.[26] Despite Fascist legislation introduced with that aim, in the immediate post-war period, as Grazietta Butazzi notes, legions of Italian couturiers were still traveling to Paris to acquire toiles to copy.[27] At the same time, however, Italian artisans had begun to carve out a niche in the market of accessories, namely shoes, bags, and hats.

The Fascist Period and the 1930s

Italian textiles have been a strong export sector in the Italian economy since the Renaissance. The manufacturing industry grew in the nineteenth century, producing domestic products that looked to France and England as a source of inspiration. During the Fascist regime, an organized effort endeavored to free Italian textile and fashion production from foreign influence and to proudly promote national products in the field. Legislation was introduced to regulate Italian fashion output through royal decrees such as the *La Marca di Garanzia* (Mark of Guarantee), aimed to incentivize the production of purely Italian creations. Following the Ethiopian war (1935) and the subsequent sanctions imposed on Italy by the League of Nations, Mussolini proclaimed the nation's economic autarky. This translated into a search for natural and man-made fibers that could replace now expensive and therefore inadequate raw materials such as silk, wool, and cotton. The regime subsidized this innovative research into textile manufacturing. The result was the so-called "autarkic fabrics," made out of either natural materials recovered from century-old traditions, such as hemp, jute, and esparto, or artificial products like rayon and Lanital.[28] This production of fabrics that were proudly Italian went hand in hand with the regime's promotion of Italian national fashion. According to this ideology, Italian fashion also had to be purged of foreign terminology, especially French. With the production and promotion of textile and fashion, the Fascist regime attempted to construct a new Italian identity based upon an ideology of economic self-sufficiency and supremacy. Although it failed to create an Italian fashion system at the time, the Fascist regime had a significant impact on the development of Italian fashion in the post-war years.

In the twentieth century, Florence was a hub of Italian craftsmanship as well as the center of Italian exports, with the headquarters of many buying offices, especially to the USA, being located there.[29] In 1950, exports to the USA of "sewn goods" amounted to $595,283 plus $364,741 of knitwear, a relatively small number destined to grow in the following years.[30] During this period, Italian fashion struggled between its search for an original style, its emancipation from the French model, and its adherence to the new modernity offered by the USA. As perceptively highlighted in an article in the Italian fashion magazine *Bellezza* from that time, although Italian fashion was gaining momentum with North American clients, the rhetoric around its attempt to substitute French fashion was risky while its success was still in its infancy.

To understand the development of a mature fashion system in Italy, it is necessary, alongside the analysis of the role played by textiles, to take into consideration the part played by North America and the interconnections between the small ateliers' practices and the streamlined processes of larger companies such as Max Mara and La Rinascente.

While Italian fashion was trying to find an independent voice, Italian textiles already benefited from a reputation of quality acquired before the Second World War, in particular the Italian silk-manufacturing industries, which supplied the French couture industry and did not cease production during the war.[31] In addition, Italian textile mills suffered little damage during the Second World War, while competing industries in Germany and Japan were wiped out.[32]

Analyzing the condition of Italian textile manufacturers after the war, economist Ivan Paris argues that they came out almost unscathed and found themselves in the situation of being Europe's only tooled-up industrial center able to provide the products needed after the end of the conflict.[33] This resulted in the textile sector being the best performing in Italy, with cotton being the department least damaged by the war and therefore the one that most rapidly adapted to the new post-war situation. This was further supported by the financing of the Allies, the removal of Japan from the list of exporting countries, and the industrial reconversion difficulties faced by the UK.[34] This was followed by the recovery of the wool and cotton industries, leading to a surge in Italian textile production in 1947.[35]

Because of the economic block that afflicted Europe during the Second World War, most countries in the world suffered a scarcity of fabrics. In industrialized countries, this led to an increase in the production of artificial fibers and later of synthetic fibers such as nylon. However, although it suffered considerably in other sectors, Italy experienced only moderate problems in its textile production. Andrea Costa, from Filande Costa, a leading producer of "raw silk and finished rayon and silks," explains in American fashion trade journal *Women's Wear Daily* (*WWD*) in 1947 how the "Italian silks mills have not been bombed, as most are located in small communities, and most of Northern Italy was untouched by the war."[36]

Italy's textile industry was therefore in a privileged situation in comparison to other countries at the end of the war. It was further supplied with fine raw materials such as cotton and wool on the condition that most of it would be exported back to its country of origin, for example the USA, in the form of finished manufactured products. Additionally, countries such as England and Switzerland bought Italian textile products in order to then re-export them to the wider market. Such countries preferred to import raw materials for clothing manufacturers rather than buy already finished products such as textiles or fashion items.

In Italy, the shift from being an agricultural country to an industrial one, along with the advent of the baby boom and the so-called "economic miracle," coincided with an aspiration to the wealth and success so closely associated with America. As fashion historian Aurora Fiorentini Capitani explains, after the liberation of the country from Nazi-Fascism, American soldiers came to be seen not only as liberators, but also as "dispensers" of new wealth and symbols of a new consumer society that was opening up for the Italian population.[37] Indeed, as Penny Sparke argues, "levels of consumption in Italy rose dramatically in the course of 1950s, . . . (so) that by the end of the decade it was possible to regard the country as a modern American-style consumer society."[38]

The last part of this chapter takes a more detailed look of the correlation between the Italian and the American paradigms of textile and fashion production, demonstrating that what became the core value of Italian fashion was the quality of its materials and its almost artisanal processes of production. This was the ideal "other" for American manufacturing: on the one hand the rich

Italian traditions were glorified, and on the other, Italian production was considered "safe" because it did not compete with American industrialized production.

At the close of the Second World War, Italy was not a modern country and did not have a modern fashion system. Italian fashion's incubation period, or, as Ivan Paris defines it, "the decade of experimentation," ended around 1958.[39] On January 1 of that year, the Treaty of Rome, which had the main objective of reducing custom duties, came into force. The duties among European countries before the Treaty of Rome were very complicated and had to be negotiated individually between each state. The formation of the Common Market liberalized trade, and measures to protect textile products from competition multiplied.[40]

Fibers and Politics

Fashion, fabrics, and textiles, like other scarce goods with a high "export capacity," were used in the post-war years as a means of exchange and often also as political tools, thereby acquiring meanings beyond their physical characteristics.[41] An article in the August 1, 1945 issue of the newspaper *Il Sole*, for example, publicizes the amount of cotton supplied to the Italian population by both Italian industrialists and the Allies and highlights the Allies' support of the exchange of raw materials.[42] In a similar vein, an article from the *New York Herald Tribune* titled "Italian Fashion Designers helped by Marshall Plan" celebrates the European Recovery Program (ERP)'s aid to Italy's textile industry and claims it has helped Italy reach a higher place in the world of fashion. The entrepreneur Gian Battista Giorgini, reporting in the article, explains that the ERP supplied the Italian textile industry with $328,700,000 worth of raw cotton in addition to providing $22,600,000 worth of machinery for the modernization of textile plants. American cotton therefore represented at the time sixty percent of the circa 200,000 tons of raw cotton Italy used annually.[43] These types of imports, according to another 1945 article from *Il Sole*, were mostly used for internal consumption but also partly used for exports on account of simplified procedures that encouraged international sales.[44]

However, as late as May 1947, *WWD* reports how Italy was the only foreign market where it was cheaper for an American tourist to buy retail than wholesale. This absurd situation was due to the fact that:

when an Italian firm ships goods to the United States, it must turn half of its dollar payments to the Italian treasury and receives liras for them at the rate of 225 to the dollar. The other half might be retained by the exporter and used to buy raw materials abroad or the dollar might be sold in the free market at whatever rate they can command.[45]

Economic considerations of this nature are relevant to the interpretation of the use, commerce, and circulation of certain fibers, their manufacturing into textiles, and finally their use in Italian fashion, because they show how the materials available to Italy's fashion designers were predicated on larger economic issues.

Italian Fashion's Materiality

Fibers, fabrics, and textiles were significant protagonists in the making and the allure of garments in post-war Italy. Consumers and producers were aware of the crucial role that they played in fashion, as highlighted in the pages of magazines such as *Vogue, Harper's Bazaar, Linea*, and *Novità*, in Italy and in the UK from that period. These pages included diverse and often evocative designations combining the name of fabrics or companies with their characteristics, such as Woollena, Costsurah, Valchiria Satinato, and Drapsusa. Fabric producers proudly promoted fashion couturiers who used their fabrics with full-page color advertisements such as Tondani's for a Vanna piece using their Wollena fabric.[46]

The International Wool Secretariat (IWS) consistently proclaimed the quality of wool fiber through a range of magazine advertisements. These included standalone ads such as the one in *Harpers' Bazaar* featuring a drawing of a sheep happily declaring: "Take it from me. Wool is the natural thing to wear. Because it is comfortable, warm, wears well, prevents chills, has elasticity."[47] Alternative approaches included adding the slogan *la lana é insostituibile* (wool is irreplaceable) at the bottom of each page of fashion magazines such as *Novità*.[48] Alongside its regular presence in the printed press, the IWS organized a fashion show around Europe every autumn. *Novità*'s report on the 1953 IWS Italian show explains that the *confezione* manufacturers (clothing mass manufacturers) and dressmakers presented their products alongside each other.[49] This coexistence of different types of production was also happening in fashion shows sponsoring artificial and synthetic fibers, as described in the following section on SNIA Viscosa.

The emphasis placed on fabrics rather than on the finished garments in fashion magazines is symptomatic of the fact that many readers would have known how to sew or knit at the time, and that most Italian consumers were purchasing made-to-measure clothes from dressmakers. The act of commissioning a garment arguably requires some knowledge of the different types of materials available, their cost, and the way in which they drape and feel on the body. The prevalent presence of fashion patterns offered in magazines for readers' private use and the regular long articles describing new fabrics, colors, textures, and properties were aimed at knowledgeable readers and catered to their needs. This is evident in the front cover announcement of "15 pages of fabric news" in the January 1957 issue of *Harper's Bazaar UK*. The editorial of that same issue, titled "The Fabric Comes First," declares that "The big news in fashion is now in the fabrics which form the basis of fashion and the galvanic inspiration of designers."[50] This quote demonstrates how, at this time, fabrics came first and were instrumental in advertising and selling fashion.

Natural, Artificial, and Synthetic Fibers

At the beginning of the 1950s, Italy was eager to be at the forefront of innovation on the one hand and as the bearer of taste, style, and tradition on the other. Accordingly, at that time, textiles using new synthetic and artificial fibers were promoted alongside more traditional natural fibers. A 1953 episode of the weekly newsreel projected in cinemas during intermissions titled *La Settimana Incom*, for example, promotes the blend of cashmere merino and angora rabbit used by Luisa Spagnoli to produce the "pure white" cardigan with the same enthusiasm as it describes the capacity of nylon to allow users to "say goodbye to ironing forever."[51] This coexistence triggers questions about the interwoven values related to the use of natural, artificial, and even synthetic fibers and about the relationships between fiber producers, markets, and couturiers.[52]

In several reports on the Italian fashion catwalk shows included in *Settimana Incom*, the innovations and advances made in new fibers, as well as their very low prices, were highlighted as a sign of modernity. For example, in the 1953 "Moda Italiana a Firenze" episode reporting on the prestigious *Sala Bianca* catwalk show at the Pitti Palace in Florence, textiles such as rayon are described and illustrated in their applications: images from the event show a variety of garments made with such fabrics, including suits, morning sleeveless dresses, and more elegant summer cocktail frocks.[53]

The aforementioned *Settimana Incom* episode, "Appuntamento Con La Moda," shows one of the many dresses, called the "Rose dress", made entirely of nylon by the Roman atelier Carosa presented at the *Sala Bianca* in July 1953. The presence of such a fiber on the *Sala Bianca*'s export platform is an indication of how the use of this new material was not limited to raincoats, umbrellas, and underwear, its predominant usage at the time, but was also extended to the more traditional cocktail and evening dresses. The Carosa "Rose dress" can be seen in the film, but also in a picture by photographer Federico Garolla capturing couturier Donna Caracciolo Ginetti fastening the dress on a model in a backstage shot (Figure 1.1). A *WWD* advertisement records Carosa as paired up with nylon producers Rhodiatoce and Chaintillon, making it safe to assume that they supplied the nylon for the rose dress of 1953.[54]

Figure 1.1 Giovanna Caracciolo Ginetti fastening the "Rose dress" made in nylon, photo by Federico Garolla, 1953. © Federico Garolla.

The widespread use of man-made fibers on the *Sala Bianca*'s 1953 catwalks aimed to cater for American demand for more practical and cheaper materials. It showcased how Italy was not only to be associated with natural and artisanal fibers, but also with modern and futuristic materials.

Foreign journalists were impressed with the results of the Italian experimentations with new fibers, as shown in a *Sunday World Herald* issue celebrating wools, cottons, and, "principal among the fabrics of combined fibers … coating of wool and silk; 'fancy cloth' of nylon, viscose and silk; and bouclé voile of nylon, curled rayon, viscose and silk."[55] This listing aptly summarizes the way in which natural, more traditional, fibers existed side by side with new, modern ones. Such a coexistence was not limited to the promotional level, but was also present at the production level, as the next section highlights.

Silk, Artificial, and Synthetic Fibers

The October 30, 1945 issue of Italian economic newspaper *Il Sole* reports on a sale to England of five hundred bales of natural silk for a value of circa two hundred million lire. This was the first export after the war from Northern Italy and the journalist emphatically states that surely more will follow.[56] In December of the same year an article from *Il Sole* explains how the Italian silk industry was one of the few that could draw from within its own borders all the raw materials needed to produce finished products for export, as most European countries needed to import yarns to feed their mills.[57] That article goes on to describe how the export of silk textiles was of much more of interest to Italy than the export of silk yarns and that, among others, the USA, Switzerland, and England were important markets for this type of business.

Italian silk was bought by the English department store Harrods from at least 1951 onwards. As demonstrated by the surviving company sample books, these purchases of silk coexisted with purchases of artificial and synthetic fibers.[58] This is important to highlight because often the same manufacturers were simultaneously producing natural, synthetic, and artificial fibers although we are not used to thinking of these productions coexisting. In the pages of the sample books, the fiber composition of the fabrics purchased is precisely stated along with other information such as the name of the supplier, the date of delivery, the cost, the width and length, and the fabric swatch's color number.[59] In the examples shown in Plate 1, it is recorded that Harrods ordered 100 percent silk shantung from Battista Clerici in December 1951, while in August 1953 the same department bought some silk and wool and silk and selon blends from Toninelli (Plates 2 and 3). The purchase of blends alongside pure silk and artificial fabric, such as rayon, is apparent throughout the 1950s.

Natural and artificial fibers were mixed together to obtain the desired effect and consistency in the production of Clerici Tessuto, a silk-manufacturing plant in the Como area. The company's sample books show that, along with 100 percent silk fabrics, blends of natural and artificial fibers such as silk and Bemberg (an artificial fiber derived from cotton), silk and viscose, and silk and cotton were also part of their range.

The coexistence of silk fabrics with artificial and synthetic ones in the production, sale, and promotion of Italian fashion, as shown respectively by the Clerici Tessuto's archive, the record of English client Harrods, and the Italian media's newsreels, which counters our understanding of the materials used so far, calls for an expansion of the investigation of Italian fashion and materiality to include a more detailed analysis of the fiber producers.

In the January 1953 issue of *Novità*, all the publicized frocks designed by Jole Veneziani were made from the Bemberg textile and shown in black-and-white photographs presenting the dresses. An emblematic picture shows a model who directly and confidently gazes at the camera; the other, seen from behind, looks at herself in the mirror, offering the reader the possibility to also peek at the dress from the front through the mirror's reflection. The ornate mirror-frame and draped fabric suggest a luxurious interior. The photograph is part of an article titled "La Stagione alla Scala" ("The Scala season") in which the journalist suggests that the elegant Milanese woman, who subscribed to the theater's program, would need at least five different evening gowns per season, one for each of the most important operas in the season. In this feature, Veneziani and Vanna's Bemberg dresses are shown in the elite setting of Milan's most important theater and are worn with confidence by young, fashionable models.[60] Bemberg is used in its many iterations, as brocade, velvet, taffeta, organza, and satin, showcasing the versatility of the artificial fiber.[61] Bemberg is also shown to be fully accepted by the Milanese elite at its most important social event, the Scala's season.

The July 1953 summer edition of the *Sala Bianca* featured several shows in which textile producers were coupled with couturiers or fashion houses who used their textiles to produce special garments. As well as natural fibers such as silk produced by Costa, wool by Line e Lane, and cotton by Legler, an Italviscosa show was also included in the program.[62] Garments were presented by fashion houses such as Antonelli, Carosa, and Marucelli with fabrics created using Italviscosa yarn made by manufacturers such as SAFIT, Mantero, SAPITI, and FISAC.[63]

It is important to highlight that most of the synthetic and artificial fiber producers, as in the case of DuPont in the USA, did not produce lengths of textiles, but only made fibers.[64] This lack of a finished product meant that it was vital for them to establish close relationships with weavers and textile producers who, by adopting the use of such fibers, guaranteed their inclusion in the market. Shows like the ones organized for *Sala Bianca* fostered these links and showcased on an international stage the competence of the new industry through the work of dressmakers and couturiers.

SNIA Viscosa and Fibers Promotion

Synthetic and artificial fibers were primarily produced by companies such as DuPont in the USA and SNIA Viscosa in Italy. These are mainly chemical manufacturers and they made fibers destined for fashion and textile production alongside other products such as cellophane.[65] These manufacturers therefore needed to collaborate with companies that could turn their fibers into yarns and then into textiles (by knitting, weaving, or blending them into fabrics), and with fashion designers and couturiers to design fashion garments using these. Because of their nature as primary products at the start of an extensive production process, the fibers could not be advertised as finished products. The same problem, although to a lesser extent, continues to afflict textile manufacturers, as Prato-based textile manufacturer Roberto Sarti explains.[66]

For synthetic and artificial fiber companies, in comparison to producers of natural fibers, there was an added urgency to make sure that consumers knew, understood, and valued the qualities and characteristics of their innovative fibers.[67] Blaszczyk's thorough analysis of the American chemical giant and fiber producer DuPont in the post-war period shows how companies sought to address this issue. DuPont employed market research technologies to connect with the final consumers and set up a public relations department to communicate, through photographs and press releases, the connections that it established with French and Italian couturiers who had been contracted to employ DuPont fibers such as Orlon and Qiana in their designs.[68]

In Italy the largest producer of man-made fibers, SNIA Viscosa, the *Società Nazionale Industria Applicazioni Viscosa* (National Viscose Manufacturing and Application Company), promoted its innovative products by including them as key players in the historical and cultural narrative of Italy through various initiatives.[69]

From the 1930s, according to Butazzi, the artificial fiber industry was considered a flagship enterprise of the Fascist regime, and Italy was highly productive in the manufacture of proudly self-sufficient autarkic textiles that bore strong and evocative names such as Viritex and Rayontex, two brands owned by the Zegna company.[70] According to historian Jeffery Schnapp, artificial textiles are privileged materials, because they are associated with ideas of happiness, utopias, and even miracles.[71] It is important to analyze how man-made fibers and modern technology in the pre-war and immediate post-war eras were used and commercialized, as this is crucial to understand the wider economic implications and connotations of textile and fashion production that were developed in this period.

SNIA Viscosa participated in this trend too. As Schnapp shows, they commissioned and published in conjunction with the regime the Futurist Filippo Tommaso Marinetti's poem "Il poema del vestito di latte" ("The Poem of the Milk Dress") (1938–9), "a poetic and typographical tour de force retracing in minute detail the making of Lanital," one of SNIA's innovative and autarkic milk textiles.[72] The poem was illustrated by the designer Bruno Munari and was published in an opulent tricolor edition. This was not the only example of Italian poets' interest in the production of modern textiles; other examples can be found in promotions of rayon in Italy in the 1930s and in SNIA's competitors CISA-VISCOSA's publicizing of their innovative fibers.[73]

In the same vein, in 1949, SNIA Viscosa commissioned a film from the young director Michelangelo Antonioni to promote the production of rayon viscose. The ten-minute-long black-and-white documentary *Sette Canne e un Vestito* ("Seven REEDS, one dress") was shot in the industrial city of Torviscosa.[74] The documentary shows how in the post-war years, as was the case during the Fascist regime with Marinetti and Lanital, artificial fibers needed a mythology or, as the voice-over describes, a "fable." In Antonioni's film the production building is described as a "*maestoso misterioso castello*" ("magical mysterious castle") and the chemical reactions are equated to miracles. The spectator witnesses the magical transformation of natural canes, through various chemical processes, into a one-hundred-kilometer length of viscose. As Alfred Gell explains when speaking about the power of art to enchant, "The enchantment of technology is the power that technical processes have of casting a spell over us so that we see the real world in an enchanted form."[75] The phases of transformation, although very technical and far from the viewers' knowledge, are shown in the film in a manner that plays with what Gell defines as a "spell" and offers the spectators a fable to be enchanted by and to believe in.

As SNIA was a producer of fibers and not of textiles, no weaving or any other techniques that transform the thread into fabric is shown in this film. This absence is key to understanding the ways in which company such as SNIA wanted to be portrayed. The film jumps over this gap and ends with a parade of models at the Milan Trade Fair fashion show, displaying the final use of viscose in action. The rhetoric and the vocabulary used in Antonioni's film is like Marinetti's earlier "Poem of the Milk Dress." Both present a modern mythology of innovative fibers and connect these fibers with dresses.[76]

SNIA Viscosa also formed alliances with silk producers to encourage them to use its new fibers. Such alliances had a double aim: on the one hand garments made with synthetic and artificial fibers were presented in the same setting as those made of silk, and on the other hand silk producers, with names already established in the eyes of the public, were justified to produce new textiles with the new fibers. A long report published in the 1954 winter edition of the magazine *Linea* is emblematic of this approach. It presents models and their garments against an identical white background so that there are no apparent differences between those made with natural silk and those made with nylon. Only the captions reveal the full information by describing the types of fibers used.

The drive to explicitly connect chemical technical procedures with the much more relatable and visual dress parade was at the basis of the marketing strategy devised by SNIA in the post-war period. In 1948, Marinotti established, along with the ex-Fascist Edoardo Alfieri, *Il Centro Italiano della Moda* (the Italian Fashion Center, CIM), drawing together in one national event the diverse initiatives of the sector with the aims of attracting the press and buyers, strengthening the relationship between fashion and textile manufacturers, and promoting the use of artificial and synthetic fibers. These events were considered important international shows, and journalists from newspapers such as the *New York Times* attended and reported regularly on the latest fashion news.[77] In 1950, Franco Marinotti also founded *Il Centro Internazionale delle Arti e del Costume* (The International Center of Arts and Costume (CIAC)).[78] This new venture operated from 1951 in the freshly restored Palazzo Grassi in Venice. The *Centro* was an ambitious endeavor; as well as organizing exhibitions and fashion shows, it published books on costume and the magazine *Arti e Costume*, and held a collection of textiles, costumes, and fashion prints, and also housed a specialist library open to the public.[79] Initially the *Centro* was meant to focus only on the textile industry, clothing, and furnishing, however, from 1951, Franco Marinotti appointed his son Paolo as its secretary to open up these other fields and include costume and art.[80]

The section that follows focuses mainly on the CIAC's activities between 1951 and 1958 to consider its promotion of synthetic and artificial fibers and its connection with the contemporary fashion scene. This is because the CIAC's concentration on textiles, fibers, and costumes diminished after 1958 to give space to the promotion of contemporary art.[81]

An article in a 1951 edition of the Swiss newspaper *Il Ticino* comments on how the CIAC's initiatives were initially thought to be purely promotions of the textile industrialists, but also underlines how the intention behind them was not merely economic, but mainly cultural, aiming to establish the history of costume as the history of civilization.[82]

The Legitimization of New Fibers

The historical and cultural legitimation of SNIA's synthetic and artificial fibers was achieved, among other initiatives, through the organization of large exhibitions that took place mainly at Palazzo Grassi in Venice. The first of these, titled *La Leggenda del Filo d'oro: Le Vie della Seta* (The Legend of the Gold Thread: The Ways of Silk), was set up in 1951. The connection with silk and its history was made explicit in this show through a combination of the history of silk and of the Silk Road with human attempts, from the time of alchemists, to produce artificial silk.[83] This kind of narrative provided synthetic and artificial fibers with a legendary connection to a mythical past.

In the 1954 exhibition *I Tessili dell'Avvenire* (The Textiles of the Future), the focus shifted from past to future. Here the aim, as declared by Marinotti himself, was to show the alliance between science and nature as the basis of every human achievement.[84] A fashion show labeled the *Parata del Tessuto e della Moda* (The Parade of Textile and Fashion) was organized at the Palazzo Grassi to coincide with the exhibition. The intention of this event was for eleven fashion houses, six fur houses and twenty-seven textile producers to demonstrate to an audience consisting of Italian and foreign journalists, industrialists, and observers, how artificial and synthetic yarns could achieve great results in the hands of Italian textile manufacturers.

Here again the materials, rather than the final fashion objects, were given central importance. Newsreel footage of the show describes it as a very persuasive display of the textiles of the future, where the use of synthetic and artificial fibers in accessories and sportswear achieves both beauty and practicality. As a result, with its translation into rayon, nylon, and Lilion, *alta moda* would no longer be a prohibitive luxury and would instead be within the reach of everybody.[85]

Two years later, having explored the past and the future in the previous exhibitions, the CIAC showcased the present in the show *La Moda nel Tessuto Contemporaneo. Prima Rassegna Internazionale dell'Abbigliamento* (Fashion in Contemporary Textile. The First International Festival of Apparel), which took place between August 21 and 23, 1956. Here the connection between artificial and synthetic fibers, textiles, and fashion was more explicit than in the previous editions, and was displayed through parades of garments by Italian and foreign designers from the USA, Spain, Germany, Japan, India, England, and Ireland, made with artificial and synthetic fibers in combination with natural fibers.

Each country presented a selection of sportswear, boutique, ready-to-wear, high fashion, and fur. The show's catalog openly legitimizes synthetic materials by thoroughly listing one by one the models presented along with an indication of materials, and, for each country, a description of the fashion and textile industry's contemporary landscape highlighting the role of synthetic materials.

The analysis of these documented exhibitions and cultural events organized by the SNIA Viscosa's CIAC demonstrates a clear intention to promote artificial and synthetic fibers in national and international contexts. It shows that these so-called "future textiles" were promoted not in isolation but in conjunction with other natural fibers such as cotton, silk, and wool. It further reveals how these new fibers were given a historical dimension by justifying their genesis through an emphasis on their relationship with the Silk Road, and by presenting them as a product of progress and modernity through their connection to scientific improvements.

Italian and foreign mass production was showcased alongside high and boutique fashions, especially in the 1956 event *La Moda nel Tessuto Contemporaneo*. This represented a clear distancing from the events at the *Sala Bianca* that foregrounded *alta moda* as the ambassador of Italian production. This is probably because synthetic fibers were much more suitable for machine-made production at the time.

In this context, not only was fashion a pretext to promote and showcase textiles and their fibers, but cultural and historical references and settings were also drawn to strongly root new materials within the country's heritage and tradition. The lack of an explicit commercial agenda for the CIAC added a further layer of legitimization.

This investigation into the materials of fashion in magazine photography for Bemberg, in the *Sala Bianca*'s promotion, and in the SNIA Viscosa parades, has revealed a more complex view of Italian fashion production. As early as 1953, Italian couturiers, fashion houses, and silk producers started to heavily employ and promote synthetic and artificial fibers through specialized shows, magazine features, and newsreels. The traditional coupling of Italian fashion and natural fibers was challenged, and synthetics, such as nylon, and artificial fibers were commonly produced, used, and exported in the early 1950s.

This chapter has demonstrated that while Italian fashion was trying to find its own voice during this period, the Italian textiles industry was continuing a path of growth and recognition almost uninterrupted since the 1930s. This was partly a result of the policy of autarky that the Fascist regime had imposed on the peninsula.[86] By unpicking the often unproblematized image of Italian post-war *alta moda,* this initial chapter has shown how beneath the surface of the glamorous gowns designed by the Italian couturiers, paraded on the Pitti catwalks and advertised on fashion magazines, a network of textile and fibers manufacturers were working to legitime and commercialize artificial and synthetics fibers.

At the same time this chapter shows how the North American influence went beyond its buying power, as we will see in Chapter 2, also impacting the methods of production, company organization, and fibers commerce.

2

The American Export Market and its Influence on Italian Design

Introduction

This chapter investigates the role textiles played in the embryonic period of the late 1940s to the early 1950s by looking at two events organized in the USA and Italy at the time. The first, the exhibition *Italy at Work: Her Renaissance in Design Today* at the Brooklyn Museum, promoted Italian goods in North America, while the second, the *Sala Bianca*, showcased Italian fashion for foreign buyers.[1]

These two events, although located as far apart as New York and Florence, reveal common roots in their export-focused aims and offer the backdrop of the case study investigated in the second part of this chapter, a silk-and-wool dress designed by Italian couturier Simonetta. An in-depth analysis concludes the section and aims to unravel the convoluted journey that Italian fashion took when exported and copied in the USA.

Chapter 2 zooms out from fibers to textiles and considers the decisive role that textiles played in export events such as the touring American exhibition *Italy at Work*. This is an original angle, as previous discussions of *Italy at Work* in the fashion history literature have focused only on impresario Giovanni Battista Giorgini's failed attempt to organize an Italian fashion show for the exhibition, an episode that encouraged him to put together the near-mythical first international fashion show in his house in 1951. This chapter also charts special promotional events from the early 1950s in the *Sala Bianca* in Florence, and shows how the USA played a crucial role in determining what Italian fashion designers and textile manufacturers were designing, producing, and distributing.

The impact of the Marshall Plan and the Americanization of the Italian market and production are key factors in understanding this period.[2] This chapter ends with a case study of the Italian couturier Simonetta, and examines how Italian fashion was exported to the USA and then copied. It explores the little-known and rarely studied commercial context in the post-war years of original Italian couture garments in the USA, where they were copied as both custom-made and mass-produced artifacts for the overseas market. Unpicking this mechanism is significant to the understanding of certain modes of ideation and production of couture in Italy and sheds new light on the origins of mass production in the country.

The complicated system of imports into North America of European original couture has been thoroughly described by fashion historian and curator Alexandra Palmer in relation to French couture and its Canadian market.[3] It has not, however, been analyzed with regard to the original Italian couture "translated" into American ready-to-wear.[4] Design historian Nicola White acknowledges such practice and describes how, in the 1950s, North American department stores spent thousands of dollars on "buying for reproduction (copying or translating) as well as the designs they bought for resale."[5] Anthropologist Simona Segre Reinach also refers to this process and explains how Italian fashion, because of its simple line, was easier to reproduce in the American mass-production system. However, no critical or in-depth analysis of this transaction has yet been carried out.[6]

Textiles Make Fashion: *Italy at Work* and *Sala Bianca*

Italy at Work: Her Renaissance in Design Today was a collaborative exhibition organized by the director of the Brooklyn Museum Charles Nagel, the curator of Decorative Arts and of Industrial Arts at the Art Institute of Chicago Meyric R. Rogers, and the *Compagnia Nazionale Artigiana* (National Artisan Company, CNA). It was made possible by Marshall Plan funds and the support of the Italian and American governments. This touring exhibition showed around 2,500 Italian-made objects such as furniture, textiles, glassware, and ceramics, and also included five designed interiors. After opening at the Brooklyn Museum in November 1950, it toured the USA for the following three years, stopping in eleven other museums and bringing Italian craft and design to the American public.[7]

The *Italy at Work* exhibition has been studied by a handful of British and Italian design and economic historians such as Penny Sparke, who, through this exhibition, describes the proto-design nature of Italian design in the post-war period, and Catharine Rossi, who highlights how this exhibition "constructed Italy as America's non-industrialized, non-modern other."[8] Rossi further stresses how "*Italy at Work* aimed to boost Italy's post-war reconstruction by presenting the nation's hand-made wear to the American consumer."[9] In a similar vein, Italian economists Merlo and Polese explain that this exhibition brought Italian skills to the attention of the American public, but also that it had the effect of helping Italian producers to understand the potential of the North American market and the "necessity of making goods to suit its tastes."[10] The connection to the Marshall Plan made *Italy at Work* more than just an exhibition: its role was closely related to wider export aspirations and to the aim of re-establishing links between Italian and American companies in the aftermath of the Second World War.

The second event takes us back to Italy, to Florence, where foreign buyers (initially only from North America) were invited to participate in collective Italian high-fashion shows twice a year from February 1951. This first took place in the exporter Giovanni Battista Giorgini's house, before moving to Florence's Grant Hotel and finally finding its permanent location in the Palazzo Pitti's *Sala Bianca* (The White Hall). Italian dressmakers and couturiers were required to exclusively showcase original creations that were not inspired by the French style. Chronicles of the success of the *Sala Bianca*, as these events became known, have been widely investigated, but the role that textiles played in them has been largely overlooked.[11]

Italian Fashion in *Italy at Work*

The primary objective of the exhibition *Italy at Work* was, according to its organizers, to "represent the first concerted effort of any group of American museums to implement the Marshall Plan by bringing to the attention of the potential buyer in America the full range of Italian contemporary achievement in the field."[12] This means that the objects included—and, indeed, the ones not included—in the show indicated the taste and preferences of the North American market in relation to Italian-made goods.

The textiles section was one of the largest in the exhibition and several designers and producers were represented, showcasing many specialties of Italian production, such as linen, wool, embroidery, and hand-painted silks. The display included a two-toned silk with a chariot design by manufacturer Guido Ravasi of Como (see Plate 4).[13] My study of the Ravasi company order books demonstrates that the same chariot silk was successfully commercialized in the United States in the 1950s. The history of this silk twill offers insight into the commercial opportunities that the touring exhibition offered within the American market and will be examined in the next section.

This section gives an account of the relationship between Giorgini and the organizers of *Italy at Work*. It explains that Giorgini's failure to organize an Italian fashion show in New York in connection with the exhibition had wider implications for the future promotion and export of Italian fashion.

A letter from Michelle Murphy, the research consultant in the industrial design division of the Brooklyn Museum, addressed to Alice Perkins of *WWD* clearly lays out that Italian fashion was not originally included in the show because the jurors did not feel they could select objects to represent the rapidly changing field.

> There will be costume accessories such as: shoes, jewelry and many examples of textiles for cloth. The jury however did not feel qualified, or they were concerned with the more rapidly changing aspects of fashion so that no plans were made for the showing of the work of dressmakers and tailors.[14]

Yet the necessity to represent fashion was felt, since there had been no major public presentations of the clothing made in Italy. The letter goes on to ask for advice regarding the idea of including current Italian models to be shown at the beginning of 1951 at the museum.

The answer from Alice Perkins came with straightforward views on the status of Italian fashion in 1950. In the eyes of the *WWD* journalist, "the majority of garments made by the Italian dressmakers are either direct copies of Paris, or Paris inspired."[15] Although she notes some exceptions, such as Marucelli, she explains that "Many Italian dressmakers admit quite frankly they copy Paris; others do not admit, but do," listing Emilio Schuberth as an example. She concludes:

> To have a sincere exhibit of Italian clothes fashion, the garments would have to be selected by someone thoroughly familiar with both Paris and Italian markets, or you would run the risk of presenting something Italian which was really Parisian – and perhaps being exposed by the Paris house. Certainly the New York trade would recognize any such plagiarism.[16]

Despite this negative assessment of the idea of an Italian fashion show, both Rogers and Nagel appeared enthusiastic when the Florentine exporter and impresario Giovanni Battista Giorgini arrived in New York in August 1950 and talked to them about the possibility of organizing a fashion show in conjunction with their exhibition.[17]

A letter written by Giorgini following this visit highlights his plan to present some Italian dresses from the fourteenth, sixteenth, and eighteenth centuries "in order to make a background of the modern Fashion Show."[18] Giorgini also wanted to know how to export all the merchandise he had assembled in Italy for the exhibition and wondered whether the objects would enter free of duty or in temporary importation.[19] The level of detail in these queries suggests that Giorgini was already trying to organize the show. However, a letter from Rogers to Giorgini dated September 20, 1950 reveals that, although he was interested, Michelle Murphy, who worked very closely with Fairchild Publication and oversaw this kind of activity for the Museum, had reservations. Rogers explains that:

> Owing to her close contact with the field she had heard that a good deal of unfavorable comment had followed the last show of Italian fashions due to the fact that certain Italian couturiers had been rather too free in adopting French designs. In the event the museum did have the fashion show they would have to be sure this source of criticism was eliminated.[20]

He goes on to describe talks involving a French representative who would go over the potential material in order to eliminate any problematic designs.

Despite these criticisms, Giorgini continued to work on developing the show and tried to convince the New York department store B. Altman to sponsor the event. But the high cost of import duties and of the models, in addition to the uncertainty about their originality and quality, prompted them to decline Giorgini's idea of a tie-in sponsorship between the museum, the department store, and nascent Italian fashion.[21]

The final letter I was able to retrieve from the correspondence between Giorgini and the Brooklyn Museum shows Giorgini trying to convince Nagel that he could sponsor the show himself without the input of Altman's. No answer to this letter has been found, but an internal museum memorandum dating from a few days earlier clarifies that the show had already been shelved.[22]

In this memorandum, Murphy explains how she met with Mr. Kellior, the executive Vice President at B. Altman.

> Mr. Kellior subsequently conferred with Violet Mason, Altman's fashion specialist and others and advised us today that the picture on the quality and variety of Italian Fashions was not sufficiently well-known nor clear to undertake by long range such a show.[23]

She goes on to say that "it does appear from the careful investigation of Altman's and the advice of Alice Perkins that the fashion show idea is fraught with hazard and that it would be wisest for us to forget about it under present conditions."[24]

The absence of Italian fashion in the *Italy at Work* exhibition, then, was not an oversight, but the result of a lack of originality and of a sense of unique identity for Italian fashion.

However, only two years later, in 1952, Bernard Sakowitz, president of Houston's Sakowitz Brothers department stores, wrote to Giorgini to inform him that the exhibition *Italy at Work* was at the Houston Fine Arts Museum and that:

> Tonight they will have a costume dance $50.00 per person to raise funds for the museum and they are also having a Style Show of original Italian dresses. These dresses were bought and imported by several stores in New York City and with special arrangements through the Ambassador in Washington, we managed to borrow these dresses for our show tonight.[25]

This letter highlights how Giorgini's idea from 1950 to have a fashion show to accompany the *Italy at Work* exhibition became a reality, but with a few variations from his original idea. Instead of having both historical and contemporary Italian fashion on show, the 1952 event showcased only Italian contemporary couturiers' creations, "the originals" bought by New York's department stores, along with a charity costume dance. This highlights how, only a couple of years after the opening of *Italy at Work*, when Italian fashion was not deemed original enough and only Italian textiles were on display, the American appetite for Italian fashion creations was growing.[26]

Giorgini dedicated the next decade of his professional life to addressing the issues raised in the exchange of letters over *Italy at Work* and perfecting a system that would allow Italian fashion to become one of the USA's favorite markets. The *Italy at Work* experience, as journalist Giulio Vergani explains, drove Giorgini to put together in a very quick span of time, from October 1950 to February 1951, a fashion show in his house specifically aimed at North American department store buyers.[27] The interest in export influenced the Florentine fashion displays and the critiques and comments Giorgini received helped him shape his catwalk show in response to the American market's needs.

In the existing literature, the above correspondence has only been considered through the copies of the letters available in the Giorgini archive, with analysis of these documents pointing to the fact that Giorgini's failure to organize a fashion show at the Brooklyn Museum became the pretext to organize the first "Italian High Fashion Show" in February 1951 in his house.[28] Thanks to the unearthing of the other set of letters from the *Italy at Work* archive in the Brooklyn Museum, a more multifaceted situation with wider implications has emerged. As shown above, the absence of fashion in *Italy at Work* was because

Italian fashion was judged too derivative of the French style and therefore not original. This is a key point to make because awareness of this weakness encouraged a change of direction in Italian fashion in the following years. On the other hand, the textiles field was acclaimed and displayed at the time, as seen in the next section.

Italian Textiles in *Italy at Work*

In the introduction to the *Italy at Work* catalog, Rogers describes the renaissance of Italian craftsmanship and production after Fascism and the destruction of the war:

> As might be expected under present conditions, the renaissance in design is finding its expression, in materials that are either basically less costly or readily obtainable from local natural resources . . . The most complete development will in general be found in those objects in which skills, imagination and a sense of the material itself are the most important ingredients.[29]

This text highlights how Italian craftsmen reached the highest achievements through creative and skillful transformation of cheaply available materials.

Although full fashion garments were not on display, and no section was specifically dedicated to fashion, the catalog and exhibition featured costume jewelry, accessories, textiles, embroideries, and ecclesiastical garments. These kinds of objects were considered worthy of being displayed due to their originality and creative use of materials.[30] As demonstrated above, at that stage the derivative French-influenced style of Italian fashion did not appeal to the Americans. But items involving close engagement with the quality and intrinsic characteristics of the materials are praised by Rogers, who declares that, "On the whole, the most successful commercial production in the field is to be found in the fashion-driven ingenuity shown by the designers of women's bags, purses, and shoes."[31] An example of this is shoemaker Salvatore Ferragamo's use of the native and traditional material of straw, which he reinterpreted to create an original and "fashionable" pair of "Valle" pink straw shoes included in the exhibition.[32]

The section on textiles and embroidery was the second largest in the exhibition after the one on ceramics. In the catalog, after giving a historical overview of the success and prestige of the textile arts over the centuries, Rogers concludes that the Italians preferred natural forms and not "radical" design, and that they mainly relied on color and greater freedom in the printed fabrics. When speaking of the work of Maria Chiara Galeotti, a producer of hand-woven fabrics and outfits better known by the brand name Tessitrice dell' Isola, besides highlighting her sensitivity to color and texture, Rogers describes how she mixed raffia with normal and artificial fibers, and indicates that hand-loomed fabrics in cotton, hemp, and linen were new to American tastes. This remark, together with the selection of the textiles and accessories displayed in the exhibition, emphasizes the selection of goods that would not compete with American production and that could therefore be "safely" imported by prospective buyers.[33]

According to Rossi, besides limitations due to economic restrictions or the favoring of contemporary design, some objects were rejected from the exhibition for "not being sufficiently craft-like."[34] This consideration was evident in the case of textiles, where preference was given to hand-woven examples in hemp and linen. Moreover, it appears that silk was present only as a craft production, whereas its industrial production, which exported to the USA most of its raw silk output, was largely overlooked. Additionally, rayon, nylon, or any other synthetic and artificial materials were barely mentioned, although they were being produced in the country from as early as 1947. This favoring of particular fibers and materials over others in the exhibition highlighted how, in the 1950s in America, Italy was still associated with natural fibers, a notion that, as seen in Chapter 1, was about to change.

The craft-like goods on display were also considered as new and "other" to bring to the attention of the museum public. For example, in July 1950, a few months before the opening of the exhibition, an article in *WWD* describes three textiles by the Italian silk mill Ravasi that were selected to be shown there.[35] *WWD* was the USA's most famous trade fashion newspaper at the time, so its readers would have been interested to know in detail what types of fabrics would soon be seen and bought in the USA.[36] The magazine describes the three fabrics chosen as: a silk twill in rust and white depicting an ancient chariot scene; a "yarn dyed, hand-loomed silk in shades of muted blue, gold and red"; and a "modern design in light blue and silvery white brocade, called 'the clouds.'" These textiles were representative, in their natural fibers and traditional manufacturing, of the types of objects displayed in *Italy at Work*.[37] Further investigations in the Ratti foundation archive brought to light a swatch of the chariot textile, reproduced in Plate 4.[38] The fabric is also present in the company order book. Here the names of the textile agents selling the piece are listed in the column near the textile swatch, and the USA is recorded in the column devoted to the countries where the product was sold.[39]

In 1954, when the touring of the exhibition ended, the Ravasi chariot swatch was acquired by the Brooklyn Museum to be part of the permanent collection, along with pieces by other producers such as Cheti and Myricae.[40] This acquisition, the archival evidence of sale in the USA, and the interest shown in the fabric and producer by *WWD* testify to the wider repercussions that *Italy at Work* had for Italian goods. The chariot textile was particularly significant as a symbol of the 'renaissance' of Italian design in America. The American trade press offered the Ravasi company, and possibly the other textile mills involved in the exhibition, a visibility that could have helped boost their sales.

This case study has given the opportunity to follow the fate of one of the textile manufacturers involved in *Italy at Work* beyond the museum realm and into the commerce and export of fabrics. In so doing, it underlines the importance that the exhibition had in terms of giving visibility to Italian mills in the USA.

Sala Bianca

The first *Sala Bianca* show is generally heralded by fashion historians as marking the birth of Italian fashion, and 1951, the year of the first Giorgini fashion show at his house, is largely seen as a watershed moment in Italian fashion chronology.[41] However, foreign buyers were visiting the peninsula before that: Italy's most famous fashion journalist, Elisa Massai, notes that American buyers were already visiting Italy to purchase dressmaking models from as early as 1949.[42]

This section focuses on the importance of textiles in the economy, marketing, and promotion of the early *Sala Bianca* fashion shows. As textile historian Margherita Rosina notes, the strength of Italy's textiles offered a way to overcome the dominance of Paris in the fashion context while fashion design was still reliant on French inspiration.[43]

A 1951 *Life* magazine report titled "Italy Gets Dressed Up," for example, stresses how even Italian cocktail dresses "were weak as compared to the French masters.'"[44] At the same time, journalist Walter Lucas explains how the Italians did not want to steal the thunder of French couturiers, but nevertheless "felt that they had something that was peculiarly their own to offer: richness of materials and color, delicacy of handwork—and price."[45] In a similar vein, fashion press authority Carmel Snow describes how "Italians have always used the very finest fabrics and lean war years have whetted this taste. Their fabrics are magnificent, woven with love and care that spring from this national craving for the best."[46]

Aware of these considerations, Giorgini encouraged and set up partnerships between couturiers and textile producers, especially in 1953. White describes these connections, but records them as arrangements whereby Italian fashion was employing only Italian textiles. She states, for example, that USA ready-to-wear manufacturers who bought Italian design for reproduction "customarily bought the fabrics from the 'linked' Italian textile producers."[47] However, as seen in the Simonetta case study below, the equation was much more nuanced. The analysis of fashion garments, labels, advertisements, and fashion magazine editorials reveals a more complex relationship. Italian fashion was not exclusively employing Italian textiles. American fabric producer Cohama, for example, was advertising Italian couture made with Cohama fabrics available in the USA in a 1951 issue of *WWD*.[48]

The Italian magazine *L'Europeo* reveals how, in the January 1953 *Sala Bianca*, each textile manufacturer had paid a large sum for each model presented and had given dressmakers the textile for free. The idea was to sell to the department stores of America, the UK, Switzerland, and Germany not only the dress to be reproduced in thousands of copies but also the textiles to go with the garments. The Italian critics at the time suggested that this might not work because it was easy to reproduce the Italian textiles elsewhere.[49] But the Americans had a different opinion, as seen in Carmel Snow's article written as a response to the same show:

> What struck me was the close collaboration of the Italian dressmakers and the fabric manufacturers. Italians have a way of blending all kinds of fibers, silk cotton, wool, rayon acetate, or anything that comes along and catches their fancy. No buyers could refrain from touching the fabrics—first, because of their beauty then because it was often impossible to know whether they were silk, satin, cotton, or wool.[50]

Once more an interest in the Italians' innovative blends of natural and artificial fibers is picked up by American observers. The journalist also highlights that this fascinating mix was the result of the partnership between couturiers and textile producers, and between beauty and technology. These would become staple characteristics of the Italian textile and fashion production in the 1960s and 1970s, as we will see in Chapters 5 and 6.

Archival research in the Giorgini papers further demonstrates that some of the more multifaceted connections between couturiers and textile producers continued well after 1953. For instance, a correspondence between Fibrafil and the *Centro di Firenze per la Moda* (Florence Center for Fashion), the organization that ran the Giorgini events, reveals a request for the speaker to announce models made in Dralon during the *Sala Bianca* show of 1961. The price was one million lire for ten mentions. The letter explains:

Moreover, we confirm that, although it was produced by Farbenfabriken BAYER AG, and is therefore of German provenance, our raw materials and the textile used for the high-fashion models will be only of Italian provenance. Amongst the weavers, we can quote Lanificio Breschei, the Lanificio Figli di Pietro Bertotto, Tessilprato and Maffioli.[51]

It is fascinating to note how the German synthetic fibers became "Italian" as the raw materials were processed by the specialized machines of the Italian textile mills. In an advertisement from the same year published in *Novità*, the fiber Dralon also has a substantial presence on the printed page as it is promoted in connection with Italian couturier Cesare Guidi and Italian wool mill Lanifico Figli di Pietro Bertotto, which was responsible for weaving the blend of Dralon and wool.[52] This advert uses a similar strategy to the one used by SNIA Viscosa for its fibers, as seen in Chapter 1. Such evidence shows how an analysis of both fibers and textiles reveals a more complex network of makers and reveals the way in which Italian products from as far back as the fifties were not exclusively "Italian" but the result of more articulated synergies.

Giorgini directed Italian dressmakers and tailors to create designs that suited America's taste, undoubtedly because the USA was a more lucrative market. A report about the eighteenth Florence fashion show (July 1959) listed how the USA represented 30 percent of the buyers, and Germany 27 percent, while the British represented 20 percent of the commercial and industrial compounds. The report emphasized that forty million lire from the guaranteed deposit amount that buyers had to pay in order to participate in Giorgini's shows were in foreign currency.[53] This detail stresses the importance of the export markets at this time and the necessity to please foreign buyers with designs and styles that would appeal to their customers. For this reason, Giorgini kept on faithfully following his American clients' suggestions, as a letter exchange with a representative of the San Francisco department store I. Magnin, a Mr. Carpenter, demonstrates.[54] Carpenter first notes that he considers the choice of the Tuscan capital good as a neutral ground, but states that it will be necessary to organize an airplane service from Paris to Florence.[55] Secondly, as a result of too many experimental models presented being deemed unsalable to American customers, he suggests that a committee be established to leave out any "freakish" models. He also indicates that he would prefer a presentation of fewer models in fewer days, and with the shows of smaller houses relegated to the end. This and other such letters show how Giorgini was regularly asking American stakeholders, including journalists and buyers, their opinions about his shows. Evidence in the Giorgini archive further shows how sometimes, as in the case of the entrance fee, their suggestions were put in practice quite literally and immediately.

The influence of America on Italian fashion has already been unpicked by Nicola White, but this study only covers the influence that America had as a market on Italian export and fashion design.[56] The next section will endeavor to bridge the gap in the literature and shed new light on this relationship by enlarging the scope of study to include the investigation into the multilayered business of transatlantic copies.

Italy and the USA: Export and Domestic Market

The Value of Hand-Made and Machine-Made in Italy and the USA

The mechanisms of clothes making in Italy in the post-war period were significant in informing the direction of made-to-measure and mass-produced fashion in both Italy and the USA. This section shows how Italian textiles and fashion have been closely intertwined from their inception. The interdependency of fashion and textiles is palpable from the ways in which Italian fashion has been produced. The considerations that follow are key to understanding the significance of textiles and their fibers in analyzing Italian fashion outputs.

"The women in Italy wear only custom-made clothes, since they have no mass production."[57] This quote from an American newspaper article from circa 1951 aptly summarizes Italy's domestic fashion market in the immediate post-war years, when very few Italian women bought ready-made clothes.[58] It is worth noting that custom-made can designate different levels of hand-made, including the dressmaker (*sarta*) and the couturier. Italian women would not always attend the atelier of the couturiers as most women could not afford such a luxury. However, they still had hand-made clothes in their wardrobes, as middle-class women would mainly purchase garments from their local *sarta*. Conversely, elite or high-society Italian ladies would be clients of French couturiers and Italian *alta moda*. The rest of the population would use second-hand clothes and garments would often be passed down through the family.[59]

By contrast, in North America, as fashion commentator Elizabeth Hawes notes in 1938, "There are only two kinds of women in the world of clothing. One buys her clothes made-to-order, the other buys her clothes ready-made." The writer states that wealthy American women could buy made-to-measure from Lanvin or Paquin in Paris, for example, or from the Bergdorf Goodman department store. Furthermore, they could buy style, while the middle classes could only buy mass-produced from department stores such as Macy's and were at the mercy of "fashion."[60] Although this statement dates from before the war, the situation in the immediate post-war years continued unchanged.

Despite the differences in the fashion systems and economic situations of the USA and Italy, women from different classes in both countries had their wardrobes made by hand. Although the results were similar, their allure was different and carried distinct values. The norm in Italy was to commission a few pieces made to last from a dressmaker, typically a low-paid worker who could do it from home. This practice was widespread and was not considered glamorous.[61] On the other hand, in the USA, the most common habit was to purchase off-the-peg standardized garments that could last the span of a season, a practice that was not considered glamorous either.[62]

Italian consumers would go to the dressmakers with the material they had purchased in a textile shop and ask them to copy items from photographs or to reproduce patterns from fashion magazines.[63] This type of hand-made fashion was not widespread even within Europe, and an article from *Novità* remarks how made-to-measure dresses in Switzerland were an exception reserved for a very small group.[64]

In 1951, an incredulous American commentator could not believe that in Italy women had their clothes hand-made.[65] In Italy, however, this was considered to be a sign of backwardness, as seen in a report from 1945 by the managing director of Lo Presti-Turba, one of the first Italian producers of *confezione* (mass production) of female garments, noting the underdevelopment of the Italian industry in this field.[66] These opposite perspectives indicate how one country had a large skilled and low-paid workforce, while the other had an abundance of consumers with high income. While Italy saw its situation as synonymous with the lack of a modern clothing industry, this translated into an admiration of Italy's artisanal skills by the USA. The hand-made origin of Italian fashion constitutes, along with textiles production, one of the principal foundations on which the Italian ready-to-wear system was built, and one of the key characteristics by which it was recognized worldwide. It is therefore necessary to reconstruct (and deconstruct) its history.

Boutique Fashion as Proto Italian Ready-to-Wear

While there is no evidence that the Italian *confezione* had any success in the American market, boutique fashion, which can be defined as the Italian equivalent of American sportswear, is presented by many scholars as the sector that differentiated Italian fashion from its French rival, a niche that Italy carved out for itself internationally and through which it reached commercial success.[67] The strength of boutique fashion relied on the price tag, the simplicity of the lines, the quality of textiles, and, as entrepreneur Gianni Ghini defines it, on being "different, novel and fantastic, though not extreme."[68] Ivan Paris also highlights how this sector combined the potential for high-volume production with the allure of known couturiers.[69] With its multifaceted nature, boutique fashion had the advantage of acting as a bridge between nascent Italian fashion and the demands of the American (and other) export markets.[70] Furthermore, both the foreign and Italian press agreed that what distinguished Italian boutique was the craftsmanship in the techniques employed to produce the pieces such as the use of knitwear or the type of fabrics employed and their designs and colors.

American sportswear originated as a type of clothing for active sports and then "evolved to encompass resort wear, town and country, and travel clothes, all of which enable ease of movement."[71] Italian boutique wear had its origins in Italy's relationship with America. Encouraged by the demand from the overseas market, Italian couturiers opened boutique branches of their ateliers to appeal to the new consumers. They even added the name "Sport" to their own brand names, such as Fontana Sport, Simonetta Sport, and Veneziani Sport. There was no direct evolution in Italy from the demand for comfortable sportswear to practice sports and its morphing into a fashion trend as happened in the USA. While some Italian brands such as Emilio Pucci designed specifically for sport with skiwear and beach ensembles, the majority of Italian "sport" boutique lines adapted the existing enterprises of hand-made couture ateliers for the demands of a different market, mainly North American, by opening new boutiques and designing for a small artisanal mass production. Despite the "sport" designation, boutique fashion labels remained prominently associated with the couturier's own luxury name in Italy and had practically no connection to the idea of sport itself.[72]

The spectrum of Italian production ranges from the hand-made tradition embedded with historical know-how and craft (high fashion/*alta moda*) at one extreme to the machine-made mass production (ready-to-wear/*confezione*) at the other. Although several nuances exist in the gamut between hand- and machine-made, boutique fashion was exceptionally well placed at the intersection between artisanal craft and industrial production, and was able to exploit the allure of Italian textiles in combination with the nascent reputation of Italian couturiers' brands. In that sense, Italian fashion historian Enrica Morini defines boutique fashion as the production of small-quantity *prêt-à-porter*.[73]

In December 1951, Jole Veneziani opened a new branch of her atelier, the Veneziani Sport boutique, in Milan with an entire new "sport" collection. According to Italian fashion magazine *Novità*, this was encouraged by the success of her sport models with American buyers in July of the same year.[74] Her stamp of originality came from new color combinations, such as green and purple, that had not been used before in sport lines, unique dyed fabrics as well as special solutions to waterproof her silk and cottons. The article concludes with the news that one of the most elegant department stores on Fifth Avenue had invited Veneziani to present one of her sport lines in New York.

The news of the opening of Jole Venziani Sport was also of interest for the trade magazine *Women's Wear Daily*, as shown by an article titled "Metallic Sweaters to Raincoats in New Boutique at Veneziani Sport."[75] The article, accompanied by a sketch of one of the products, describes how the boutique was opened on the fashionable Via Montenapoleone in Milan with a press party. The shop, it explains, was conveniently located near the Veneziani Couture House so that the two "branches of Mrs. Jole Veneziani's activity will be more differentiated than they have been in the past … The boutique displays and sells slacks, raincoats, skirts, sweaters, and accessories to wear with separates and sportwear."[76] *WWD*'s report describes in detail the type of products on offer at the shop, such as skirts in "beautiful hand-printed white satin" sold with matching scarves "with splashes of colors like moss green, rust, and gold." Raincoats represented an important product of the boutique, and they epitomized Italian ready-made production in synthetics and artificial materials. The careful consideration given to the models, also represented with a sketch, and to the accessories, along with the detailed description of the boutique's interior, emphasize how attentive the American press was to the news of products that could appeal to their readership.

These two reports, one in the Italian and one in the American press, demonstrate once more that the materials of Italian fashion had much more impact on American clients than their line. Boutique fashion was acting as a great ambassador for promoting and selling materials such as silk with its inventive prints, and the wool and cottons that Italy was very skillful at producing. Its intrinsic quality was mostly bestowed by the materiality of its products rather than their style.

The Mechanisms of Copies: Italy and the USA Between "Made in Italy" and Export

"Made in Italy" and Export

Giorgini's correspondence with Houston-based department store owner Bernard Sakowitz reveals that "Made in Italy" labels were very important in the early 1950s in the USA and were requested to certify the provenance of the merchandise. In a letter dated January 24, 1952, one of Bernard Sakowitz's employees complains to Giorgini that the Italian company Nicky Chini had shipped an order of ties with only the Sakowitz labels and not the "Made in Italy" ones. They therefore requested to have the missing labels urgently shipped separately so that they could sew them in.[77]

Another letter from Sakowitz's auditor to Giorgini reveals more about the import/export laws of those years. The letter regarded an issue with the invoice from La Rinascente to Sakowitz in which a home value in lire was indicated next to the goods.[78] It transpired that if the value in lire was indicated, then the reference "made solely for export" would have to be omitted. In that case, if the goods were not exclusively for export, they incurred a three percent addition in duties for the importer in the USA. This probably means that, at least until 1953, garments in the USA with a "Made in Italy" label were made especially for export and not available on Italian soil. This suggests that Italian fashion history could develop in a different way if analyzed through objects made for the USA as opposed to (or in comparison to) those made for internal consumption in Italy.

The idea of "Made in Italy" has had a fluid definition since the 1950s. The widespread notion that Italy was producing beautifully made garments and accessories has been built in an irregular way. Italy was not exclusively producing fashion in the country in the 1950s, just as it is not today. Even when self-sufficiency (autarky) was the priority of the Fascist regime, not everything purchased by Italian women was made in Italy and the Italian elite was still buying elegant gowns in France.[79] Therefore, the idea that Italian fashion was always made in Italy in the period I am considering, 1945 to 1985, can be disproved.

This section challenges, through a series of examples, the traditional understanding of the 1950s "Made in Italy" label and presents evidence of the existence of a more complex network of relationships between makers, designers, creators, manufacturers, and distributors. As Paulicelli states, "On closer inspection, what is known as 'Italian style' or paraded under the label of 'Made in Italy' often turns out to be more multinational and less purely original than its name suggests."[80]

A French article from the 1950s reports that the Italians had an attractive business on their hands. Salaries in Italy were less expensive than in France: for example, Anny Blatt, a designer who had launched the fashion of the knitted jumper in Paris, had all her pieces made in Italy and then imported back to France and still achieved strong savings despite the custom duties. Furthermore, labor was abundant in Italy, and an order could be executed in one week, while in France the same work would take at least six weeks.[81] This article highlights an important point: the mechanism of delocalized production that we have witnessed in the last forty years in Europe was already in place in the early 1950s. As we shall see in Chapter 5, fashion production moved from Western Europe to east European countries in the 1970s, then later moved to China. As anthropologist Simona Segre Reinach aptly puts it: "The act of questioning or examining the concept [of 'Made in Italy'] in depth addresses what is in part a history of fashion, and in part still a living market."[82]

The Transatlantic Commerce of Italian Couture: Simonetta's Case Study

This case study addresses the mechanism of transatlantic copies and garment translations. It aims to understand the various stakeholders, modus operandi, and repercussions of these processes on the creation of Italian fashion in the 1950s. This is an important area of interest for this research as it highlights the difference in material quality between export goods and domestic ones and demonstrates the direct influence of foreign markets in shaping Italy's fashion output.[83] These aspects, along with the previous section's analysis of the meaning of the "Made in Italy" label in the immediate post-war period, provide a rounded vision of the role that Italian textile and fashion played in these years.

The beginning of this investigation is an object: a short evening dress by Italian couturier Simonetta Visconti held in the Costume Institute at the Metropolitan Museum of Art of New York (Figure 2.1).[84]

The archival study conducted in the Giorgini and Simonetta archives in Florence revealed the existence of several photographs, drawings, and reproductions of the same dress, sometimes also called "Cheese Basket" dress, in Italian, American, and English newspapers and magazines.[85] The examination of these copies, or translations as they were called by the American department

Figure 2.1 Simonetta Visconti, short evening dress, also known as "Cheese Basket dress", 1950, wool and silk, gift of Janet A. Sloane 1982, Metropolitan Museum of Art New York: 1982.427.6a, b. Image copyright The Metropolitan Museum of Art/Art Resource/Scala, Firenze.

stores, offers initial insight into the ways in which Italian couture was exported into the American market, an area so far underexplored.[86]

The dress was donated in 1982 by Janet A. Sloane, a stylist for millinery company Madcaps Inc., a regular at European fashion shows and one of the earliest patrons of nascent Italian fashion.[87] Madcaps was featured in *Vogue US*, and her hat designs were sold in the 1950s in department stores such as Lord and Taylor, Bergdorf Goodman, and Saks Fifth Avenue.[88]

As noted in the previous section, in the early 1950s, even before the exposure that Giorgini offered through his collective shows, Simonetta Visconti was already a well-known name in the American and British markets, and pictures of her works were featured in the pages of UK *Vogue* as early as 1948.[89]

Research in UK *Vogue* has brought to light an image of the aforementioned Simonetta dress in the September issue of 1951. In the black-and-white photograph (Figure 2.2), the dress is worn by a model resting on a travertine wall probably located either in Rome, where Simonetta had her atelier, or in Florence, where the fashion show took place. The picture was part of an article reporting on the latest Italian fashion show in August 1951 and titled "Italy Shows a New Trend in her Fashion Trade."[90]

The success of certain Italian fashion designers in the post-war years can be attributed to many factors. What emerges in the study of the relationship between North America and couturiers such as Simonetta is the fact that she agreed to sponsor, like many others such as Veneziani, Noberasko, Fabiani, and Pucci, all sorts of different products and lines. This included nylon socks, Cohama fabrics, underwear, and artificial and synthetic fibers.[91]

This consideration is twofold: the immediate success of designers such as Simonetta and Pucci in the post-war years exposed them to a visibility that was unprecedented for Italian designers and that contributed to the popularity of Italian fashion more widely. On the other hand, this overexposure might have been too much too soon for some of them. Journalist Gloria Braggiotti Etting reported in September 1951 on how the Italian "unspoiled designers said 'Yes' to anything anyone asked them," referring to the enthusiasm that followed the Grand Hotel's fashion show in Florence in August 1951.[92] This unquestioning consent might have contributed to the rapid disappearance of some of these designers' names. Indeed, the businesses of almost all the couturiers who were active and hugely popular in the early 1950s, apart from Emilio Pucci, were discontinued past the 1960s mark.

Most of the designers that made the "international jump," such as Vanna, Noberasko, Marucelli, Simonetta, Fabiani, and Mirsa, were also the ones that

Figure 2.2 A model wearing the "Cheese Basket" evening dress by Simonetta, photography by Henry Clarke, *Vogue UK*, September 1951, p. 103. Henry Clarke, British Vogue, © Condé Nast

regularly participated in Giorgini's and other fashion shows both in Italy and abroad. Giorgini was a buyer for many American department stores, including I. Magnin and B. Altman, and his first export office opened as early as 1923.[93] As demonstrated above, Giorgini catered mainly to the needs of the US market in the 1950s, therefore designers working with him were more likely to collaborate with American companies. Any deals sealed would benefit both the designers and Giorgini, since he was charging the buyers a commission of seven percent on every sale.[94] Doing business with American department stores was very lucrative as the case of the Rome-based menswear tailor Brioni illustrates. In 1952, Brioni's men's suits were paraded in the third *Sala Bianca* show, after their debut there in 1951, and gained international success. As a result, the New York department store B. Altman bought the whole evening collection, and the orders that followed the show increased the company's sales by 52 percent from 1951 to 1952.[95]

Italian fashion designers were keen on signing exclusivity deals and rights to reproduce and copy abroad as the case of Simonetta has shown. In Italy during the 1950s, no such deals existed, and textile producers, couturiers, and clothing manufacturers were fighting their corners. A 1954 report by Enzo Picone, a cultural clerk at the Italian Embassy in the USA during the *Congresso Internazionale della Moda, del Tessile dell Abbigliamento* (International Congress of Fashion, Textile, and Apparel) in Naples, candidly describes how Italian fashion had enjoyed the exclusive privilege of free advertisement in North America worth several dozen millions of dollars until the mid-1950s. This is followed by a warning that this tide was turning in 1954, and that it was therefore necessary to act quickly and coordinate efforts in order to preserve the advantages and privileges till then freely obtained.[96]

The early success of Italian fashion in the USA was in its infancy and, as the report above stresses, there was a need to institutionalize and consolidate the singular designers' advertising deals and success. This need is also expressed in the words of a journalist from Houston declaring in the early 1950s:

> Although 90% of the fabrics used by French designers are woven in Italy, the Italian original model prices are from 30 to 50% lower than the French. The next problem they are tackling is to increase production enough to make prices even lower so that original models may be sold here. Now the models are purchased primarily for copying.[97]

The quote highlights two key aspects when considering this period: the importance of the Italian textiles even in the French production of fashion, and issues related to copying and mass-production that will be examined further in the next section.

Ready-to-Wear versus Couture

As curator Andrew Bolton puts it: "Since its birth in the mid-nineteenth century, haute couture has been defined by the tension between the model and the multiple, between the original couture dress and the mass-produced copy."[98] Bolton explains that "this tension between originality and reproduction intensified between the years 1900 and 1929, a period that saw a rapid growth in the ready-to-wear industry and a concomitant growth in the department store." He describes how couturiers at the turn of the twentieth century employed strategies like those of fine artists to highlight the idea of the uniqueness of couture. These included featuring the couturier's signature on labels, giving names to dresses, and organizing mannequin parades.[99]

The tension described by Bolton was also notable in Italian fashion during the 1950s. A letter from Giorgini to Bernard Sakowitz presents a deal for an Italian manufacturer from Milan to export large quantities of ready-to-wear to the USA at competitive prices:

> Count Borletti, owner of "Rinascente" of Milan, has organized a wonderful factory with American machinery and they are now making dresses in American sizes designed by one of the leading dressmakers of Milan.

Giorgini states that he was impressed by the dresses and notes that the ones in Italian pure silk average at around 19 to 30 dollars in price. He then continues regarding the cotton dresses:

> I do not know if the cotton dresses may compete in prices with your home-made ones, but being imported, you would have special designs and colors which your competitors would not carry.[100]

The letter is very interesting because it reveals the intention of exporting large quantities of Italian ready-to-wear as early as 1953. Moreover, the letter concludes with the following: "Besides, having the Manufacturer a very large collection [*sic*] any model at our Florence Fashion Show could be copied by this Manufacturer in quantities, in all sizes at extremely low prices."[101] What is revealed here is extraordinary: while on one hand Giorgini was promoting Italian couture on the catwalk of the *Sala Bianca*, on the other he was also advertising to his clients in the USA Italian manufacturers such as the Rinascente who could directly copy and manufacture couture items, using Italian materials and American machinery, for the US market. This would have probably undermined Italian couturiers, especially if rights for reproducibility were not paid to them, but it would have benefited Italian textile manufacturers who would be guaranteed orders for hundreds of meters to satisfy American demands for high numbers.[102] This deal further highlights how Italian fashion, influenced and tooled by the USA, was developing its weaker side in the mass production of clothing.

Although it remains unclear whether Altman, Magnin, or Sakowitz ordered any of these ready-to-wear dresses, the fact that Giorgini offered such a deal demonstrates a change in the promotion of Italian fashion abroad and highlights the growing importance and desirability of Italian fashion design, which now almost equaled the established desirability of Italian-made fabrics.

The next section delves into the mechanisms of copying and translating original Italian garments and into the shifting relationship with their materiality as they moved from Italy to the USA.

Italian Originals, American Copies

Photographs and illustrations of the Simonetta Metropolitan Museum dress were published in 1951 in a number of American and Italian newspapers and magazines, demonstrating the circulation and success that this dress had among the press and buyers.[103]

In a *Town and Country* article titled "Florence in Fashion," the couturier herself is photographed full-page, modeling her dress and posing similarly to UK *Vogue*'s photograph of the same dress (Figure 2.3).[104] The dress appears again half sketched in an unidentified American article titled "Fashion" where the copy declares:

> At Bergdorf Goodman they're understandably proud of having secured a fashion collection, designed for themselves alone by Italy's Simonetta Visconti. The clothes are all made to order, of, of course, the most magnificent fabrics, and are to be had nowhere else.[105]

A further article from New York's *Herald Tribune* features a picture of Simonetta's cheese basket dress with the caption: "Short evening dress has checkerboard skirt of contrasting squares of shirred black velvet and plain jersey. By Simonetta Visconti. From a collection of Italian Imports at Bergdorf Goodman." The article explains that Bergdorf Goodman was ready with an edition of the recent fall fashion openings in France and Italy:

Figure 2.3 Simonetta Visconti wearing the "Cheese Basket" evening dress, *Town and Country*, September 1951, p. 138–176. Published in *Town & Country* magazine. Written by Gloria Braggiotti Etting. Photography by Jerome Zerbe.

Eighty-eight imports, hand-picked by Andrew Goodman, catch all the highest, youngest moments of the French and Italian designers. Many of them are exclusive with the store and will never come face-to-face with less expensive ready-to wear duplicates.[106]

This press coverage indicates that the department store Bergdorf Goodman acquired the exclusive rights to reproduce an original import designed and worn by Simonetta. According to journalist and writer Guido Vergani, this practice was carried through to 1952 when the collections of Fabiani and Simonetta were purchased outright by Bergdorf Goodman.[107] The original dress was probably imported into America and then, according to the orders, reproduced in a large number of copies.

A *WWD* article on Simonetta's collection gives further insight into the deal by specifying that the collection was "designed exclusively for their custom-order department" and that customers had the choice to request garments made in the original fabrics or choose domestic ones.[108] The option for the clients to select either Italian or American materials exposes an important shift in the relationship between Italian textiles and fashion. Italian couturiers were gradually gaining celebrity status, as illustrated by the numerous interviews, TV appearances, and profiles of Simonetta, including a full-page color portrait in *Vogue US*.[109] The predominance of Italian textiles in those years, which initially differentiated Italian fashion, started to make way for the emergence of the names of couturiers. Italian fashion did not suddenly substitute the allure of Italian textiles, but a shift in that direction happened in a slow and uneven manner. The coexistence of different practices of export and consumption of fashion and textiles is further demonstrated by the availability of thirty-five original garments from Simonetta's collection at Bergdorf Goodman: the stored planned to sell both originals and reproductions.

A series of drawings in the Bergdorf Goodman custom salon sketch folder in the Fashion Institute of Technology (FIT) archive in New York help clarify further the nature of the transactions between Italian couture and the American department stores. Among these drawings, signed mainly with the names of Italian couturiers such as Simonetta and Fabiani, a pink and cerise drawing inscribed Schuberth (Plate 5) is particularly informative.[110]

A comparison between this drawing and those produced by the Schuberth atelier demonstrates that the American sketch was not made by the same draftsperson who usually worked with the designers associated with the atelier in Italy.[111] Instead, its style is similar to other drawings marked Schuberth and many others marked Simonetta conserved in the same folder, which suggests a continuity of hand. All these drawings are fully executed and include details such as the model's hairdo, jewelry, gloves, and details of constructions, such as back shoulder straps.

These drawings were probably commissioned and designed in Italy and functioned as illustrations for reports on the couture collections that were sent to Bergdorf Goodman and became part of the company's internal records.[112] It is therefore possible that they were shown to clients of the department store as a catalog to survey the collection and select pieces in the absence of originals or ahead of their public display.

A Schuberth dress in the Metropolitan Museum of Art collection (Plate 5) bears striking similarities to the one depicted in the Bergdorf Goodman drawing, which is also portrayed in a black-and-white photograph published in *Harper's Bazaar UK* (Figure 2.4). The gradient pink to cerise silk fabric and the black lace decorations are identical. However, the cut and shape of both the skirt and the bodice are very different: the first dress features a full skirt and shoulder straps, while the second has a very narrow tailored skirt and is strapless. The Met dress bears the label "Emilio Schuberth, Roma," suggesting that it might have been ordered as an original through the Bergdorf Goodman couture department and modified at the request of a specific client.[113] This is indicative of the mediating role that the store's couture department played in the transatlantic "business of copies," on one hand commissioning drawings to report on the latest Italian shows, and on the other working with local clients to provide customized modifications of original pieces.

A *New York Herald Tribune* article from September 1951 reports on Italian couturier Micol Fontana showing her new fall collection in the US West Coast and explains that the orders she received in America would be made in Rome according to individual measurements. The house of Fontana was used to "this rarefied kind of custom mail-order business."[114] The Simonetta collection purchased by Bergdorf Goodman was similarly all made to order.[115] These examples show how Italian fashion garments could be bought in New York by American clients and still be hand-made in Italy. This gave American customers the opportunity to purchase originals without having to go to Rome in person. The department store experience was different from visiting a couturier's atelier in Italy, an exclusive practice which was limited to celebrities like Ava Gardner, who is known to have developed a very personal relationship with couturiers such as Sorelle Fontana. Department store custom-made purchases were probably less expensive, but they still retained a foreign allure and they were explicitly aimed at what *WWD* termed a "sophisticated audience whose wardrobe needs include many gala occasions and varied settings."[116]

It is worth noting that the Bergdorf Goodman copies of Simonetta's and other couturiers' designs, despite being reproductions, still retained a sense of exclusivity due to their connection with the "original" as previously discussed, but also because no cheap ready-to-wear copies were allowed for production. As proudly stated in the caption from the *New York Herald*'s article quoted above, such models were exclusive to the department store that sold them. This system was in place across North America, as demonstrated by a deal signed between

Genevieve Naylor

Italian Evenings

Shuberth (above) : the pinks of wine from *rosé* to deep claret
seen through grilles of black lace. The skirt, the new length—north
of the ankles—a buoyant, beautiful dress of lights
and shadows, a really remarkable sight on a dance floor.
Simonetta Visconti (opposite) : black taffeta and never before so much of it
in one evening dress, the bodice poured in thick folds,
the skirt, a terrace of wild roses spelled out in velvet. These intricate
dresses are the amazement of the Roman collections.

55

Figure 2.4 An Emilio Schuberth evening dress, *Harper's Bazaar UK*, November 1952, p. 55, photography by Genevieve Naylor, Genevieve Naylor/Courtesy of Hearst Magazines UK.

Simonetta and the Canadian department store Holt Renfrew for the exclusive rights to reproduce in Canada.[117]

These exclusive practices were, however, not the only ways through which Italian fashion garments could be obtained in the USA. As White explains, "It is apparent from *WWD* coverage, that from 1951, US ready-to-wear manufacturers (predominantly from Seventh Avenue) come to Italy in increasing numbers to buy both boutique and couture designs for translation and 'volume reproduction.'"[118] These models, once in North America, would be copied or, as the Americans described this procedure, "translated" for both mass production and the tastes of the US market. This usually meant simplifying the lines, and in many cases replacing natural and more expensive fabrics with more easily available and often synthetic ones. Such changes in material are well illustrated by the case of a Fabiani suit originally made in silk as shown at the Italian collective high-fashion show of July 1951 and documented in *Life* magazine, which was then translated into synthetics for the American market where it could be purchased for ninety dollars.[119] This kind of production is also in evidence in a 1951 advertisement by the Russek Designer Shop on Fifth Avenue at 36th Street that features Fabiani's Double Silhouette Dress for sixty-nine dollars nighty-five in crisp, black rayon taffeta faille, in sizes ten to sixteen.[120]

A further type of mass reproduction, described as "Literal American Translation," was available in a price bracket ranging from less than forty dollars to 150 dollars. This compared to European originals that would cost from 450 to 1,100 dollars.[121] The US department store Macy's referred to this type of reproduction as "line-for-line copies," as seen in the advertisement for a Simonetta Visconti line-for-line copy in black silk available in sizes ten to sixteen and costing sixty-four dollars and ninety-five cents.[122] The advertisement of cheaper copies indicates how couturiers like Simonetta did not reserve their creations for the upper-end markets, but also disseminated their brand names through cheaper mass-produced imitations targeted at the American middle class.

The Seventh Avenue ready-to-wear manufacturers who carried out the high-volume production of copies did not always change the fabrics to domestic and synthetic ones: they were also able to buy textiles from the Italian mills linked to the couturiers.[123] "Linked" in this context refers to agreements between textile manufacturers and couturiers whereby, for example, textiles would be provided for free to the designer and advertisements for the garment with the textile producer's name would be paid for by the textile manufacturers. Such arrangements served to associate the Italian textile producer with the allure of a couturier's name, and American industrialists often emphasized this prestige in advertisements of their American "'translated" models.[124]

Finally, US department stores could also purchase Italian textiles and produce garments in the USA without a specific designer in mind. A letter from Sakowitz to Giorgini illustrates this practice as he requests, in relation to the pure silk fabric he purchased in Milan: "Please place the order for delivery as soon as possible as it is our intention to manufacture shirts with this fabric in New York."[125] An article from *WWD* also highlights this in its report:

> Fabrics will get the bulk of money spent in Italy. Most manufacturers and designers have been at the fabrics centers before coming to Florence and others plan to visit them before taking off for Paris. One Seventh Avenue coat man declares he has spent $40,000 for fabrics alone for the next spring's line.[126]

Arrangements such as the one between Simonetta and Bergdorf Goodman probably had a time limit, as demonstrated by an article in the May 1953 issue of *WWD*.[127] Here, the model Illiria Pompilli is once again parading the Simonetta dress in Chicago, but this time alongside Italian menswear and womenswear made by Bartlay Ltd. for Jerrems clothing. The durability of this copy demonstrates how a dress originally created in the 1950s could still be reproduced, photographed, and commercialized three years later in a different American city by a different department store. The longevity of this type of design is testament to the long-lasting appeal of the Italian couturiers' names.

The in-depth study of the "cheese basket" dress, as it was also known, and of its copies, has shown a complex and multileveled engagement between American department stores, mass producers, and Italian original designs. As we have seen, Italian originals were copied in the USA as part of an institutionalized system in which various levels of reproduction coexisted without necessarily competing with one another, as they catered to different types of customers. A picture reproduced in *WWD* which shows representatives of high-fashion stores, big volume retailers, and Italian couturiers posing together in Florence attests to the openness about such arrangements in Italy.[128]

The Value of Copies

In the case of clothing, normally the translation or copy was aimed at adapting garments to different tastes and body shapes, and it was a practice regulated by US government standard pattern measurements. However, Alberto Fabiani and other Italian designers sometimes also designed patterns for American seamstresses in a different way: instead of adhering to standard patterns, the sizes were cut to their own measurements, which were probably based on Italian sizes.[129] Such practice shows how American clients could be exposed to different, more European, ways of fitting garments.

The US fashion industry openly copied Italian fashion, but at the same time dictated, through its buying power and the profitable practice of mass producing original Italian designs, a type of fashion that would be easier to copy. In this way they almost "imposed" a style upon the Italian designers who were eager to sell to the lucrative American market.

This section has established the circumstances and characteristics of the Italian–North American copy–translation business. This practice could be described as the production of what I term "valuable copies" because of their monetary value and legitimacy, and in order to distinguish them from what could be called "clandestine copies" which were not regulated by an agreed system and were therefore illegal. The matter of copies was not a new one in nascent Italian fashion, and it worked in both directions. As previously mentioned, Italian couturiers looked to France for inspiration in order to meet the demands of their domestic clientele. This practice, although forbidden by the Fascist regime, picked up again at the end of the Second World War and filled columns of French and Italian newspapers with news of arrests and conspiracies of Italians spying on the French couture shows to illegally copy their creative models.[130]

On the domestic front, Italian couture houses were very attentive to how their original models were photographed and shown as a preventative measure for the risk of illegal copies by the *confezione* (Italian mass production) and other couturiers. One letter in particular reveals how the distinction between what I described as a "valuable copy" as opposed to a "clandestine one" manifested in the Italian fashion system. Dated January 13, 1951 and addressed to Giorgini, it confirms the participation of the Sorelle Fontana atelier, along with the other Roman houses of Schuberth and Carosa, in the collective fashion show organized for North American buyers in his house in February 1951. In the letter, the couturiers specify two conditions: first, at least seven or eight buyers of American houses would have to be present at the show; and second, journalists, photographers, and other Italian observers who were interested in Italian fashion would have to be excluded from both days of showing.[131]

The second condition highlights how the Italian domestic fashion system, unlike the American one, was not regulated enough to prevent unapproved or illegal copies of original designs. The Fontanas knew that the Americans would pay for both their original creations and for rights to reproduce them. An article by renowned Italian journalist Elsa Robiola also points to these distinctions, as she explains how the Italian fashion collections of 1951 were inaugurated earlier in the year than the usual presentations of fashion.[132] Robiola reveals that the Giorgini fashion show was kept secret at the request of the American buyers to enable them to export the dresses to America before the press and public were informed. After this secret preview, the normal fashion show took place in March and was documented in the press as usual. This meant that the press and public were only able to see the dresses months after they were made. This delay had a double aim. On one hand, Italian *confezione* could not illegally copy couture garments before they were exported to America, and on the other hand Italian models were shown at the same time as the French couture, and therefore could not be derivative copies of French models. This meant that American buyers had the reassurance that could buy some of the best and original European production. Toward the end of the article, Robiola puts forward an important question about the difference between models made for the American market and those produced for Italian use, but suggests that at that stage, the experiment was too small for its impact to be assessed. We now know, as seen above, that in the long run the experiment had a significant impact on both Italian and American fashion output.

The starting point for this case study was the Simonetta short evening dress in the Met collection. The so-called cheese basket dress is made of natural textiles such as silk velvet and sheer wool. It was "Made in Italy," as indicated by the label attached within it, and was probably produced using Italian silk.[133] It is therefore most likely an "original" that came from Italy in 1951, either purchased directly by the donor in Italy or bought from a range of originals on sale at Bergdorf Goodman.[134] Irrespective of the details of its biography, from the moment it was created to the moment it reached the Met collection, the dress offers through its materiality a valuable means to understand the "translation" business between Italy and the USA and its influence on the future development of Italian fashion.

The first part of this book has highlighted contrasts and extremes that coexisted in the 1950s Italian fashion system. Through an analysis of the core material of fashion, namely fibers and textiles, it has demonstrated how post-war Italy was Janus-faced not only in its relationship to modernity, but also within its fashion and textile industries. The coexistence of craft, hand-made, and couture, along with the drive toward reproducibility fueled by the success of boutique fashion and the transatlantic business of copies highlighted through the Simonetta case study, has presented a complex and multifaceted Italian textile and fashion manufacturing industry.

This complex layering was also carried through in the combination of natural and artificial materials which were often used in the same piece of textile or promoted alongside each other, as seen with SNIA Viscosa's promotion strategy for its synthetic fibers. A study of the goods presented at the exhibition *Italy at Work* proved that the USA was mainly interested in acquiring textiles new to them, such as hemp and other natural fibers. However, as seen in the discussion of the business of copies, when translating original couture Italian garments, Seventh Avenue manufacturers often replaced natural materials with synthetic and artificial ones.

Right after the end of the Second World War, it was Italian textiles, rather than Italian fashion, that first offered a way for Italy to step out of France's dominance. At the same time, the American export market, with its influence and buying power, played a decisive role in determining what Italian fashion designers and textile manufacturers were producing. The investigation into *alta moda* and its boutique equivalent mainly created for the American export market has presented an important precedent of mass-produced quality garments to the Italian ready-to-wear trend that would explode in the 1980s.

The Simonetta case study has put forward the challenges presented to Italy's textile manufacturers by the transatlantic business of copies, whereby Italy's fashion designs could be easily copied in the USA using local synthetic fabrics that were not made in Italy to create a cheaper hybrid. Further research into transatlantic exchanges, however, also showed how Italian textiles were simultaneously being sold to Seventh Avenue manufacturers with no connection to Italian fashion design. These various relationships complicate the idea of "Made in Italy," notably challenging the notion of Italian fashion as mainly associated with natural Italian textile and fibers.

It has been shown how Italian manufacturers used innovative strategies to promote their textiles, including pay-per-mention arrangements at fashion shows and free advertising through American department stores. While these initiatives were not part of a formal strategy, Chapter 3 will show how, through the *Camera Nazionale della Moda Italiana*, a clearer plan was later devised to organize the Italian fashion and textile industries, with the Italian fashion–Italian textiles combination presented as the winning formula to promote a unified Italian system.

3

The 1960s, a Decade of Metamorphosis in Italian Fashion

Introduction

In a double-page spread published in American *Vogue* in October 1967, seven models descend the iconic Spanish Steps in Rome wearing creations made by seven Italian couturiers: Lancetti, Galitzine, Forquet, Antonelli, Fabiani, Sorelle Fontana, and Carosa. The captions name the types of textiles used, as well as details of the textile companies that made them or commercialized them such as Faudella, Nattier, Gandini, and SANET, including the names of the cities where they were based, such as Turin and Milan. The bold photograph with vivid hues depicts a young and fiery image of Italy, fully in tune with international fashion codes.[1]

The use of Rome's iconic Spanish Steps as the backdrop for these modern and colorful outfits shows once more how Italy's heritage was used to promote Italian products abroad. Compared to earlier black-and-white Italian fashion photographs which used the national historical setting of the 1950s, this image, with its bright colors and low perspective, offers a modern image of the 1960s Italian fashion system. The models were not only observed by the magazine readers, but they were also scrutinized by a large group of bystanders visible at the edge of the picture. The presence of this audience suggests the theatricality and the staging of the photoshoot and how the location was consciously used to promote the new system.[2]

The models in their dynamic poses gaze down at the viewers, confidently occupying the center of the frame. This image, as with other similar photographs created in the 1950s, still relies on the allure of *alta moda* as an ambassador of Italy's taste and beauty. However, now the names of textile producers, as well as *carnettisti* (a type of wholesaler discussed in detail in Chapter 4) such as SANET and Nattier, are placed beside the names of the couturiers, some of which had already been famous for a decade, such as Alberto Fabiani and the Sorelle Fontana.

However, in this chapter the couturiers are no longer the subject of the investigation. New forms of production that combined industrial manufacture and *alta moda* were emerging to accommodate the rise of different types of consumers: for example, the new industrial working class, young students, and even children. Developments such as industrialization, migration, and increased disposable income for the working class were factors that contributed to make a wider slice of the population more fashion-conscious.[3] These new consumers viewed *alta moda* as a desirable product, but turned to mass-produced garments to express their fashionability. The buying power of the new consumers encouraged various players in the fashion industry to cater to their needs: these included magazines, TV shows, and manufacturers such as the *Gruppo Finanziario Tessile* (Financial Textile Group, GFT), who in 1965 opened alongside their other lines a fashion range aimed at younger consumers called *Ventanni* ("twenty years old"). I will analyze some of the factors that contributed to this rise in fashion consumption; the agency of these new players is important and needs to be taken into consideration. However, it will not be the main focus of this chapter. I will instead focus more on this decade's experiments in new types of mass production, such as *alta moda pronta*, boutique fashion, and ready-to-wear (*confezione*), and how these were challenging *alta moda*'s undiscussed leadership. These were new ways of collaboration between industry and *alta moda* that laid the foundations, in the 1970s and 1980s, for the new powerhouse of Italian *prêt-à-porter*.

Although fashion exports were important for Italy in this decade, the domestic market also began to grow and take shape. It is therefore critical to investigate how the domestic market operated. As the caption of the image discussed above showed, more players, such as textile manufacturers and wholesalers, were coming into the limelight, and their role needs to be assessed.

This chapter provides an overview of the years from 1958 to 1972 and gives examples of innovative collaboration between *alta moda* and industry. Furthermore, a case study of Cleonice Capece investigates a first attempt to combine ready-to-wear with the allure of a designer at the helm.

The period between 1958 and 1972 is characterized by the expansion of the embryonic Italian textile and fashion industries. In the 1950s these were still in a phase of experimentation. Their rise culminated in the 1970s—"the decade of consolidation," as Economic historian Elisabetta Merlo describes it—which saw "Milan emerging as the new fashion capital" and the establishment of an Italian fashion system with industrial and economic significance.[4]

The years between 1958 and 1963 have been traditionally defined as the Italian "economic boom."[5] In this period, the Italian Gross Domestic Product

(GDP) reached 6.5 percent of growth and 8 percent for the industry, a historic record for Italian economic development. In this five-year period, exports grew by 14.5 percent and, more importantly, private domestic demand grew by more than 8 percent in 1963, thanks also to increases in salaries.[6] New products such as cars, motorbikes, white goods, and fashion represented a new material culture, and played a crucial role in building new identities. As consumption historian Emanuela Scarpellini explains, "material culture plays an important part in constructing new identities and materializing values and behaviors, becoming the means of determining how one relates to society and tries to be part of it."[7]

However, historian Silvio Lanaro prefers to define this period as an acceleration rather than an economic boom, and the result of an expansive process already started around 1951–2. The changes that transformed Italy in this period were the result of earlier phenomena that continued to produce their effects until the 1970s.[8]

Writing in 2011, Scarpellini reminds us how this period is presented by researchers and journalists as a sort of golden age, in contrast with contemporary sources which had a different tone. These were also the years of mass immigration, with its consequences of unpleasant living conditions and speculative building. Scarpellini's analyses of Italian family consumption rates conclude that the Italian "miracle" came later than in other European countries, and that when it did arrive it was selective, since it did not apply to all levels of the population. Therefore, "at the 'height' of the miracle, it was the middle class that made great leaps in consumption, while many urban and rural workers were largely excluded."[9]

Both the economic continuities and the radical economic shifts between the 1950s and 1960s, and the coexistence of different cultures of consumption, can be traced in the development of the textile and fashion systems during this period. Despite academic disagreement over the nature of the socioeconomic shifts that occurred in the late 1950s and 1960s, it is still clear that they had a big effect on fashion. As Italian economic historians such as Ivan Paris note, the 1960s were a crucial decade for the rising Italian fashion industry in ways that were fundamentally different from the fifties.[10] The innovations and changes developed in the sixties brought the country to establish a fashion system both vertically and horizontally integrated; an "authentic fashion system" as he defined it, as we will see in Chapter 5. Paris describes these as the years of the metamorphosis of Italian fashion, when the increase of demand triggered changes that profoundly impacted supply.[11] Merlo is also convinced that the mid-1950s and the 1960s were crucial years in the history of Italian ready-made clothing. Many firms modified their production. For example, textile producers

Marzotto and Lanerossi became a vertically integrated producer of clothing, a term that describes how the supply chain was owned by the same companies that were producing the final garments. Furthermore, ready-to-wear manufacturers Max Mara and Lubiam became synonymous with industrial manufacturing, and even small firms ventured into the clothing business.[12]

The year 1959 became the symbol for the start of a new era in Italy, rather than the closure of a decade. Between 1958 and 1962 fashion production rose to represent 17 percent of all the country's manufacturing activity, becoming a very important player in the Italian production system. By 1965 the clothing industry was responsible for 56 percent of all Italian consumption; a decade earlier the proportion was only 22 percent.[13]

American fashion trade magazine *Women's Wear Daily* reported in 1962 that the annual growth in Italian apparel was estimated at 25 to 30 percent, the highest among western countries. It was thought that the reason for this fast development was connected more to "booming exports rather than the rising of the domestic demands."[14] By the end of the 1960s, alongside the increase in importance of the export market, the domestic market also started to become significant.

Treaty of Rome and Export

From January 1, 1958, the Treaty of Rome, which was ratified the year before, started removing customs barriers between European countries. On the one hand, this opened markets such as France to easily exported Italian goods. On the other hand, it put Italy in direct competition with European countries, such as Germany, which, especially in the field of clothing manufacturing, were much more technologically advanced and streamlined in their production processes, and therefore could offer their clothing at lower prices. Ginsborg believes that the Italian industry had now reached such a level of technological development, and differentiation in the production of a range of goods, that it was in a position to react positively to the Common Market.[15]

As Ginsborg reports, in the so-called miracle years between 1958 and 1963, "export became a driving sector behind expansion with an average increase of 14 percent per annum." The role of the Common Market in this growth is clear: the percentage of Italian goods exported to the EEC increased from 23 percent in 1955, to 29.8 percent in 1960, to 40.2 percent in 1965.[16] Furthermore, a 1961 dossier on Italian exports produced by the magazine L'*Abbigliamento Italiano* reported that between 1958 and 1960 the value of Italian exports of ready-to-wear and knitwear to EEC member states increased by more than 130 percent.[17] As early as 1958 the CNMI was also seeking to quantify export outputs and its foundation document highlighted that the value of exports was around five hundred billion lire, of which two hundred billion were earned from textiles.[18] This data shows that export-driven sales were substantial in this decade and need to be taken into consideration when valuing fashion and textile production and output.

The *Camera Nazionale della Moda Italiana* (CNMI) and the Promotion of High Fashion

This period also saw an intensification of the activities of the CNMI, which was established in 1958 as the *Camera Sindacale della Moda Italiana* (Union Chamber of Italian Fashion). This body was created by the same group of couturiers who joined Giorgini's venture in Florence in 1951, discussed in Chapter 2. However, this new entity, created on the model of the *Chambre Syndicale de la Couture Parisienne*, was inactive until 1962. That year the name was changed to *Camera Nazionale della Moda Italiana* to mark its changed aims; the CNMI then started to organize multiple national efforts and to promote Italian fashion in collaboration with parliament, government, ministers, public bodies, and trade associations.[19]

The CNMI strategy was to organize a close relationship between the textile sector and all the other fashion players, with *alta moda* and its original creations at the helm. This was justified because *alta moda*, with its history and the fact that it successfully challenged the traditional hegemony of French fashion, was recognized as the sector that opened doors internationally for other fashion ventures to flourish.[20] The CNMI relied on a certain idea of the "trickle down" theory by economist Thorstein Veblen. In his 1889 book, *The Theory of the Leisure Class*, Veblen regards fashion as a phenomenon generated between innovators and imitators, in which the newly affluent imitate the original styles of the upper class. Furthermore, the CNMI based its action on the premise that the international success of Italian *alta moda* influenced the success of the Italian textile industry.[21] Therefore, the duo of Italian fashion and Italian textiles was considered to be the natural combination for a swift development and domination of the foreign markets.[22] The CNMI's official document that set out this vision highlighted how the Italian internal market had a problem of domestic distribution.[23] Although no further details were given, this clearly hinted at the activities of the *carnettisti*, their role and the complex mechanisms of production they were responsible for, as we will see in Chapter 4.

The CNMI set out to "elevate the quality of textile production and strengthen Italian high fashion."[24] It therefore promoted convergence between the textile and *alta moda* sectors, through several initiatives: among them, the establishment of a fashion design prize; the coordination of advertising between the two sectors; and the requirement that *alta moda* use at least 50 percent of Italian textiles in their seasonal output. These ideas were intended to have three effects: first, to spur the Italian textile industry to devote at least a part of their quality production to the Italian high-fashion sector; second, to establish a stricter connection between textile manufacturers and couturiers so that they could guide their respective productions; and third, to help finance the *alta moda* houses to acquire high-quality fabrics and therefore drive national and international promotion.

These endeavors were developed under the auspices of the *Ministero del Commercio con l'Estero* (Italian Minister of Trade and Foreign Affairs), while the prize was managed by the *Mercato Internazionale del Tessile per l'Abbigliamento e l'Arredamento* (International Market for Furnishing and Fashion Fabrics, MITAM). The latter consisted of a total prize of eighty million lire to allocate to the best women's fashion designs presented to national and international press and buyers. Eligible designs had to be made exclusively with Italian textiles. No single fashion house could receive more than three million lire in prize money. A key part of the prize stipulation was that the link between textile producers and fashion houses had to be mentioned in every phase of presentation, description, promotion, and sale of the outfits.[25]

However, this promotional plan, as admitted by the CNMI itself in 1966, proved difficult to carry out, because it came after "decades of complete disorganization during which had been accumulated misunderstandings, polemics, mistrust."[26] As we will see in Chapter 4, the Italian fashion system in the 1960s was a complex network of companies, institutions, and players. The CNMI's efforts did not always result in immediate changes and success, but they set the basis for a more unified system in the 1970s, as Chapter 5 will investigate.

It would be restrictive to think that the CNMI had the strength to command such deep changes in the Italian fashion and textile panorama on its own. It must be considered that other agents helped to drive change. Changes were commended by an interaction between production, the mediation of such institutions as the CNMI, and the demands of consumption.

New Ways of Production, with New Products and New Ways of Consumption

Outside Italy, especially in the USA, Germany, and other more industrially advanced nations, mass production of women's clothing had begun in the middle of the nineteenth century. Even after the Second World War, there was scarce production of women's ready-to-wear in Italy, although the male counterpart was already available. As highlighted in Chapter 2, in the 1950s made-to-measure was still the mainstream method of clothing production in Italy. Fashion historian Rietta Messina argues that even in 1959 the Italian ready-to-wear industry was less developed than that of other European countries. Italy was only mass-producing one-and-a-half million women's dresses while the Netherlands was producing four million, France twenty million, and Germany twenty-seven million.[27]

Although the CNMI believed *alta moda* had to be promoted as the pinnacle of taste, Ivan Paris states that the course of change in the 1960s was set not by *alta moda* but by the industrial mass-production sector, and by advances that pre-date the decade.[28] He identifies two innovations originating in the period before the Second World War that facilitated change in the 1960s: the development of ready-to-wear and advances in synthetic fibers. These had the effect of "radically transforming the traditional character of the textile and clothing industry."[29] This was the case with the ready-to-wear company Max Mara, based in Reggio Emilia. In the period from 1951 to 1965 Max Mara was sourcing its fabrics from Italian companies. However, initially the fabrics produced were not suitable for industrially mass-produced clothing. Max Mara's problem was that the delicate fabrics manufactured in Italy were not suitable for the new industrial steam press.[30] As textile producer Roberto Sarti explained, in the 1950s the textile manufacturers were catering mainly to dressmakers and couturiers who created made-to-measure garments by hand or with sewing machines. With the advent of ready-to-wear and its mechanized industrial system, the textiles were undergoing a heavier treatment under industrial steam machines that could shrink the wool cloth by two or three percent, impacting on the size of the garments. In response, the textile industry adapted to produce a new "stabilized cloth" which would not shrink in the steam.[31]

By 1959, consumers were fully supportive of both synthetic fibers and ready-to-wear, as demonstrated by a consumer survey that indicated the public preferred "skirts made from synthetic fibers as opposed to those made from wool, silk and linen."[32] Additionally, Italian expenditure on ready-to-wear apparel grew by more than 30 percent in the course of the decade and its ready-to-wear production at the end of the 1950s equaled two million units.[33] This consumer direction emphasized how mass production was taking over the center stage previously occupied by *alta moda*.[34]

Textile historian Margherita Rosina notes that in this period there was a split at the production level in terms of the type of fabrics used: on the one hand silk production for *alta moda*, and on the other hand, synthetic fibers such as Lilion, Rhodainzino, and Rilsan nylon as well as Lurex and Terital (also known as Terylene) for the nascent *prêt-à-porter*.[35] However, *alta moda* houses, both Italian and from other countries such as Germany, the UK, and Switzerland, participated in shows organized to promote the use of the new, modern fibers. *Alta moda* was experimenting with new materials and not relying only on silk. An example of this, separate from events organized in the 1950s and discussed in Chapter 1, comes from the event set up by the *Centro Internazionale delle Arti e del Costume* (CIAC) of Palazzo Grassi in Venice, from September 8 to 11, 1960. Entitled "Images of a Century," this was a play that told the story of the technological advances and changes in the last century that had transformed everyday life, such as the telephone, the first flight, and the phonograph. Among these there was the invention of rayon, the first artificial fiber, which in 1889 was introduced into the clothing world. A fashion show followed the play, consisting entirely of dresses in new fibers. The names of couturiers who participated were Capucci, Fabiani, Fercioni, and Veneziani Antonelli, as well as leaders of English high fashion Frederick Worth, Norman Hartnell, and Hardy Amies.[36]

The *Sala Bianca*, which was traditionally associated only with *alta moda*, started to adopt new strategies to develop links between Italian *alta moda* and the apparel industry. On October 13, 1962, during a meeting between representatives of these two sectors, it was decided that, starting in January 1963, the Italian industrialists (*confezionisti*) could attend the Palazzo Pitti fashion shows.[37] This marked a change of tendency compared to the early 1950s when Italian *confezionisti* were banned or discouraged from attending the catwalks in the *Sala Bianca* in favor of buyers from overseas (as seen in Chapter 2). This was because it was feared that Italian manufacturers would copy the couturiers' designs illegally without paying royalties. A decade later, as the system was regulated by the CNMI, the industrialists were encouraged to participate and, from March 1963, to forecast trends for the following seasons. In July 1964, the list of buyers at the *Sala Bianca* fashion show included the usual buyers from North America, Great Britain, Japan, Germany, and Switzerland, as well as Italian buyers from clothing manufacturers and retailers such as Cori, Max Mara,

Rosier, Rinascente, and Pirelli Confezioni. Pirelli, a company today mostly associated purely with rubber tires, had been producing overcoats, capes, and military uniforms alongside haberdashery and medical supplies since 1877.[38]

The privileging of these industrialists over overseas buyers attested to a growing domestic market. This move was also connected to the fact that, later in the 1960s, the fashion shows at Palazzo Pitti became more and more associated with boutique fashion and ready-to-wear. As will be shown in Chapter 5, the new protagonists who emerged at the beginning of the 1970s were the clothing manufacturers working in collaboration with fashion designers, in what became known from 1978 as the Italian *prêt-à-porter*.

During the sixties consumers of mass-produced objects took into consideration factors including price, material characteristics such as fabric and cut, and adherence to the high-fashion trends of Paris, Florence, and Rome, as part of a desire to project social values through clothing. An increased awareness of fashion, also gleaned through a wider readership of fashion magazines and television shows and the increased industrialization of *alta moda* production that made available luxury and fashionable garments to a wider slice of the population, all played a role in what has been defined as the "democratization of luxury." Here luxury means fashionable garments in conformity with prevailing trends and image content that equaled the embodiment of lifestyle suggested by the garment's designer.[39]

Paris states that "the centrality of demand, in the form of new consumers and modes of consumption, was a determining factor in the radical transformation of the Italian Fashion Industry."[40] Migration played a big role in these shifts. Aside from migration overseas to Australia and the USA and to Europe, mainly to Switzerland and Germany, between 1955 and 1971 around nine million Italians were interregional migrants. Many of these people were moving from rural areas to industrial cities, such as Milan and Turin.[41] In this context of national changes, Italians also transformed their mores, cultures, and family life, and the population used their growing income to buy consumer durable goods for the first time.[42]

Paris believes that even at the beginning of the 1960s the Italian clothing industry, both mass production and *alta moda*, lacked the understanding to react effectively to contemporary socioeconomic changes.[43] I would suggest that this is also because institutions such as the CNMI continued to see *alta moda* as the point of reference of the market, on which all the other sectors, such as textile and mass manufacturers had to "depend."[44] The CNMI, which aimed to defend and develop Italian fashion as an economic sector, believed that *alta moda*, with its prestige, tradition, and original creations, had to lead all the other strands of the wider sector of fashion and apparel.[45] This approach assumed that the upper classes, the only people able to afford couture, would "dictate" the direction of the Italian fashion system in a Veblen manner. Another implication of the CNMI's aims was the assumption that only *alta moda* created original pieces. This assumption of superiority of the craft and artisanal products implied that the industry of mass production could not lead on creativity. This was reinforced by a habit that persisted in some strata of the population during the sixties, to go back to the dressmaker and obtain a hand-made special piece to add to one's wardrobe.

However, *alta moda* was not always the product the new emerging consumers wanted or could afford. This challenged the entrenched hierarchy. As Scarpellini highlights, this period in Italy also saw the rise of a "revolution fashion" or anti-fashion. With these terms, she referred to fashion trends made popular by a variety of youth subcultures, mainly of foreign origins such as the beatniks, the yé-yé, hippies, mods, and teddy boys. These youth movements came with their specific fashion codes that challenged the middle-class fashion system and embraced clothing as a new way of expressing their personalities and beliefs.[46]

Some of these tendencies found their apex in the iconic boutiques that opened in these years in Milan and Rome. These new retail spaces tended to feature innovative shop designs and they often mixed Italian-designed ready-made garments with imports of products from abroad, mainly inspired by the fashion tendency in London and Paris. They were located mainly in Milan—such as Cose, Gulp!, La Drogheria Solferino, Carnaby Street, and Fiorucci—but also in Viareggio where a boutique selling miniskirts, handbags, and scarves by Paco Rabanne, Cacharel, and others was placed inside the Piper discotheque.[47]

Industry and *Alta Moda*

In this panorama in which industry and *alta moda* were mainly divided and working on parallel lines, new ventures and ways of producing that attempted to bridge the gap were undertaken in various part of Italy.[48] I will explore here a sample of three different types of experimentations: the GFT–Biki agreement; the Sorelle Fontana-owned factory for *alta moda pronta*; and Brioni's industrialized craftsmanship. These examples highlight different ways of collaborating between designers and manufacturers, a collaboration that Merlo defines as "one of the pillars of the Italian fashion's ascendance to international standing."[49] As we have seen in Chapter 1, a sporadic dialogue between fashion designers and textile and clothing manufacturers had started in the 1950s. In the 1960s such ventures continued to evolve and, as we will see in this section, took on a different shape. They did not always last for a long time: when the political, social, and productive environment changed, they became obsolete.

The pioneer was the GFT–Biki project. In 1957 the Milan couturier Biki, who had established her brand in the city in 1934, partnered with Turin-based industrial textile and clothing manufacturer GFT. Biki was associated with the allure of Milanese high society and was well known for her close relationship with the Greek opera soprano Maria Callas.[50] Her glamorous creations for the famous singer, with the high quality of the materials and precise tailoring, made these garments that the opera star wore off stage very exclusive.

The fact that such an accomplished and renowned couturier signed a deal with a mass manufacturer is indicative of a certain shift toward integration between industry and creativity. However, in 1957 there were no standard procedures in place: the roles and responsibilities of the two parties were defined as a work-in-progress and changed through the years. In 1957, according to the first deal with GFT, Biki was responsible for designing a number of sketches for garments that might subsequently be mass produced by GFT. The industrialist would then select some sketches to prototype and those suitable would be produced on an industrial scale using GFT fabrics.

In this first stage, twelve sketches were prototyped and five were produced. However, these were put into production without having been previously tailored by Biki. This meant less input from Biki into the final garment, which would have resulted in a lack of wearability. This happened because, according to Merlo, the couturier was not keen on working in her atelier on designs that would subsequently be mass produced by others. Such an attitude testified to the belief that industry and *alta moda* were still two separate entities.

This deal continued up to 1959, during which time Biki designed five collections in this way. The agreement was modified in 1960 to add, on top of the designer's creativity, also her name. Therefore, each product made by GFT featured a label stating "model designed by Biki for Cori," where Cori stood for Confezioni Rivetti, the owners of GFT. This contract lasted only one year as Biki wanted to renegotiate the terms; she felt the deal did not adequately take into consideration the fact that the Cori line was benefiting from her fame. She then proposed to be involved in the manufacturing process with her son-in-law and the co-designer of her lines, Alain Reynauld. The couturier had probably understood that there was much profit to be gained if she was involved in the production. After Biki, more Italian couturiers got involved with industry and this practice slowly started to be considered a normal way of working rather than the exception.[51]

In response to the designer's requests, Rivetti increased the minimum number of prototypes they would buy from Biki and agreed to pay for the use of Biki's name with three percent of the Cori–Biki line revenues. However, the involvement in production did not last long, and GFT continued producing the Cori–Biki line in a way that the couturier thought poorly represented her *alta moda* creations.[52] In different forms, the deal continued until 1972.

This was one of the earliest experiments undertaken to regenerate Italian women's ready-to-wear clothing.[53] Merlo, in her analysis of the GFT–Biki association, argues that although this was a milestone in the relationship between fashion and industry, it was not a commercial success.[54] She believes one of the reasons for failure was that the Cori–Biki style was not considered fashionable by clients. Furthermore, GFT's attitude of not entirely involving the designers in the manufacturing process, and therefore not fully exploiting Biki's creativity, resulted in concentrating on mass production aspects such as standardization and the sizing system rather than on working toward customizing the industrial product with the aid of a couturier, to make it more appealing.[55] The results of this collaboration can been seen in an advertisement in the magazine *Amica*.[56] Here it is evident that the glamour associated with Biki's *alta moda* creations did not necessarily translate into the GFT garments. The Cori–Biki coat seen in the editorial, was not fitted and was worn quite loose on the wearer without highlighting her figure. Despite the striking difference between the Biki for *alta moda* and the Biki for GFT, the collaboration with the industry made previously very exclusive designs available to a wider public, making luxury seem more available and therefore democratic. The move of couturiers toward the industry can be ascribed, among other factors, to the new middle-class and working-class demand in this decade.

Although, as Merlo states, "the partnership … never really worked," this archetypal relationship formed the basis for the 1970s collaborations between GFT and designers such as Emanuel Ungaro and Giorgio Armani, which have been considered by many to mark the start of the Italian *prêt-à-porter*'s success, as we will see in Chapter 5. While in the association with Biki her creativity was considered only on a marketing level, in the partnerships that followed there was deeper collaboration, and GFT transformed "from a production-driven company into a designer-driven business."[57]

Following the Cori–Biki partnership, more and more ready-to-wear experimentations sprung up through the country. In Rome in 1966 the couturiers

Sorelle Fontana started the *Fontana Alta Moda Pronta* (Fontana ready-made couture), a ready-to-wear production in Cecchina, near Rome. Thanks to funds from the *Cassa del Mezzogiorno* (Fund for the South), three hundred workers were employed in the automated system of production of garments that applied "American production practice using Italian Necchi sewing machines and complex patterns."[58]

In the television show *Linea Contro Linea* aired in October 1967, the Sorelle Fontana extensively illustrated the difference between couture and ready-made couture. One of the sisters compares *alta moda* garments with similar ones produced for the couture ready-to-wear. The same tweed textile was employed for both ensembles. However, with a shorter length, fewer seams and details, the "*alta moda pronta*" garment, reproduced in hundreds, if not thousands of copies, would cost the consumer a third of the price of the more refined *alta moda* garment.[59]

The Sorelle Fontana *alta moda* creations version is shown being paraded in the sisters' traditional salon, which recalls in its style a French haute couture atelier. One of the sisters, talking to a renowned actress, highlights how *alta moda pronta* and *alta moda* catered to different types of women, with different needs and economic means. The Fontana stress how it had become necessary to industrialize *alta moda* as it was fundamental to redistribute the high cost of research and design of the *alta moda* collections not only to the few exclusive clients that could afford it, but to the ready-to-wear realm.

The film has a cutaway, and from the elegant salon the viewers are catapulted onto the Sorelle Fontana's factory floor where machines and employees are seen working at the pace of a faster and robotic music. Here the technical characteristics of the ready-to-wear versions are unpicked. The way in which the ready-to-wear garments are described is all to do with finding ways to reduce the number of hours of work, and therefore decrease their prices. The juxtaposition of the glamour of the atelier, with its unique creations with a higher price tag, and the efficiency of mass production and consequent availability of the garments for a wider clientele, aptly stresses the tension between the two types of production.

The fact that such a program was aired on television, at a time of rising TV ownership, suggests the will to expose Italian TV viewers to a new kind of product: one not hand-made but instead machine-made.[60] In this context, the industrial product was not demonized, but instead accepted and promoted as a vital aspect of a new kind of society. At the same time, although machine-made, it was associated with the allure of a quality product via the prestige of the Sorelle Fontana, traditionally known for their couture output.

Despite the encouraging outlook and the Sorelle Fontana plant producing more than two hundred dresses daily, the venture closed in 1972. This, according to fashion historian Cinzia Capalbo, was caused both by the Italian economic crisis and by union protests.[61] As we will see in more detail in Chapter 5, production-line workers were coming together to demand fairer treatment, and they took control of the factories.[62] For small enterprises in particular, which could not afford to stop production for a long period, such as the fashion enterprises of the Sorelle Fontana and Cleonice Capece, this had the consequence of closing down their workshops and factories.[63]

In the menswear sector, Brioni represented a successful example of merging the quality of couture with industrial organization. In so doing the company increased the growing demands for its suits. The approach adopted by Brioni was defined by sociologist Massiono Sargiacomo, who studied it in depth, as "tailors and industry" or "industrialization of craftsmanship," which he defines as "a combination of the principles of industrialization to achieve high productivity while retaining high-quality craftsmanship and maker creativity."[64]

In Brioni's case, a menswear atelier originally set up in Rome by Nazareno Fonticoli and Gaetano Savini in 1945, the production was moved in 1960 from Rome to the small town of Penne in Abruzzo in central Italy. The region was a historically recognized supplier of skilled labor: since medieval times it had had a reputation in tailoring, and generations of tailors and seamstresses had their workshops in the area. The Brioni plant resembled a large-scale tailoring workshop but was organized in an industrial fashion.[65] Furthermore, Swedish serial production was introduced together with the adoption of the Anglo-Saxon sizing system, which offered a "more efficient regime for measuring, cutting and assembling suits without losing the sartorial character of each garment."[66]

This system resulted in an increase in production and in 1961 Brioni started to distribute in the USA through the concessionary Cezar Ltd.[67] The 1960s export sales were between 70 and 80 percent of the total, of which 40 percent went to the USA, and 20 percent of the sales were absorbed by Italian clients. This integrated system of craft and industry proved successful and in the 1970s Brioni ventured into production of ready-to-wear suits.[68]

The above examples were not the only businesses experimenting within this sector. *WWD* reported how in March 1967 the Italians were the new challengers in European ready-to-wear (rtw): "Italy is ready-to-go ... ready-to-wear ... Italy is on the rtw rise. Her rtw exports to the United States jumped from $2,500,000 in 1965 to $4,600,000 in 1966."[69] The article gives a list of the ready-to-wear brands showing in Florence, and detailed information on names, places of production, and trends. For example, Antonelli Sport is described as a pioneer of couture ready-to-wear, with its collection designed by André Laug and made in a factory in Bologna, where the less expensive Mary Antony collection was also produced. Other designers involved in ready-to-wear were Enzo, already onto his third rtw collection made in Nerviano; Alberto Fabiani, whose rtw line was made by Camel of Turin; and Pino Lancetti with two collections: one couture ready-to-wear, made by Genoese manufacturer Ci. Bi., and the other of printed knits made by Icap of Perugia.[70]

A few months later, in October, *WWD* reported again on the Italian *alta moda pronta* which they translated as "de Luxe rtw," this time investigating more of the inspirations for the ready-to-wear collections. The Italian trend was to "pull the best from their high fashion collection and put it on the assembly line for the volume sales." For example, Irene Galitzine, who started her ready-to-wear only the previous year, was translating "all the best sellers from her couture collection in a more simplified way, using high fashion fabrics" and manufacturing them in Turin using the Camel company.[71]

These experiments in mass production relied on the experiences in the previous decade of couturiers who had developed the Sport lines for the American export markets, as analyzed in Chapter 2. Luciana Antonelli, who started her ready-to-wear collection seven years earlier (known as Antonelli Sport), declares in her interview with *WWD* that before designing a new collection she traveled around shops and stores in Italy and Europe to understand what women liked. She continues: "I watch them at the restaurants and on the streets to get the feeling of their mood. Then I go back to the factory in Bologna and I design for young, chic, modern women at reasonable prices."[72] The words of Antonelli foreshadow, by a few years, the modus operandi of the Italian fashion designers of the next generation that were active in the 1970s and found their habitat in the city of Milan, as we will see in Chapter 5.

Boutique of Ready-to-Wear

An alternative avenue of production to the partnership between *alta moda* and industry during the 1960s was offered by the boutique of ready-to-wear. This kind of business, unlike the Biki–GFT agreement and the Brioni or the Sorelle Fontana ventures, did not have any connection with *alta moda* and was only mass produced. This new avenue of fashion manufacturing combined the allure of a brand name, a boutique in a prestigious street near other high-end fashion businesses "where buyers used to orbit," participation in the Pitti *Sala Bianca* shows, and a production in series although not in high numbers.[73]

The Italian designer Cleonice Capece epitomized this new way of making Italian fashion. Capece recalled how she was not formally trained in fashion business or design, a characteristic she shared with many Italian couturiers of the previous decade. She described the beginning of her venture as quite fortuitous. She opened her boutique in the prestigious Roman Via Gregoriana where she had a shop with a workroom. The name on the door read: "Cleonice Capece Ready-to-Wear Couture."[74] The English words were a very interesting choice for the Italian fashion panorama of the 1960s. This was due mainly to her foreign, rather than domestic, clientele. The production in series of her garments had an artisanal nature. Capece would design her collection and have the models parade at the Palazzo Pitti fashion shows in front of press and buyers from all over the world; she would then meet buyers at Florentine Palazzo Strozzi where the orders would be placed. These orders were reproduced in series by a circuit of off-site workers, mainly women who would specialize in one sector of production—for example shirts, skirts, trousers, dresses, swimwear, or embroidery—and they were always done fully by one person or small workroom. They would be paid at *cottimo* (piece rate) and the final product would come back to the Via Gregoriana atelier, for quality control, labeling, and packing to fulfill the orders.[75]

An example of the type of clients and quantity Capece was dealing with is given in a group of invoices submitted to the CNMI.[76] These numbers are far from the quantity the big ready-to-wear manufacturers were producing, but nevertheless produced an important export revenue.

According to Capece, the number of pieces reproduced rose exponentially when the model was bought in by a manufacturer, as was the case in Japan, for example. When a Japanese mass manufacturer bought a style to be reproduced and distributed in Japan, Capece was requested to make a prototype and a paper pattern in a Japanese size. She would fly to Japan to supervise and approve the prototype before production commenced. This would become a Cleonice Capece "Made in Japan" collection, distributed by the company Intermode and the department stores Isetan and Matsuya.[77] This ready-to-wear collection would be sold at a cheaper price to Japanese consumers than the Cleonice Capece "'Made in Italy" line.

Capece was not the only Italian designer collaborating with Japan in these years. As early as 1959 the Isetan store was presenting Italian fashion.[78] In 1963 *WWD* reported on the news that a joint Italian–Japanese venture had been launched to promote Japanese dress fabrics on the world markets. The new company was called Lucrezia and had its headquarters in Palazzo Corsini in Florence. The players behind this venture were "Isetan, Asahi Chemical Industry Co. Ltd., Osaka, one of the leading producers of acrylic fibers in Japan, and G. B. Giorgini." The capital for such a collaboration was provided by two Japanese companies, while Giorgini was in charge of marketing know-how and recruiting and managing staff. The *WWD* article described in detail the aim of the Italo-Japanese operation:

> Initially the new firm will concentrate on producing a line of apparel, principally in the boutique and couture sportwear category, featuring Japanese fabrics, although some European fabrics will be used as well. Isetan will supply fine quality silks, cottons and blends, including kimono silks cut to dress widths and some hand-made fabrics. Some of these fabrics will be aimed at the home furnishings field. Asahi Chemical will furnish acrylic fabrics. The line will feature between 300 and 400 original models, according to present plans. Models will be sold mostly to stores but a small boutique shop will be maintained at the Palazo [*sic*] Corsini site. Faustino Gonzales has been engaged to produce about 40 models per season.[79]

It is very important to emphasize that this new venture was planning to promote Japanese fabrics through the creation of a fashion brand because there were restrictions in place in Italy on the import of goods from Japan.[80] Therefore it was easier to bring into Italy raw materials for manufacture in Italy, and then to "partially re-export" the resulting products. The further aim for the Japanese was, once the restrictions in place were eased, to shift the emphasis onto selling fabrics directly to manufacturers and couturiers. Furthermore, "Although Italy is the headquarters of the company, the aim is to sell to all of Western Europe and eventually to enter the American Market through buyers who visit European fashion showings."[81]

The Cleonice Capece collaboration with Isetan and Giorgini's venture between Italy and Japan highlights a very key factor. Italian fashion and textiles were putting in place international collaborations and projects aimed at expanding their export appeal further than the North American focus explored in the previous chapters. In the 1960s, collaborations intended to mass produce and distribute Italian design were set up not only nationally, as seen with the examples of Biki and Sorelle Fontana, but also intercontinentally, such as the Japanese example has shown.

The Cleonice Capece label started as an export-focused enterprise, but in 1969 the *Salone Mercato Internazionale dell'Abbigliamento* (International

Clothing Show, SAMIA) opened a section called *Moda Selezione* that took place right after the Pitti Fashion shows in the *Sala Bianca*. It was dedicated to show ready-to-wear with a high fashion content and the buyers invited opened the Italian market for Capece.[82]

Capece's label was a successful international business. However, it was not initially recognized as worthy of being part of the CNMI and despite her attempt to become a registered member, her application was rejected several times.[83] This is probably because Capece was operating more on a mass-production level, and using not only Italian materials, and CNMI wanted to promote and highlight the *alta moda* as the ambassador of Italian fashion together with Italian textile exclusively.

The case of Cleonice Capece, a lesser-known protagonist of Italian fashion, highlights how in the 1960s in Italy although there was no well-organized national system of mass production that was satisfying the national clientele, the boutiques, designers, and some segments of industry were still managing to experiment by adopting new design, production, and distribution solutions. Some of these, such as the GFT collaboration with couturiers of the likes of Biki, would fully develop and institutionalize in the 1970s (with the collaboration with fashion designers such as Armani and Ungaro) and would form the basis of the Italian fashion system, as we will see in Chapter 5.

As seen in these examples several attempts were undertaken to connect high fashion with the ready-to-wear industry in the 1950s and 1960s. However, most of these experiments did not have a long-lasting life beyond the early 1970s. There were many reasons for this, such as changing consumer tastes and behaviors.[84] Furthermore, many couturiers who had previously had success in the 1950s with the American market then disappeared from the Italian fashion scene at the beginning of the 1960s. This was mainly due to their incapacity to adapt their production to the shifts in consumption, and their unwillingness to collaborate with Italian industry. As couturier Jole Veneziani argued in an interview in 1969, the price the fashion industrialist would pay to collaborate with high-fashion couturiers, which amounted to five million lire at the end of the 1950s, was considered too little for the contribution the couturier would make with her or his brand name and creativity.[85] This lack of synergy was caused by both the couturier's inability to adapt to the new environment, the new society and new consumers, and also the choice of the industrialists who would not pay enough for the visibility that the association with a label would give them. As described in the case of GFT–Biki line, the industrialist at the beginning of the venture was not paying royalties to use the couturier's name.[86]

In this period, the couturiers still carried the allure of a trusted brand. Their names, such as Biki in the fifties, were associated with tradition, elegance, and taste. According to Merlo, the use of these attributes formed the strategy GFT employed to ennoble their ready-to-wear. Female consumers, although increasingly likely to embrace the new fibers, were still doubting the adoption of off-the-peg garments and nearly 65 percent of them still relied on dressmakers for made-to-measure dresses.[87]

Biki, like many other couturiers such as Sorelle Fontana, was working simultaneously for exclusivity in their *alta moda* ateliers and for the mass production of their line through industry. This stresses how, in this decade, the craft-based exclusivity of *alta moda* and the industrialization of mass fashion coexisted. The distinction between the two was nebulous and it was not evident which direction fashion would take: some couturiers, such as Barocco, even declared to *WWD* that their *prêt-à-porter* line was so similar to their couture line that they could not sell the two in their shop together, otherwise nobody would have bought any more *alta moda*.[88]

The fact that *alta moda* could not be distinguished from an industrialized product at this time makes sense in this period of experimentation as new forms were tried out and not fully institutionalized. Scholars also disagree on the best key to use to read this period. On one hand Merlo thinks that the driving force is industry, in the form of players such as GFT trying to broaden the appeal of the industrial product by involving the allure of the couturier. Conversely, Paris states that consumer demand for new products was driving the changes. This contrast highlights an issue of agency. There is no definitive answer to what caused the changes in this decade and it cannot be stated with certainty if it was production or consumption-driven, or both. What is certain is that these forces contributed to the shaping of this decade. Surely these different actors were interacting and, as we have seen, CNMI tried to interpret this panorama and put in place initiatives that could benefit the sector through a more partnership-based approach.

Mass manufacturers clearly emerged from this panorama as the new players in fashion production. However, they did not yet possess the allure of their *alta moda* counterparts. Their collaborations, although not entirely successful or well developed, laid the basis for a more sophisticated integrated system between industry and design in the 1970s and 1980s.[89]

Chapter 3 has investigated CNMI's agency in shaping the direction of fashion and textile production in the 1960s. The existing literature had not previously investigated the role of this governmental body, and this suggested a lack of importance. However, my archival research shows that CNMI policies and initiatives had an important impact on the existing system. With the advent of ready-to-wear in the late 1970s, CNMI became an important and recognized player in the Milanese ready-to-wear system.

This chapter has also explored early attempts at cooperation between couturiers and mass production. Some aspects of these early ventures, such as the collaboration of designers with a manufacturer such as GFT, as seen in the Biki example, survived into a series of collaborations that, during the 1970s, shaped the success of Italian ready-to-wear.

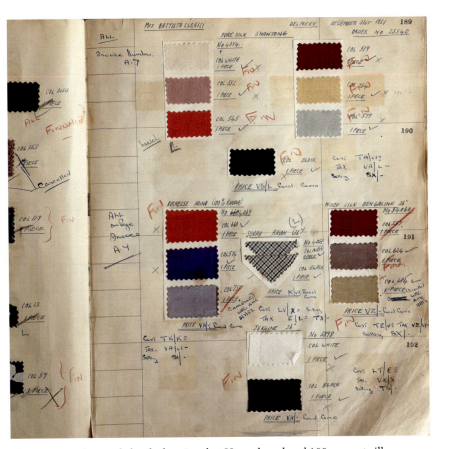

Plate 1 Harrods sample book showing that Harrods ordered 100 percent silk shantung from Battista Clerici in December, 1951. Courtesy of Harrods Company Archive and Simone Morciano Photography.

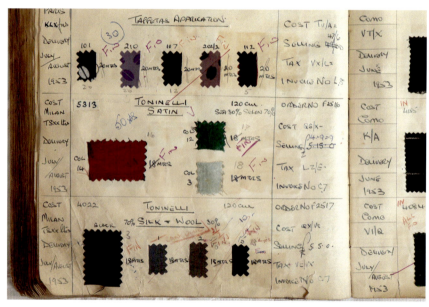

Plate 2 Harrods sample book showing that Harrods ordered from Toninelli a silk and wool blend (70% – 30%) and a silk and selon blend (30% – 70%) in August 1953. Courtesy of Harrods Company Archive and Simone Morciano Photography.

Plate 3 Swatch of 'Chariot' textile, Guido Ravasi, 1949, Fondazione Antonio Ratti, cat. CP 4-2214. Courtesy of Fondazione Antonio Ratti.

Plate 4 Sketch of Emilio Schuberth's dress, circa 1952, from Bergdorf Goodman custom salon collection, 1939–69. Images courtesy of Fashion Institute of Technology|SUNY FIT Library Special Collections and College Archives.

Plate 5 Emilio Schuberth, evening dress spring/summer 1952–3, silk and cotton, Metropolitan Museum of Art: C.I.55.76.12a–d, Gift of Mrs. Byron C. Foy, 1955. Image copyright The Metropolitan Museum of Art/Art Resource/Scala, Firenze.

Plate 6 Brenda Azario with her two daughters wearing matching Ungaro outfits, 1966. Courtesy of Cristina Azario.

Plate 7 Alberto Fabiani, dress and jacket, spring/summer 1967, wool, Victoria and Albert Museum: T.322 & A-1978. ©Victoria and Albert Museum, London/Alberto Fabiani.

Plate 8 Drawing by Ricci Modelli of a Fath original design, 1950s. Courtesy of Centro Studi e Archivio della Comunicazione, Università degli Studi di Parma.

Plate 9 Italian drawing of Patou's ensemble, 1960s. Author's Private collection and courtesy of Alessandra D'Innella photography.

Plate 10 Emanuel Ungaro, coat made with Sonia Knapp wool for Nattier, 1968, wool, The Museum at Fashion Institute of Technology, FIT: 72.112.73, Gift of Rodman A. Heeren. ©The Museum at FIT.

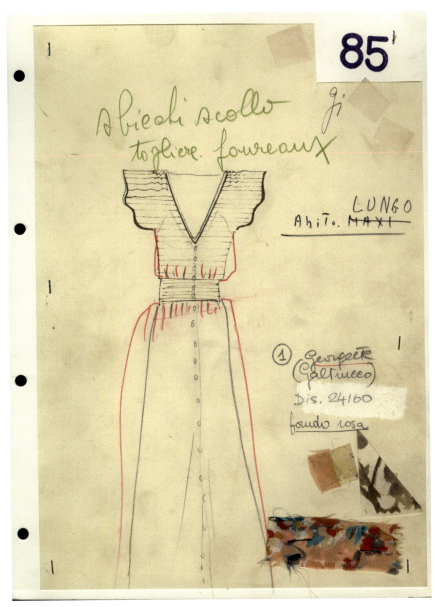

Plate 11 Krizia, working fashion drawing for a long dress, 1975. Courtesy of Centro Studi e Archivio della Comunicazione, Università degli Studi di Parma.

Plate 12 Walter Albini for Krizia, working fashion drawing for a cotton t-shirt, 1965–70. Courtesy of Centro Studi e Archivio della Comunicazione, Università degli Studi di Parma.

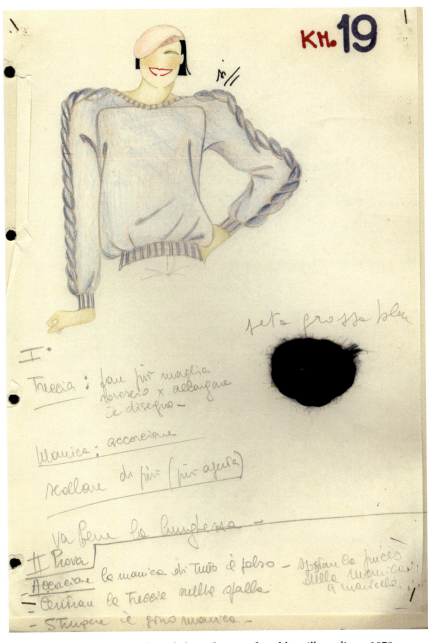

Plate 13 Krizia Maglia, working fashion drawing for a blue silk cardigan, 1979. Courtesy of Centro Studi e Archivio della Comunicazione, Università degli Studi di Parma.

Plate 14 Krizia, working fashion drawing for ensemble with cuff links, 1971.
Courtesy of Centro Studi e Archivio della Comunicazione, Università degli Studi di
Parma.

Plate 15 Krizia, working fashion drawing for ensemble with beret, 1971. Courtesy of Centro Studi e Archivio della Comunicazione, Università degli Studi di Parma.

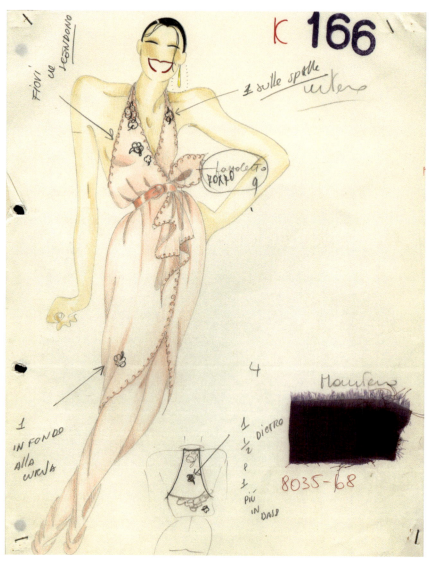

Plate 16 Krizia, working fashion drawing for pink dress, 1979. Courtesy of Centro Studi e Archivio della Comunicazione, Università degli Studi di Parma.

Plate 17 Krizia Maglia, working fashion drawing for a knitted dress 1979. Courtesy of Centro Studi e Archivio della Comunicazione, Università degli Studi di Parma.

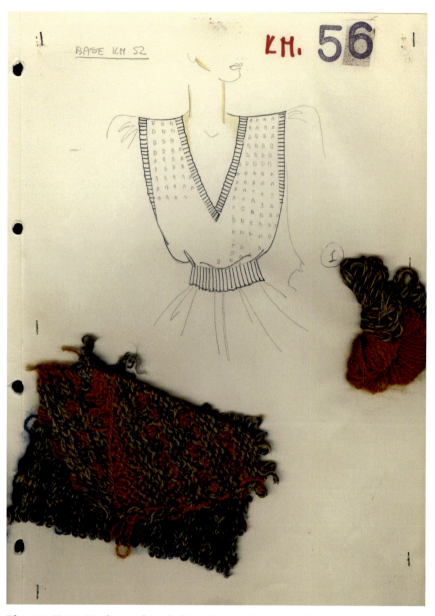

Plate 18 Krizia Maglia, working fashion drawing for a knitted vest, 1979. Courtesy of Centro Studi e Archivio della Comunicazione, Università degli Studi di Parma.

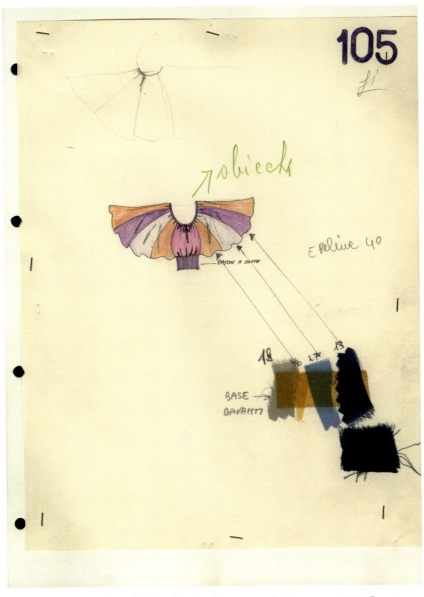

Plate 19 Krizia, working fashion drawing for a rayon shirt, summer 1975. Courtesy of Centro Studi e Archivio della Comunicazione, Università degli Studi di Parma.

GIACCA COME MOD. 23

24
4108

FILA ART 555.000

Plate 20 Gianfranco Ferré, technical drawing for jacket, model 32, *prêt-à-porter*, spring/summer 1984. Courtesy of Centro di Ricerca Gianfranco Ferré, Politecnico di Milano.

CREPE DE CHINE STAMPATO STUCCHI ART 4026

DIS.18640

Plate 21 Gianfranco Ferré, technical drawing for skirt, model 32, *prêt-à-porter*, spring/summer 1984. Courtesy of Centro di Ricerca Gianfranco Ferré, Politecnico di Milano.

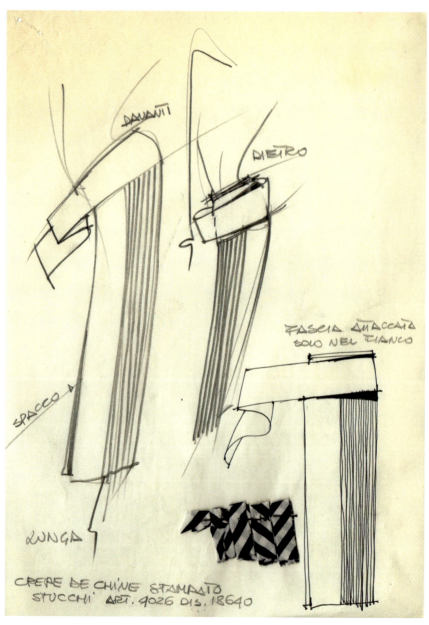

Plate 22 Gianfranco Ferré, second technical drawing for skirt, model 32, *prêt-à-porter*, spring/summer 1984. Courtesy of Centro di Ricerca Gianfranco Ferré, Politecnico di Milano.

Plate 23 Gianfranco Ferré, model 32 being paraded during *prêt-à-porter* fashion show, *prêt-à-porter*, spring/summer 1984. Courtesy of Centro di Ricerca Gianfranco Ferré, Politecnico di Milano.

Plate 24 Gianfranco Ferré, *scheda colori*, *prêt-à-porter*, spring/summer 1984. Courtesy of Centro di Ricerca Gianfranco Ferré, Politecnico di Milano.

Fashion Meets Industry: The Role of *Carnettisti* in Domestic and International Markets

Chapter 4 focuses through an in-depth case study on the role of the Italian textile wholesalers: the *carnettisti*. These little-studied intermediaries had well-known company names, but they acted behind the scenes of the Italian textile–fashion system. The assessment of their story and an investigation into their role reveal the wider impact of the *carnettisti* on the development of Italian domestic and foreign markets and their contribution toward building an established and highly regarded Italian production system.[1]

The *carnettisti* belong to the category of new players who, although already active during the fifties, came to the fore in the sixties. The *carnettisti* were a well-organized cog in the fashion–textile mechanism, and the investigation into their genesis, their modus operandi and function within Italian fashion's production and promotion system reveals the existence of a complicated network of suppliers, small companies, and studios.

This chapter acts as a case study and delves into the mechanisms of production and commercialization of textiles in Italy during the 1960s. It investigates the role played by the little-known intermediary, the *carnettisti*, who worked behind the scenes in Italian fashion and textile production. Their companies acted as a bridge between the many textile producers and the couturiers and dressmakers scattered around Italy and beyond. In their role as intermediaries they used their technical knowledge of production, as well as their understanding of the fashion market. Their main function was to choose fabrics from many manufacturers. The result of their selection was a *carnet* signed with their name. They attempted to sell these textiles to couturiers and, as we will see in the latter part of the chapter, also to dressmakers and department stores. While originally the *carnettisti* mainly acted as agents, some of them started to produce their own textiles, blurring the differentiation between manufacturing and commercialization. The term *carnettisti* has been translated in the English literature as both "textile converter" and "wholesaler." This ambivalence can be attributed to the multifaceted and often ambiguous role of *carnettisti*, which this chapter investigates.

The *carnettisti* represented a driving force in the late 1950s to 1960s Italian fashion system, and my exploration of their role shows how textiles and their commercialization had a greater relevance than has been previously acknowledged in the literature. This chapter explores the role of the *carnettisti*, from a position of relevance and prestige at the beginning of the 1960s, to a deep crisis at the beginning of 1970s that led to profound changes in their role and visibility.

In fact, the role and functions of the *carnettisti* have deep historical roots. A similar function to the *carnettisti* was performed by the *marchands merciers* during the French *Ancien Régime*. According to historian Carolyn Sargentson, the *marchands merciers* played a crucial role in the French luxury market in the late seventeenth and eighteenth centuries, mainly marketing "imported and exotic goods, fashionable and novelty items."[2] Unlike the *carnettisti*, the *marchands* were prohibited from manufacturing, and their main strength was in marketing. The *marchands merciers'* history goes back as far as the twelfth century. By the fourteenth century their trade focused on silks, and by the late seventeenth century their trading practice became capital-intensive. Although they were not allowed to manufacture, the *merciers* could finish products. This practice enabled them to offer a wide variety of products, and Sargentson explains that "such flexibility in the finishing process is typical of luxury production, producing a high degree of variation and individuality, association of novelty and fashion and a significant element of consumer choice."[3] These characteristics of capital, luxury, variety, and trend, as we will see, had much in common with the *carnettisti*.

Italian textile historian Chiara Buss believes that the role of the *carnettista* started in France in the mid-1800s and was a progressive mutation of the figure of the wholesaler. She defines the *carnettista* as an intermediary between the manufacturer and retailers or fashion houses, who offered an added service of "selecting from each season's vast production those fabrics which, because of their pattern, weave and color, will best represent the 'latest fashion.'" The *carnettisti* displayed their selection in a pattern book, called a *carnet*, from which they could work out their orders. Among this earliest type of *carnettista* was the Parisian firm Claude Frères, who supplied Lyon silks internationally, combining them with the allure of Paris haute couture.[4] Firms continued to trade in similar ways for many decades: Brenda Azario cites as a much later example the French

Pierre Besson, a supplier of textile for haute couture active in the 1960s and 1970s.[5] This name was included in a 1969 advertisement in *Vogue Italia* and his name remained present until at least 1971.[6]

Anecdotal evidence suggests that similar figures to *carnettisti* existed outside Italy and France, at least in the 1960s. Franco de Felice, a former sales representative for the Como-based silk manufacturer Clerici Tessuti, states that *carnettisti* were also present in this decade in Belgium, the Netherlands, and England, and Brenda Azario remembers *carnettisti* in Spain in the same period too.[7]

The section that follows examines in depth the general characteristics of the Italian *carnettisti*. This offers a background to analyze the development of one *carnettista* company, the Italian firm Nattier.

Carnettisti in Italy

Especially after the Second World War, the *carnettisti* in Italy were not only selecting for their catalogs from existing production but actively setting up their own manufacturing companies, called first a "studio," then, more generically, *seteria* (silk mill). This shift toward production widened the range of services they could offer. In this setting, some *carnettisti* designed their own silks, either with the aid of designers within the firm or by outsourcing the textile drawings to professional textile design studios. These were then manufactured by external weaving factories or home-weavers, and/or printed by printing workshops.[8]

Some of these companies developed beyond the *carnettista* phase to become manufacturers, such as the companies Mantero and Ratti, who became major producers of Como silks. This probably happened because they found it more profitable to invest in production, or because they had at their disposal larger capital to invest in more expensive machinery. Other *carnettisti*, such as Lucchini, Sisan, and Gandini, maintained their "stylistic" role, more attuned with the selection and forecasting side of the business. In this role, they became better known than the producers that made their textiles.[9] Some *carnettista* companies became "converters," a type of operator who could either totally plan and design the collection of fabrics, or simply select already manufactured products. The same degree of differentiation happened to manufacturers. Some simply produced items instructed by designers or converters, while others developed their own collections to be offered to buyers.

Distinctions among these various players were further complicated because all the companies in the silk sector used the name *seterie* (silk mills) whether they were physically producing silk or simply selecting a carnet of silks from manufacturers. Furthermore, when these companies were advertising their products, they all indiscriminately used the formula "fabric by."[10] Distinguishing between textile producers, converters, *carnettisti*, and wholesalers, when they use very similar names, is very complicated and it might seem superfluous. However, as Buss declares, "it is essential to make this identification in order to understand where a piece of silk with all its connotation came from" and also to understand the structure of the Italian fashion industry, and how these different actors shaped it.[11] Buss specifically reconstructs the role of the *carnettista* in the Como area, a region traditionally dominated by silk production. However, the *carnettisti* were also active in other sectors, such as wool production.

In Italy, the names of *carnettisti* first appeared in the press around the 1950s and by 1959 they jointly sponsored a ball in Florence's Boboli Gardens in honor of the buyers at the eighteenth edition of the *Sala Bianca* fashion shows.[12] Their involvement in this important event reveals their status at the time, their economic ability, and their strategic positioning within Giorgini's enterprise. In 1958, the year of foundation of the CNMI, the *carnettisti* together with textile manufacturers, centers of fashion, chambers of commerce from associated cities, and representatives of the high-fashion houses, all became associates of the CNMI and they were represented in the board meetings, on the board of directors, and in the study commissions.[13] The fact that the *carnettisti* were part of such an important association from the day of its inception demonstrates that these little-known players in the market had already established their role and its centrality by the late 1950s.

De Felice recalled that the silk mills and the silk printers' roles developed at the same time. He remembered that in the 1960s many silk producers started making their own printed silks. In his interview, De Felice often calls these companies "weavers" because at the time they were mainly weaving silk and not designing, finishing, or distributing it. A few had their own printing facilities within the factories and many subcontracted to other producers. Often the designs for the patterns came from the style offices within the silk mills, which acquired them from external design studios. At that time, the profession of the pattern designer was external to the silk manufacturer, whereas nowadays it has been incorporated. De Felice explains that around twelve girls were employed in each of these design studios to paint and design patterns. They were coordinated by a head designer, who would tour the world with files containing hundreds of drawings on paper with various patterns, in order to sell them to silk manufacturers. The companies Boggia, Spadacini, and Gualdo Porro, an independent studio for woven silk design, were some of the names in the Como area.[14] New drawings were developed each season and were priced at around two hundred and fifty thousand lire each. Each drawing was unique and once purchased it became exclusive to the buyer, and could not be reproduced by others.[15] After selecting the drawings, the silk mill commissioned an external engraver to translate the initial patterns into a screen that was then sent directly to an external printer.[16] The weaver's style office, in contact with the printer, tested colors on small pieces of textile to create printed proofs ("maquettes"). Once the final print, the *pezza tipo*, was approved, the whole production, including variations and at least seven colorways, could start. The final printed collection consisted of around fifty or sixty designs that together with block color fabrics and jacquards completed the seasonal collection of a silk mill. This network of small, highly specialized, often family-run companies, all working together in synergy to produce one final product, has been defined as *distretti industriali* (industrial districts). The *distretti industriali* have been heralded as the distinctive characteristic of the Italian industrial system and basis of the success of the "Made in Italy" label in the 1980s, as we will see in more detail in Chapter 5.[17]

De Felice believes that, in the post-war period, the textile producers were not very important strategically: they simply manufactured textiles, while the wholesalers/*carnettisti*, with their communication strategies, oversaw the commercialization and distribution of the final products, and often directed the weavers by commissioning specific types of textiles. De Felice pinpoints the distinction that, although the wholesalers and the *carnettisti* had similar roles, their customer base was different: the wholesalers had a much more ordinary clientele, while the *carnettisti* supplied the higher-end sartorial customers and presented their products with photographs and special editions that increased their desirability. The *carnettisti* were not only salesmen. They also invested substantial capital because, as Azario recalls, they had to buy the full bolt of fabric produced by the manufacturers. This represented an advantage for the producers as it guaranteed that their products were sold without having to worry about the distribution.[18] The *carnettisti*, as Sarti explains, presented the fabrics to dressmakers and couturiers, cut the lengths of textiles ordered, and finally distributed them.[19]

While in the 1950s the wholesaler/*carnettista* was considered the *deus ex machina* of the textile operation, the silk producers were often small family enterprises, awaiting orders from the *carnettisti*.[20] Azario agrees that the manufacturers produced without any sense of direction, as they were simply making what people asked them to. The *carnettisti*'s role in directing style had a direct impact on production. Their function was to give the textile an identity, what we would call nowadays a brand identity. For example, a Nattier fabric would be associated with quality, bold colors, and modern design.[21]

Sarti confirms that the wool producers were considered simply as mechanical weavers of the textiles, with no ambitions of being identified as creative "authors." It was the *carnettisti*, with their sophisticated approach, who were more oriented to the presentation and commercialization of the products. While these roles were distinct, there was also a dialogue between producer and *carnettista* about what products to develop. Decisions were taken because either a couturier had expressed interest in a specific fabric, or because they had seen a fabric in Paris which they wanted to be reproduced. Sarti confirms that textile mills and *carnettisti* worked together, and were not competitors.[22]

This intermediary role meant that the *carnettisti* needed to interpret how each textile could be commercialized, and to what kind of clientele. For example, if a textile with a specific design was published in a magazine as used in a couturier's model, this increased its visibility and encouraged more dressmakers to order the same fabric.

Rosina, however, prefers to translate the term *carnettista* as "converter and distributor," highlighting their role in choosing the fabrics that met the "mood" of the season from silk mills they were in contact with. They therefore made what she defines as a "collection of collections" branded as their own, which could help the couturiers navigate the massive seasonal production. As seen above, they became increasingly influential toward the end of the 1950s, and Rosina believes this was due to their ability to fulfill the needs and the demands of fashion houses and dressmakers thanks to their position as intermediaries between the manufacturers and the consumers. This included their competence to pre-select from a vast range of fabrics and therefore save their clients the time to view and negotiate with too many producers.[23] Although many of the *carnettisti* did not have their own weaving, printing, or design studios, they became the virtual producers of fabrics, so much so that they marked them with their names on the selvedge and are accredited in fashion editorials and advertisements near the name of the couturier.[24]

In the post-war period, the term *carnettista* was widely recognized and used in everyday fashion language and official reports. Nowadays it is very obscure and almost no longer in use. This is probably due first of all to the disappearance of such companies from the system and the evolution of some of them, such as Lucchini, into different realms.

As we have seen, the term *carnettista* has been translated in many ways, as wholesaler, distributor, converter, and also sometimes as silk mill. In this chapter, the term *carnettista* follows the more general set of meanings used by the industry in the 1960s, the decade of interest here. It stands for a group of companies with a spectrum of functions beyond mere textile production; a spectrum including converters and wholesalers. The CNMI did not distinguish among them even if they performed slightly different functions. As seen below, they were grouped together under the official name of *Assortitori Tessuti Novità* (Sorters of New Textiles), but they continued to be called *carnettisti* in correspondence and among industry specialists.[25] The spectrum ranged from *carnettista* companies turned converters, such as Gandini, to Nattier, which was a textile-producing company that doubled up as its own *carnettista*.

The *Assortitori Tessuti Novità* (Sorters of New Textiles)

In May 1965 an exchange of letters between Ferdinando Chiri, the spokesman for eight *carnettisti*, and Amos Ciabattoni from the CNMI demonstrates the *carnettisti*'s desire to establish a recognized body, *Assortitori Tessuti Novità* (Sorters of New Textiles), that could protect their "elevated category of textile sales."[26] In response, the CNMI asks them to draw up a statute that would define their role and regulate the acceptance of other companies that wanted to be part of the new group.[27] The creation of a register of "approved" companies was, in CNMI's view, a way to establish a more direct rapport between the *carnettisti* and high-fashion creators.

The rules, however, remained vague. The companies eligible to be part of this register had to fulfill four characteristics: they had to be enrolled at the *Camera di Commercio* (Chamber of Commerce); they had to mainly do business with high-fashion dressmakers and couturiers at a commercial and national level; they had to present a selection of new textiles with a carnet or pattern book at least twice a year to the creators of high fashion; and finally, they should not have in their collection copies of other Italian or foreign textiles belonging to other *assortitori*.

Not everybody agreed with the proposed rules and at least one letter details some remonstrations. The 1965 letter from Walter Pession to Ferdinando Chiri highlights some of the problems with these regulations. Pession is especially concerned with the non-copy clause and with the choice of name for the new body, believing that the name *carnettisti* would have been much more recognizable and familiar than *assortitori*.[28] Despite the different opinions, the CNMI established the register of the *Assortitori Tessuti Novità* with an official document dated October 9, 1965, and later published a full-page advertisement in *Linea Italiana* with all the names of the companies in the sector.[29]

Until the set-up of an official body, the *carnettisti* had been free from a strict organizational structure and their role was mainly unknown to the general public. However, from the mid-1960s, the names of *carnettisti* such as Satam, Gandini, and Nattier started appearing more prominently. National and international fashion magazines such as *Novità, WWD, Vogue US,* and, later, *Vogue Italia* mentioned *carnettisti* in editorials, captions, and articles, to identify the provenance of the fabrics. The text accompanying the images did not normally make a distinction between textile manufacturer and *carnettisti*. Furthermore, from around 1966, a few full pages of mainly black-and-white advertising started to appear in *Vogue Italia* showcasing the work of the *carnettisti*.[30]

An advertisement for the *carnettista* Bruno Sassi in *Vogue Italia* shows how his name was associated with *tessuti novità* (new fabrics), *seterie* (silk mills), and *lanerie* (wool mills), making it very difficult for the general public to understand the difference between the producers and the *carnettisti*.[31] This lack of clarity was probably not perceived as a problem and only the industry specialists knew the differentiation between the real producer and the *carnettista*. For the magazine's readers, the important message was that the name associated with the fabric was synonymous with quality and innovation.

The black-and-white image of this advertisement, depicting a seated female model, also reveals a hierarchy between the *carnettisti* and fashion designers. The *carnettista* Bruno Sassi's name is prominently placed at the upper-left corner of the page, with the writing even overlapping the image of the model. The name of the couturier Lancetti is only indicated after the address and telephone number of the *carnettista*. The font choice and its size are also telling of the companies' relative importance. Bruno Sassi's logo is a signature, rather than a plain capital letter font as for the couturier. The *carnettista* in this instance is seen as the creator, who, like an artist, signs the product of its labor: sourcing and commissioning the fabric, the primary material of fashion.[32] The caption continues by mostly describing the fabric type and its color, rather than lingering on the design characteristics of the day suit. From this analysis it is clear that the material, rather than the design, is given priority in this instance. The role of the textile, however, is not evident at first glance, and the general public would still probably see fashion as the protagonist here. The subtlety of the message testifies to the technical role of the *carnettisti*, often far from the limelight. This advert also had a double aim: to showcase the final product, fashion, and to bring visibility to an otherwise obscure intermediary such as the *carnettista*.

This type of page was not an isolated occurrence and similar adverts were featured in *Vogue Italia* in the mid-to-late 1960s. These images are similar in composition, color scheme, and caption hierarchy.[33] They demonstrate what the *carnettisti* wanted to be known for and associated with. From the near-anonymity of their name buried in the captions of fashion magazines, they emerged with full-page images, which also represented an important financial investment. When shown these pages, Brenda Azario, owner of the *carnettista* Nattier, was convinced that this type of full-page advertisement would have been paid for by the *carnettista*.[34] In addition to paying the magazine, the *carnettista* also had to pay the couturier, as revealed in a CNMI document which indicated that couturiers should request a payment of 200,000 lire when advertising one of their models with producers of high-fashion textile and textile manufacturers.[35]

These images depicted female models in black and white on a neutral background, standing, walking, or posing while wearing high-fashion garments. The only text information emerging from the monochrome pages were the name of the *carnettista*, sometimes with their addresses and telephone numbers, and the names of the couturiers. The textile, although it was the main product the *carnettisti* were handling, was not necessarily in the foreground or explicitly highlighted in the image. The focus appeared to be the connection to the final products, the garments, and their desirability and fashionability.[36] These adverts functioned as a manifesto for the *carnettista*: they stated their role and made more explicit the connection between high-quality textiles and high fashion. Although featuring different *carnettisti* and couturiers, these pages have in common the same language and communication strategy.

From the above analysis, we can conclude that the *carnettisti* offered a varied and complex service and were not acting as a mere intermediary. Firstly, their position of connection between manufacturers and dressmakers offered a link between two industries which often did not have a direct contact. The *carnettisti* were able to define styles and trends for each season and commission products from the manufacturers, thanks to their knowledge of the needs of the couturiers and dressmakers, and of their markets; and equally their knowledge of the textile producer's side of the business.

During the 1960s fabric trends were an important side of the fashion business, and trade magazines such as *WWD* reported on them on a regular basis. For example, an article in the February 1963 issue of *WWD* described all types of fabrics used in the Paris haute couture shows from linens to woolens to silks, together with names of the producers and *carnettisti*, such as Nattier and Forneris.[37]

The *carnettisti* also acted as representatives of the manufacturers, providing branding and marketing, and thereby offering a face to an otherwise anonymous product. Furthermore, the *carnettisti* bore the cost of distribution around Italy and abroad through their national and international offices. This cost included the overheads for a wholesale stock room in which to cut the fabric ordered before distribution. This infrastructure demanded an investment of capital, and the acquisition of large stock involved further risk-taking.

These characteristics depict the *carnettista* as a flexible figure able to communicate effectively with technically skilled people in production; to answer to the demand of couturiers offering solutions to their requests; and to promote, distribute, and market an otherwise anonymous product such as a textile and transform it into a luxury and exclusive item.

Nattier

As we have seen earlier in this chapter, the *carnettisti* played an important role in the Italian fashion system, especially in the 1960s. In this context, investigating the story of Nattier—one of Italy's most successful *carnettisti* during the 1960s—exposes the relationship between Italian textile manufacturers and couturiers/ dressmakers and exemplifies ways in which taste and materials used in the making of Italian fashion were produced, selected, and commercialized.

The short-lived Nattier company (1962–73) epitomized the experimental, young, and courageous attitude typical of the 1960s economic boom in Italy and its rapid decline from the beginning of the turmoil of the *anni di piombo* (years of lead). An examination of Nattier's history exposes mechanisms and partnerships essential to an understanding of the fashion system of this decade, for example the closed collaboration between Nattier and high-fashion designers (such as in the case of the Fabiani striped suit in the next section), marketing strategies used, the type of advertisements, and relationships with clients.

The story of Nattier starts in the Piedmont region of Northern Italy, where the Azario family owed a textile company called Litex, *Lanificio Italiano Export* (Italian Wool Mill Export) in Strambino, near Turin. The family business was established by Vittorio Azario's grandfather in the 1920s and it initially produced average-quality tweed for the Italian men's mass clothing industry. Vittorio Azario was trained at the Biella Textile School and in the late 1950s took over the family business.

In 1959 Azario and his then fiancée, Brenda Tandy (later Brenda Azario), an Englishwoman who had a job as a radio announcer, began producing women's fabrics. According to Brenda Azario's 1980s recollection, Vittorio Azario did not belive the production of ordinary men's fabrics would keep his interest and he thought that "for a factory of our size, there was only one way to go and that was for the top." The later decision to undertake men's or women's business was probably taken "on the roll of a dice."[38] So, from 1959, they specialized in wool fabrics for womenswear.[39] Brenda Azario recalled in a 2013 interview that, at that time, "it was unusual for textile manufacturers to be in direct contact with fashion houses."[40] Since the market was dominated by fabric distributors and *carnettisti*, the Azarios tried to sell their new products to the leading Italian *carnettisti*, such as Satam, Sassi, Gandini, and Bises—but without much success. According to Brenda Azario, these *carnettisti* preferred to buy from manufacturers that were already selling to French haute couture houses and enjoyed their "stamp of approval."[41] This attitude revealed a well-established mode of collaboration in which links had been created in the past and newcomers were not easily accepted.

While Litex and the Azarios were struggling to find recognition, Rodier was a well-known Paris textile manufacturer founded in 1852 that worked with many couturiers, such as Poiret, Chanel, and Dior. When Rodier closed in 1962, the Azarios bought part of the company's archive and hired one of its former employees, Roger Dietsch, a so-called *placier*, a key man in the business who had the role of getting the fabrics into the couture houses. In a period when business was done in person and agents established long-lasting relationships with designers and couturiers, a man like Dietsch was key to the development of a relationship with French couturiers and he acted as a consultant for the Azarios. Dietsch also helped to bring on board other experts, such as the so-called "loom fixers," technicians able to modify the old looms to produce complex structures and special design elements.[42]

In 1961 the Azarios, encouraged by sales achieved in America, decided to open their own carnet with the French name Nattier, to distribute only the vanguard of women's fabrics produced in Italy by Litex, and that would mainly be associated with couture. The Azarios' decision to become *carnettisti* acknowledged the importance and position this sector of the business had at the time.

Nattier became the name behind the bold, inventive fabrics mainly sold to the couture houses of Italy and France, and "Litex manufactured both the luxury fabrics and the less expensive textiles destined for a less specialized market."[43] For the first years of business the Italian owners remained in the shadow of the French name, putting French representatives in charge and not revealing the real "nationality" of their fabrics. The reason for this concealment was because "there was a great resistance to these Italians knocking on doors."[44] At first they used the Parisian distributor/*carnettista* Pierre Besson, but they later opened their own Nattier office at 220 Rue Rivoli, Paris.

In the 1960s the Azarios bought several other archives of French textile companies that were closing. Part of the Nattier archive of historical sample books is today conserved in the private archive of Cristina Azario, one of the daughters of Brenda and Vittorio. A close analysis of this archive established the presence of several French textile sample books dated from the late 1880s to the early 1930s, among them one book dated 1930s with Rodier textile samples. In an interview with the author, Brenda Azario explained how techniques and effects they found in the French sample books inspired many Nattier textile "innovations" in the 1960s.[45] As Azario stated in a talk she gave at the Victoria and Albert Museum in 1982, 'We started by emulating others."[46]

Back in Piedmont, Vittorio was responsible for manufacturing. According to the English textile and fashion trade magazine *Trends Fabrics and Fashion*, in 1966, at the height of Nattier's success, Vittorio Azario was a "superb technician" who created double, triple, and even quadruple layer gabardines.[47] Vittorio, with the aid of his technicians, studied the structure of the oldest fabrics, yarns, and special effects of the 1920s and 1930s and tried to emulate them.[48]

In her interview, Brenda expressed the belief that Vittorio's technical knowledge, his ability to exploit the old machinery's capabilities, and his risk-taking made it possible for Nattier to reform the look of fashion fabrics in the 1960s. In Brenda's words: 'We innovated by breaking the rules'. Her husband, although warned by his workers of the impossibility of some of his requests, wanted to experiment and would try different combinations directly on the machines.[49] Brenda also recognizes that, in order to innovate, they relied on the skills and knowledge of very experienced textile workers. For example, although at Litex they did not do a lot of yarn spinning, they specialized in twisting and finishing of the fabrics.

> In yarn, one is blessed in Italy to have a lot of other producers around, and I remember that one of our great successes was a tweed for which we used old English spinning machinery lying around in Italy, lying idle when we found it. It was a stub yarn, where, because the machinery was old, the thick was thicker and the thin was thinner. You got regularity that you cannot get on modern machinery, and that gave a character to our fabrics that we didn't have to worry about anyone copying it; they were miles away from it.[50]

Nattier was encouraged by customer demand also to invest in research and experimentation. Brenda recalls how customers did not want cheaper fabrics, they wanted better, and the quality was made to measure and made to last.[51]

In relation to textile production, Nattier's innovations included a brushed mohair bouclé yarn and a triple gabardine which, according to Brenda, revolutionized the way garments were made. The fabrics available until then were made with lining and interlining and these internal constructions caused flaws in the external appearance of the textile. The French designer André Courrèges asked Vittorio Azario to produce a textile that could be sculpted and that had equal strength in each direction. This is how Nattier started to experiment and produce triple and later quadruple gabardine. Weighing up to eight hundred grams per meter, these fabrics were very thick and stable and did not require internal padding. They started first with the plain fabrics and then they continued by adding patterns to them, printing on them and also embroidering and brushing them. The name Nattier became synonymous with these multilayered gabardines so heavily used in 1960s sculptural dresses both in Italian and abroad, as seen for example in the Ungaro outfit in Plate 7.[52]

While Vittorio supervised the technical side of manufacturing, Brenda was the face of the business. She oversaw sales, and one of her strategies was to always wear couture garments made from Nattier fabrics. This included a wool gabardine light blue and green striped 1966 Ungaro outfit matching the ones worn by her two daughters (Plate 7). A significant part of her job was to open new markets and acquire new clients. At the height of Nattier's success, she was responsible for sixty percent of the sales.[53] Her marketing strategy was based on a one-to-one approach. She recalled how she would go to a new city such as Berlin, Barcelona, or Tokyo. Having researched fashion and textile magazines, she knew which brands and shops to visit. She might also decide "in the moment," while she was on the high street, based on the type of products a shop had in its windows. She would walk in, ask to see the manager, and when encouraged to show what she was selling she would simply reply "what I am wearing." She believed that the trick was very effective, since nobody refused to see her and discuss further business.[54] Azario's schedule was very hectic: she used to take a plane on Monday and come back on Friday night. In this way, she would visit all possible markets in Europe and Australia that could buy their fabrics. However, this was only one part of the business. Many of Nattier's clients were couturiers and small dressmakers, as will be analyzed in the next section of this chapter.

By the mid-1960s Nattier was a very successful enterprise and there was no need to hide the identity of the Italian owner any longer. Strong from their success, Brenda and Vittorio were now featured in articles in English magazines such as *Trends Fabric and Fashion*.[55] Furthermore, in 1967 one of their fabric designs was featured on the cover of the March issue of the important English trade and export magazine *The Ambassador*.[56]

The company expanded and had up to two hundred employees. It opened offices in New York and contracted representatives as far afield as Beirut and Japan. Nattier's US presence was key, and the company was supplying the most important American manufacturers of the time, such as Ben Zuckerman and Originala, and also designers such as Geoffrey Beene and Oscar de la Renta. The names of both Litex and Nattier were featured in editorials in many issues of *Vogue US* and *Vogue Italia*. For example, Litex was featured on the *Vogue US* cover in August 1963, depicting a ready-to-wear Ben Zuckerman suit made with a Litex wool textile.[57] In the early 1960s the Neiman Marcus department store also became a client and the owner himself was the first to ask the Azarios to advertise in *Vogue US*.[58] The result was an Italian issue in 1960 that saw Litex advertised in conjunction with the car manufacturer Fiat, liquor producer Strega, airline Alitalia, and Italian couturiers such as Pucci, Sorelle Fontana, and Fabiani.[59] The collaboration with such important Italian companies marked a crucial moment for the Azarios' visibility and success.

The occasion of such extensive coverage was the "Italian Fortnights at Neiman Marcus," a two-week program of events and performances at the Dallas department store. Attractions included a charity ball honoring the Italian ambassador, an Italian film festival, a concert of baroque music on Stradivarius instruments, and even Italian police to direct traffic. In conjunction with the exhibitions at the department store, which included among many other things Italian sculpture, Capacci and Lucenti ceramics, Fiat cars, and Franchi guns, special Italian exhibitions were organized around town in the city museums, such as *New Generation of Italian Artists* at the Dallas Museum of Fine Arts and the *Italian Sculpture Show* at the Museum of Contemporary Craft.[60]

The eight-page 1960 *Vogue US* advertisement is titled "Italy via Neiman Marcus." It depicts black-and-white images of Italian life, in which models wearing Italian fashion ride in Fiat cars, with Italian cities and their historic buildings as backdrop. The atmosphere in these shots is refined and classic, very different from the way in which Italy was depicted in earlier images. Azario's Litex is described: "LITEX of Torino, designers and weavers of couturier textiles, creates a trend-setting sculpture wool and mohair fabric … selected by CAPUCCI for his town and travel suit." Evidently the emphasis here, as in the *carnettisti*'s advertisement previously analyzed, is on the fabric and the producer rather than on the name of the couturier.[61]

Distribution of Textiles in the 1960s

This section uses extensive archival material, and the recollection of Brenda Azario, to understand the market destinations of the products that the *carnettisti* commissioned and bought from Italian mills scattered around the country. The detailed recollection that follows, generated by a Nattier textile employed in the making of an *alta moda* red-and-blue striped suit by Alberto Fabiani (Plate 8), observes how the textile was further advertised and used by other segments of fashion production.

This system worked like a pyramid. At the top was *alta moda*, with few clients, therefore absorbing only a few meters of fabric. This section follows the path of one fabric as it was sold in progressively larger quantities to dressmakers, textile retailers, and department stores associated with a wider middle-range customer base. This demonstrates how, although *alta moda* bestowed the kudos and glamour to the textiles commissioned by the *carnettisti*, its limited market did not guarantee the sale of enough meters to cover the expenses of such exclusive textile production. Such a precise analysis is important because it acknowledges the presence of layers of fashion production (or reproduction) that although not as recognized and studied by the literature, contributed equally to the development and survival of the system of distribution and consumption of Italian textiles during the 1960s.

The Journey of a Textile: A Fabiani Striped Ensemble

Brenda Azario recalls how she would target big couturiers in both France and Italy as possible clients for Nattier fabrics. For example, she used to visit the master couturier Cristóbal Balenciaga in Paris, and she would bring with her a suitcase with large textile samples of around half a meter that could be easily examined and touched to feel the way they would drape. Although both French and Italian couturiers used the same textile suppliers, such as Nattier, even by the 1960s Italian couturiers did not yet have the same status and the French were considered to be the makers of taste.

Similarly, Mrs. Azario would visit Italian couturiers such as Alberto Fabiani. These Italian and French clients, however, would buy only around twenty to fifty meters of a particular fabric because they only produced a few items for the catwalk shows. They chose existing fabrics in the collection, or they could request a custom-made design. This would be the result of discussions between the *carnettista*, who knew what was technically possible to make, and the couturiers. Once the textile was sold, it was used by the couture house to make a specific model that was then paraded on the catwalk of the *Sala Bianca* in Palazzo Pitti.[62] An example of such a production is represented by the Alberto Fabiani red-and-blue suit now in the Victoria and Albert Museum collection (Plate 8).

The specialist press, such as *Amica*, published reports from the catwalk shows, as well as publishing fashion photographs. The caption describing the photograph normally mentioned and described the fabrics, naming the textile manufacturer or more often the name of the *carnettista*.[63] This was a weekly magazine launched in 1962 and associated with the newspaper *Corriere della Sera*. It mainly heralded ready-to-wear fashion, although articles on couture fashion were also present. Fashion photographs of *alta moda* would appear in the press only several months after the deal was made between the *carnettista* and the couturier, and after the fashion show at Palazzo Pitti. Only if the couturier sold more than one model, which was not always guaranteed, would he or she order more of the same fabric. This system meant that only a very small quantity of fabric was sold to the couturier. The couturier represented a small market, but, as we have seen in the *Vogue* advertisement pages analyzed in the previous section, generated good visibility in terms of image for the *carnettista*, and provided kudos for the textiles.

However, the few meters sold could not absorb the cost of production which included setting up the looms and machines and the investment in the research for the product. More meters needed to be sold and, as this chapter goes on to demonstrate, the dressmakers and textile retailers fulfilled these requests.

Copying Couture: Selling Fabric to Dressmakers

Nattier's books testify how the textile employed in the making of the Fabiani suit would have a second life. These volumes, similarly, to the ones produced by other *carnettisti*, contain hundreds of pages filled with stamp-sized textile samples. These colorful fabrics are identified only with a number, and they are often associated with names of couturiers, such as Balenciaga and Fabiani. In order to understand the function of these books it is necessary to examine the dressmakers' businesses in more detail.

In the 1960s, French couture was still a source of inspiration for Italian dressmakers. Brenda Azario recalled how the Paris and Florence fashion shows came first, then, after about a month, more shows took place in Milan. The *modellista* Rina Modelli showed the French and Italian models she had acquired from the couture fashion shows and sold their equivalent paper patterns or cotton *toile* to the Italian dressmakers.[64] This practice was widespread and Christian Dior himself talked about a system of record keeping in which "for professional buyers, the file shows whether they purchased the paper pattern, canvas, or the original dresses."[65]

The pattern maker and dressmaker Enrichetta Pedrini, the owner of Rina Modelli, was one of the few *modelliste* in Italy, together with Guidi in Milan and Ricci in Bologna. Their role was to go to Paris and acquire the exclusive rights to reproduce in Italy some garments, and to sell the toile (*tele*) to more than one dressmaker. Exclusivity, together with the right to use the Parisian couturiers' name, was bought at a high price.[66] This is probably the case for the models by Madeleine de Rauch reproduced in the February 1952 issue of *Bellezza*.[67] The captions that accompany the photographs of the French models associate the name of the couturier with a garment from Rina Modelli's collection. According to the fashion journalist Maria Pezzi, Rina had very refined taste, and she bought up to 250 models per season in Paris.[68]

This system of authorized copying of French couturiers through their drawings and patterns started in the interwar period and continued in the 1950s.[69] An example of drawings reproducing French design is shown in Plate 9. Here a Jacques Fath model is reproduced with all its details, and was sold by Modelli Ricci. Many of these drawings, or *croquis*, have been found in Italian couturiers' ateliers such as Schuberth, Sorelle Fontana, and Antonelli.[70]

Fashion historian Gloria Bianchino defines the *croquis* as:

> design on thin pasteboard, in tempera or watercolor, that faithfully reproduced the original French model and bearing the stylist's name at the bottom, with a few directions for sewing—more often these are merely suggestions for the material. For the most part, the designs are almost identical—as if they were traced—with the female figure always reproduced in the same position, always almost frontally ... On a croquis, the design had to be clearly legible for the dressmaker to decipher it, and conventions were codified, such as the use of opaque tempera for heavy materials or very diluted for transparent ones. Often, these designs were shown to prospective clients so that they could choose their model.[71]

This business of copies and French inspiration, however, did not stop in the 1950s with the advent of Giorgini's fashion shows aimed at showcasing only Italian models. It continued at least for the duration of the 1960s, as the drawing in Plate 10 shows. Here a 1960s Jean Patou ensemble, composed of an orange coat and a purple/orange patterned mini dress, is reproduced in detail providing the dressmaker with three different views, and a description of its construction, in Italian, on the reverse of the page.

In Milan in the 1960s, between five and six hundred dressmakers from every part of Italy flocked every season to Rina Modelli's workshop and salon in the central Via Manzoni, at the corner with the fashionable Via Montenapoleone.[72] First, in the morning, they bought paper patterns to reproduce in their ateliers for their local clientele, then, in the afternoon, they attended the fashion show where they could see the original models parading. According to the account of a dressmaker from Rimini, Ilva Semprini, the dressmaker could not afford to buy more than a couple of models as they cost a few million lire. It was also usual for a couple of dressmakers from the same city to buy together up to four models that they would then exchange.[73] In Rina Modelli's account books, the names of couturiers such as Carosa and Curiel have been found alongside those of local seamstresses.[74] This indicates how the business of French copies was not only relegated to local makers, but also involved high-end Roman couture houses.

After purchasing patterns or *toiles*, the dressmakers went to Nattier, located a few minutes' walk away from Rina Modelli in their central offices in via Santo Spirito. There, they consulted the sample books and bought the fabrics corresponding to their paper patterns. In this instance, the fabric was automatically allocated according to the model already purchased. The textile sample surviving in Nattier's book is therefore small, a mere reference, as it does not need to showcase its quality, pattern, and feel. Sometimes instead of the sample fabric only a small photograph is present.

These books became a record of the Nattier textiles employed in each season and they were specifically produced to fulfill the dressmaker business, which, according to Azario, was a big source of revenue for a *carnettista* like Nattier. Although they did not sell many meters to each dressmaker, their total number was high enough to represent a very important market outlet for the *carnettista*.[75]

Looking through these books it is noticeable that on some occasions the same textile with the same code was sold to more than one couturier. This was the case for the white and bright green striped fabrics number 2855/63 sold to both Lapidus in Paris and Ektor in New York.[76] This duplication was not just a coincidence or a mistake, but a normal practice in textile and fashion dealings. A textile, unless bought "in exclusivity," could be sold to more than one client. Publications like *WWD* would report how a particular Nattier stretch gabardine in Madras coloring, first shown in Italy, was then used by French couturiers like St. Laurent, Balenciaga, Venet, and Ricci.[77] On the other hand, when a textile was exclusive to one designer this was clearly stated and advertised as in the case of the Nattier fabric "Feathers and Flowers." exclusive to Valentino.[78]

Although couture was at the forefront of the fashion image, the most profitable sales for Nattier were made in this second stage, when garments were reproduced for a wider public. Couture models would offer visibility and allure to a design and to a fabric, but not all the population could afford the exclusive models.

Fabric Shops

A further layer of sale, but no less important for a *carnettista*'s fabric, was to the textile retailers or fabric shops. Rosina states that:

> In Italy, a country where artisanal traditions had always been very strong, seamstresses and small dressmaking shops survived much longer than elsewhere, encouraging the growth of a large number of drapers' shops where it was possible to buy Italian and foreign fabrics by the meter.[79]

The *carnettista* sold their fabric in these kind of shops after six months from the date of the production. This type of business was a common feature on Italian high streets. Rosina believed that the survival of this kind of outlet in Italy, longer than in other countries, was due to Italy's ongoing artisanal tradition and the widespread presence of small ateliers of seamstresses and dressmakers. These businesses had guaranteed the growth of drapers' shops where Italian and foreign textiles could be purchased by the meter. These shops were regular features of the main Italian shopping streets, and catered to a large market of tailors and dressmakers who were key producers of clothing at the time. By 1957 an ISTAT (*Istituto Nazionale di Statistica*—National Institute of Statistics) study showed the presence in Italy of thirty thousand textile shops.[80]

One of the best-known chains of fabric shops was Galtrucco, which had branches in several Italian cities.[81] As De Felice remembered, the *carnettista* usually added thirty percent to the price of sale of a given textile; and textile retailers such as Galtrucco would then double this price. Such an increase was due to the fact that the retailers were the last links of the chain and if they did not sell, they would be left with the stock unsold.[82] These retail outlets had very nice shops in central locations, like the Galtrucco headquarters in Milan's Piazza Duomo, or Bassetti and Polidori in Rome. The latter company engaged in two types of distribution, one as a wholesaler/*carnettista* and the other as a retailer.[83]

While the visual identity of the *carnettisti* was closely associated with the fashionable final product, retail textile shops like Galtrucco aimed at showcasing their variety of textiles, patterns, and quality. In such shops, consumers could find the striped red-and-blue Nattier fabric, and thanks to the patterns published in *Vogue*, they could commission local dressmakers to reproduce the *alta moda* ensemble.[84]

Textile Designers, Department Stores, and Other Outlets

Nattier did not only sell textiles manufactured by their own Litex plant. As they catered to designers' needs, they commissioned and produced fabrics that designers requested. Therefore, they collaborated with a variety of textile designers, printers, producers, and yarn spinners.

One of their younger clients, the French designer Emanuel Ungaro, requested some fabrics to be designed by his then girlfriend Sonia Knapp, a talented graphic designer. A collaboration started: Knapp designed; Nattier executed with the aid of external printers such as Savinio, Jermi, and Bellotti. This is how many of Nattier's most "iconic" printed fabrics were created, such as the wool in dark blue and turquoise with a wavy motif, reproduced in Plate 11.

The fabric could then be sold to North American department stores, which acquired the exclusive right to reproduce the models; in their turn, they advertised the model in the pages of US *Vogue* specifying that the wool was by Nattier (Figure 4.1).[85] The American market guaranteed the *carnettisti* the sale of many more meters of a textile originally created for a French couturier.

Finally, as the fabric was exclusive to Europe for only six months, Nattier also sold to big Japanese wholesalers such as ITOH, who could buy more meters. This expansion of the market beyond the western borders would allow Nattier to sell more of the fabric that it had invested in producing in the first place; but these sales would also lengthen the fabric's "life" beyond the season in which it was made.

As seen in the journey of the Fabiani–Nattier striped red-and-blue wool, a fabric in the *carnettista*'s portfolio could gain second and third lives thanks to its different uses, retail, and marketing. Through these practices, "unique" couture models were made reproducible and their copies, with the same textile quality, would be available to a broader sector of the population. The *carnettisti* were the orchestrators of a complex mechanism linking consumer, producer, and designer.

Figure 4.1 Ungaro–Bonwitt Teller coat with wool designed by Sonia Knapp for Nattier, *Vogue US*, September 15, 1968, p. 114 photography by Irving Penn, *Vogue*, © Condé Nast.

Carnettisti in the CNMI: Toward a Codified Role and Crisis

Toward the end of the 1960s, the *carnettisti*'s existence was under threat, and within a few years they would either change their nature radically or disappear. As we have seen, the Italian fashion market was changing, and *alta moda* was giving way to ready-to-wear fashion. The *carnettisti*'s role started to be tarnished, and their key services were gradually substituted by a more direct relationship between high fashion and textile manufacturers—a link that the CNMI was actively promoting.

A sign of the shifting times is an exchange of letters dated early 1967, between Roman couturier Patrick de Barentzen, Dr. Amos Ciabattoni, the then CEO of CNMI, and Como silk manufacturer Tessitura Serica Bini. The correspondence started because de Barentzen called upon Ciabattoni to help him establish contact with textile manufacturers for his growing production of ready-to-wear. The request of such an intervention came because two manufacturers, Bevilaqua and Verzoletto, had turned down a request to collaborate directly with de Barentzen because of their pre-existing rapport with the *carnettisti*.

In response to this call for help, Ciabattoni wrote letters to all the textile producers de Barentzen listed, to facilitate a meeting between de Barentzen and the producers. The aim would be to establish a direct collaboration for the supply of textiles for de Barentzen's growing line of—as Ciabattoni calls it—the "prêt-à-porter Italiano di Alta Moda."[86]

The most telling response to this request came from Tessitura Serica Bini, clearly explaining the reasons for their refusal to collaborate. The problem for de Barentzen began because more and more couturiers, as seen in Chapter 3, had started developing *prêt-à-porter* lines. Serica Bini did not have distinct pattern books to offer to the *carnettisti* (who catered for *alta moda*) and to the producers of ready-to-wear. This meant that if Serica Bini was to have a direct relationship with de Barentzen this would compromise the existing relationship with the *carnettisti*, which represented one of their major sale outlets.[87] This is a clear sign of how highly the textile mills regarded the role the *carnettisti* played in their business: they were keen to maintain the relationship even though this would mean rejecting a new partnership with ready-to-wear business.

These letters highlight a series of interesting points on the role of the *carnettisti*. Firstly, the *carnettisti* and textile producers by 1967 had a longstanding and mutually profitable relationship. In fact, the *carnettisti*, working as a bridge between producer and couturiers, selected and bought large quantities of textiles and offered them to the high-fashion designers who, as we have seen, purchased them in limited quantities due to the nature of their business.[88] This system worked for many years as the three players were satisfied by the deal: the producer sold large amounts to one client, the *carnettista*; and the *carnettista* achieved its profit by offering the products to couturiers and, as we have seen, progressively in larger quantities to dressmakers, textile shops, and department stores. Finally, the couturiers were satisfied, because by consulting the *carnettista*'s stock, they could easily select the best of the textile production without having to search the output of many manufacturers around Italy.[89]

In this correspondence, the silk manufacturer expresses clearly the very tight relationships with the *carnettisti*, and condemns a Milan newspaper that attributed the success of the Rome fashion show to direct contact between high-fashion houses and textile manufacturers. The Serica Bini silk manufacturer expresses the belief that all the fabrics seen in the Roman fashion show were supplied by the *carnettisti*, with the small exception of two or three textile producers who eliminated the *carnettisti* intermediary and were in contact directly with dressmakers. The letter continues to highlight the exclusive and important role played by the *carnettisti*, who owned a vast variety of new fabrics (*tessuti novità*)—buying many meters of these with their own capital and at their own risk in advance of the fashion shows, so that the high-fashion designers could use what they needed at a later stage. The biggest merit that Serica Bini attributes to the *carnettisti* is their quick response to the demand of couturiers and dressmakers. Therefore, they owned a large stock that often remained unsold, and therefore in so doing they bore the financial risk.[90]

What follows is key to understanding the *raison d'être* of the *carnettisti*. Serica Bini makes it clear to Ciabattoni of the CNMI that the *carnettisti* performed the key role of liaison with designers and consequently they were a source of continuous orders. Serica Bini was aware that this relationship came with the loss of visibility for the manufacturer in terms of advertising.

> This state of things leads me to fully recognize the utility of the *carnettisti* and to use a decisive policy to protect them: it would be highly acceptable to us as well, clearly, to be able to work directly with the dressmakers, in order to be considered a direct supplier and therefore have the advertisement advantages that this entails, but it is obvious that one has to give away something in comparison with the advantage of dealing with the *carnettista* who offer early and remarkable orders.[91]

Ciabattoni's response to Serica Bini further clarifies the situation of the *carnettisti* in the mid-1960s. In this letter, the CEO of the CNMI takes the time to analyze the relationship between couturiers and *carnettisti*. Ciabattoni recalls how the *carnettisti* "in the past" were almost exclusively the vehicle for the couturiers to obtain textiles. However, their *carnet* (selection of fabric) was often composed of non-Italian textiles, mainly French. The CNMI wanted to change this tendency and promote Italian textiles, and therefore, as previously seen, they set up prizes for those fashion houses that employed at least fifty percent Italian textiles in their collections.[92] This did not mean an exclusion of the *carnettisti* from the system, but it was a change of rules that was not in their favor. The CNMI's policy, as we will see toward the end of this chapter, meant the inclusion in advertisements and specialized press of three players: the designer, the textile manufacturer, and the *carnettista*.

Furthermore, in the considerations highlighted in the Serica Bini exchange of letters a new definition of "Made in Italy" emerged. In fact, the monetary prize established in 1964 by the CNMI to promote the use of Italian fabric by Italian couturiers suggested, by its very existence, the reason for its introduction: that in the years up to 1964 the *carnettisti* were supplying Italian designers with materials that were not necessarily Italian. There were two possible reasons for this. First, perhaps Italian textiles were considered so prestigious that they were primarily sold to the more lucrative export markets, leaving the Italian market with only a partially Italian supply chain. Or perhaps Italian fabrics were not deemed good enough, and the more prestigious French textiles were supplied through preference to Italian couturiers. Second, the CNMI was aware that the "Made in Italy" brand needed to be protected. *Alta moda* was therefore chosen as the ambassador to bring prestige to the entire Italian clothing system.

The CNMI's intention to connect high-fashion producers directly with textile manufacturers had the consequence of redefining the role of the *carnettisti*. The types of services that the *carnettisti* had been offering, as the Nattier example has shown, included bearing the financial burden of buying meters of fabrics from the producers, responding to customers' demands by producing new exclusive fabrics, opening new markets and partnerships, and being in charge of sales, marketing, and advertising. The CNMI perceived them only as the middleman and therefore responsible for inflating costs, and in the 1970s all these activities were brought in-house by the textile mills themselves. Silk producers like Clerici Tessuto developed an in-house *ufficio stile* (style office) to select fabrics that would become part of the collections. This was akin to what the *carnettisti* were doing with their carnet. Furthermore, commercial representatives were hired to travel from market to market to place their products, a responsibility similar to that of Brenda Azario at Nattier.

In 1970, the trade magazine *L'Abbigliamento Italiano* published an investigative report across five articles, by journalist Laura B. Piccoli, scrutinizing the crisis of the *carnettisti* during the previous few years. Each article contains interviews with representatives of the *carnettisti*, such as the owner of Sassi or the CEO of Seletex. The problems highlighted in the articles are mainly related to the new tendency of *alta moda* to have direct relationships with textile producers in order to obtain lower prices. This development diminished the role that the *carnettisti* had played until that moment. Piccoli's investigation suggests that the real reasons for this new alliance were not connected to choices of taste, or the needs of professionals, but driven by the implementations of national agreements. Probably this conclusion refers to the activities of CNMI, which, since 1964, had been aimed at encouraging a direct relationship between textile producers and couturiers. This, according to Bruno Sassi in his interview with Piccoli, deeply subverted the textile and fashion productive system in place until that moment.[93]

In the new 1970s panorama, couturiers, instead of buying textiles from the *carnettisti*, preferred to buy directly from the textile producers. Sassi says he believes that this was not only a matter of substituting the *carnettista* with the textile manufacturer, but that couturiers tended to choose a supplier only because it offered them free full-page advertisements in specialized magazines. Such an agreement offered the couturier visibility at no extra cost. However, Sassi laments that this often results in the advertising of fabrics chosen not because they were in tune with the season, but merely to look good on the page. In Sassi's opinion, advertising ephemeral or non-existent fabrics bewildered the consumer and unbalanced the productive circle, because the fabric had no commercial life beyond the page and the catwalk.[94]

Notwithstanding the reasons so far listed, the factor that most challenged the *carnettisti's* role was the progressive disappearance of dressmakers' and seamstresses' businesses, and the parallel success of *prêt-à-porter*.[95] In the aforementioned interview, one of the solutions to the *carnettisti's* crisis, suggested by Sassi, was for the *carnettista* to supply not only high fashion but also *prêt-à-porter*, albeit with a less prestigious and less expensive selection of textiles. However, many *carnettisti* were not able to adapt to the new system and the changing market that was emerging. Furthermore, the shift was already taking place, as seen in the case of Cleonice Capece, who produced only ready-to-wear. She already bought, as early as the 1960s, directly from fabric manufacturers and *carnettisti*.[96]

Although many *carnettisti* closed after the crisis at the beginning of the 1970s, some remained and continued their activities, such as Gandini, Lucchini, and SATAM.[97] As described above, multiple reasons contributed to the gradual disappearance of the *carnettista* and each company followed a different trajectory. For Nattier, the period of success came to an end in 1969. The Azarios borrowed heavily to buy new machines to modernize some of the production. Brenda recalled how at the time the interest rate was seven percent, but that it quickly rose to fifteen percent and the business suffered as a result. The already unstable financial situation was aggravated by personal circumstances, especially the accident that in 1969 caused Brenda to be hospitalized for two years. Her prolonged absence had an immediate negative impact on the sales for which she was responsible. Nattier-Litex was put into receivership in 1971 and closed the following year.[98]

Ciabattoni's reply to Tessuti Serica Bini's view of the *carnettista's* dilemma is revealing in terms of the direction that the next decade took.[99] Although the CNMI did not aim to explicitly exclude the *carnettisti*, it wanted to include a third protagonist, the textile producer, in the system of promotion of Italian textile and fashion. This meant that the names of fashion creator, textile manufacturer, and *carnettista* had to be compulsorily presented and clearly stated in the presentation of the fashion collections, in the specialized international press, and in the advertisement.[100]

The *carnettisti* were reluctant to adopt the new system, because if they openly revealed their sources it would cause the loss of many revenues and invalidate most of their work behind the scenes. Although not all the *carnettisti* complied with the rules, many did, as demonstrated by the advertisements and editorials in the spring/summer 1966 issue of *Linea Italiana*, where both the *carnettista* and the producer were mentioned. In a 1966 advertisement for Seletex and Tita Rossi, the name of the *carnettista*, Seletex, is prominent and clearly connected to the image of the model descending the stairs, and the name of the designer (Tita Rossi) and of the producer of the tartan wool (Ferrarin) are listed in the caption describing the image.[101]

Ciabattoni believed that the promotion of the nascent Italian *prêt-à-porter* could only be achieved with a precise "policy of prices" and the increased involvement of the textile producers. This resulted in the direct connection between fashion brands and textile manufacturers or the involvement of *carnettisti* willing to follow the demands of the new system. Examples of adaptable *carnettisti* were Lucchini and Gandini, who survived the change because they managed to collaborate with *prêt-à-porter*. The shift in the panorama of the Italian textile and fashion system during the 1960s from couture to *prêt-à-porter* inevitably resulted in the disappearance or change of role of the *carnettisti*.

The 1968 spring/summer issue of *Linea Italiana* features eighteen pages of advertisements for the couturier Biki. The numerous pages include black-and-white or color photographs representing models either in full page, three-quarter, or shoulder height in a variety of poses wearing Biki's creations. The pages are introduced by a frontispiece designed by the Italian illustrator Brunetta, while the eighteen pages of photographs are united by the same graphic treatment. This consists of a full-page picture with four beveled corners on a white background, the logos of the products advertised at the bottom of the page, and Biki's signature on each page reversed out in white either at the top right or top left corner of each picture.

Linea Italiana's glossy pages, its editorials' standpoint, and the fact that it was translated at the back into French, English, and Spanish, pointed, according to White, to a middle-to-high market level and a mixture of trade and public consumption.[102] The magazine first appeared in 1965 and it was a biannual publication. As fashion historian Gabriele Monti states, it was a crucial publication that in its pages celebrated the qualities and characteristics of Italian fashion.[103] The magazine was the official mouthpiece of the *Centro Italiano Tessili Abbigliamento Alta Moda* (Italian Center of Textile, Ready-to-Wear and Haute Couture, CITAM) and the Ministry of Foreign Commerce. It had the aim of supporting cooperation between textile manufacturers, couturiers, and garment makers, and promoting abroad the union between Italian fashion and Italian textiles.[104]

Biki's multipage advertisement, among many similar others included in *Linea Italiana*, visually summarized the effort the CNMI had put in the previous year to create a much more organic and united fashion–textile system. Textile producers, *carnettisti*, and designers were advertising side by side with other fashion-system companies such as make-up brands, sewing machines, and fiber producers. The *carnettisti* who decided to play by the rules of the new system foreseen by CNMI, and to reveal their sources, managed to adapt their role and continued their business. These pages attempted to offer the readers and trade the impression of a fully organized and organic fashion system. This approach would continue and be refined in the following two decades, as will be highlighted in Chapter 5.

This chapter has investigated details of the mechanisms, commission, and promotion of textile production for *alta moda* through the *carnettisti*. During the 1960s this sphere of fashion was still influential and considered the pinnacle of taste. As we have seen, although a textile was initially created for *alta moda*, it "trickled down" to fashion productions that reached a wider number of customers. During the 1960s the *carnettisti* became more visible to the eyes of consumers, through full-page advertisements and debates on their role in the specialized press; yet at the same time their position of leadership was threatened by changes in the fashion–textile system. The period under consideration here ended with a crisis in the system, and the advent of the new powerhouse of ready-to-wear, which the majority of *carnettisti* seemed unable to cater for.

There were signs that *alta moda* was about to give way to the new *prêt-à-porter*. Not only was *alta moda* venturing into synthetic fabrics, but for several seasons *prêt-à-porter* used the same textiles supplied to *alta moda*, especially woolen ones.[105] What seems to be a contradiction is well explained by Rosina, who highlights how, in this decade of changes, *alta moda* "was losing the leading position it had enjoyed in previous decades, unable to transform itself from a creator of unique garments for the elite into a creator of prototypes for industry."[106] Gradually, as we will see, Italian textile manufacturing decided to supply the luxury ready-to-wear businesses, as they would order a higher number of meters compared to *alta moda*. Furthermore, the manufacturers gradually retreated from the market of retail and drapery shops, because many *stilisti* who started to work for the industry requested exclusive use of the textiles.[107]

Chapter 4 has been dominated by the relationship between *carnettisti*, textile producers, and *alta moda*, but in the next section, and the next decade, the trio will be the *stilista*, the textile producer, and the clothing manufacturers. As the relationship between production and consumption shifted, the system reshaped itself by focusing on new players and intermediaries.

5

Milan and the *Stilisti*

Introduction

In the early 1970s, Italy was deeply entrenched in a period of workers' protests, political terrorism, and, like most of the western world, was also involved in the oil crisis.[1] Despite the political and economic situation, Italian fashion was living through a moment of deep changes that would lead to the affirmation of a mature fashion system.

The years between the beginning of the 1970s and the mid-1980s were a period that saw the establishment of a solid industrialized Italian fashion system mainly associated with the *distretti industriali*, also known as *distretti produttivi* (productive districts) in the center-north of Italy. The city of Milan sits at the core of this fashion and textile network of small and medium companies. Although Milan was part of production even in previous decades, the city now rose to national and international attention as the capital of Italian *prêt-à-porter*.[2]

I have chosen to analyze the productive system of the *distretti industriali* because of its innovative structure based on clusters of small companies localized on the Italian territory. However, this kind of industry did not start up suddenly in the 1970s. The system had its roots in the years after the Second World War and it reached obvious statistical significance by the mid-1970s.[3] As a result, several economic studies have been written about this period, as analyzed in detail in this chapter. Although I mentioned the districts in Chapter 2, I investigate this typical Italian economic model here for two reasons. The first is that in the 1970s and 1980s there was a proliferation of international interest from economists, sociologists, and anthropologists in the Italian manufacturing model. The way in which Italy was producing goods, including fashion, seemed to offer something for other nations to learn from. Secondly, this model has been heralded by fashion scholars as one of the pillars of the success of Milanese ready-to-wear. Anthropologist Simona Segre Reinach, for instance, believes that the industrial districts, along with design, manufacturing, service industries, and communications (TV, press, advertising agencies, and PR), were the key ingredients of Milan's success.[4]

The seventies, in terms of Italian fashion production, have been defined by economic historian Ivan Paris as the period of consolidation and maturation of the previous decades' experimentation and metamorphosis. This resulted in the establishment of an "authentic fashion system" that saw Milan become the stronghold of Italian fashion, affirmed as one of the top four worldwide fashion centers, together with New York, Paris, and London.[5] Although Paris in his paper does not define this "authentic fashion system" directly, he is probably referring to what historian Rietta Messina had previously described as

> an organic and integrated relationship between the various components of production and services, in the textile sector as well as in that of clothing and knitwear, which made it possible to cut down on the time required to bring in innovations, to expand the choice of materials and to increase the range of products.[6]

By the early 1970s the designer Walter Albini, together with the labels Krizia and Missoni, had left the *Sala Bianca* in Florence to present their mass-produced collections in Milan. This was the start of a phenomenon that saw a growing number of designers getting together in events such as *Milanovendemoda* and *Modit*. *Milanovendemoda* was started in 1969 by the agents and commercial units of the garment sector. The idea was to initiate a direct dialogue with buyers in the city of Milan, where more and more designers had chosen to locate their headquarters. Nine years later, in March 1978, *Modit* took place in the *Fiera Campionaria* of Milan. This event was organized by the *Associazioni Industriali dell'Abbigliamento e della Maglieria* (Association of Garment and Knitwear Industrialists) together with consultant Beppe Modenese. This show was a catalyst for the relationship between the *stilista* (designer) and industry, and it consecrated Milan as its capital.[7]

Segre Reinach argues that between the 1970s and 1980s Milan did not become the capital of fashion, but specifically the capital of *prêt-à-porter*.[8] This is a key distinction to make as Italy continued to have a larger fashion landscape not limited to Milan. From 1967, when an agreement was signed between the *Centro di Firenze per la Moda Italiana* and the *Camera Nazionale della Moda Italiana*, couture fashion shows moved to Rome, while Florence maintained its role in representing the *moda boutique* and knitwear production. Furthermore, in 1972 Florence also became synonymous with menswear fashion with the debut of the Pitti Uomo shows.[9]

As *prêt-à-porter* became the new language of fashion, it is the center of this investigation. This chapter will return to another facet of this book's argument, namely the important role that production played in Italy's history of fashion and textiles. Here I survey economic theories that define the Italian network of production in the form of the *distretti industriali* and how they supported the development of *prêt-à-porter*. I investigate the city of Milan and how it acts as the helm of widespread regional production. Here the *stilisti*, a new breed of designer/entrepreneur/creative intermediary, found the ideal place to establish their headquarters and the studios from which they could design their collections.

The Rise of Milan

The city of Milan becomes important for this research in the early 1970s because the media, such as magazines, the main fashion shows, and trade fairs, were located here in this period. While in the previous chapters I have focused on production and how this has driven Italian fashion, there has been a shift from production to mediation as the key driver of the fashion industry since the 1970s that has made Milan the center of attention for this investigation.

In 2002 the volume *Moda a Milano: Stile e Impresa nella Città che Cambia* was published to promote the role that Milan and Lombardy played in the success of the Italian fashion system.[10] From its first pages, it highlights how fashion in Italy is an industrial product. Such a statement was obvious by 2002, but at the beginning of the 1970s industrialized fashion was a phenomenon that had just started to develop.

This chapter brings together secondary sources to demonstrate the importance that Milan assumed in the fashion panorama from the beginning of the 1970s. It sheds light on what has been traditionally considered the "rise" of Milan as a fashion city and its establishment as the center of a regional hub of industrial districts. As seen in previous chapters, Milan was already part of the Italian fashion landscape throughout the period analyzed so far. However, it was only in the early 1970s that the city took center stage of a new phenomenon, a new system, that saw the designer of *prêt-à-porter* gaining "international commercial and media success."[11]

Segre Reinach has widely written about Milan as a fashion city, arguing that the relevance and role of Milan in fashion history is strictly connected to the arrival of "a particular model of production and consumption: fashion designers' *prêt-à-porter*."[12] Segre Reinach establishes that until the 1960s Milan did not play a major role in fashion. The only exceptions she mentions are the 1906 Milan International Expo (as mentioned in the Introduction to this book), when Rosa Genoni exhibited, thus encouraging Italian couturiers to free themselves from the dictates of French haute couture; and the 1948 Expo, when the *Centro della Moda Italiana* opened (see Chapter 2).[13]

However, economic historians Elisabetta Merlo and Francesca Polese believe that the economy of fashion in Milan goes back at least to the late nineteenth century and the beginning of the twentieth century:

> During these years, Milan boasted a well-developed, diversified economy of fashion in which all elements were present, from production and distribution of fabrics, to complete garments, to the entire range of accessories, and finally, with decorations such as ribbon, lace and bows.[14]

This system had its historic roots even further back. For example, in the mid-1500s the term "millinery" was derived from *Millaners*, which indicated merchants from Milan who traded in northern Europe in silks, ribbons, gloves, and Florentine straw hats.[15]

Furthermore, after Italy's unification, Milan also became the capital of the fashion press. Merlo and Polese point out how the presence of a specialized press highlights the strict connection between fashion and industry in Milan, as many magazines were backed by the city's clothing and textile manufacturers. Between 1861 and 1920 seventy-five of the one hundred and forty-nine Italian fashion magazines were published in Milan.[16] This increased with the launch, between 1920 and 1945, of another fifty-two new magazines in Milan.[17] In 1945 *Bellezza*, which until that moment had been based in Turin, was transferred to Milan where it remained till 1970.[18] Finally, in the 1950s, two more specialized magazines, *Linea Italiana* and *Novità*, appeared in the Milanese panorama. The latter was bought by Condé Nast and became *Vogue Italia* in 1966.[19]

Moreover, Milan was not only synonymous with the fashion industry: it was an economic city. As historian John Foot describes, it was the "central market city, a place of exchange and finance dealing for buyers, producers, mediators."[20] The "market" locations were concentrated mainly in the Stock Exchange, the *Camera di Commercio* (Chamber of Commerce), and the *Fiera Campionaria*. In September 1946 the *Fiera*, as it came to be known, was the second biggest universal fair organized in the world, after the one in Paris in August of the same year. Three thousand six hundred exhibitors from every production sector were represented. During the 1950s and 1960s the results of each edition were spectacular. Italy's main architects designed unique buildings viewed by millions of visitors.[21] This was one of Europe's most important industrial and commercial exhibitions and all the fashion players, from *alta moda* to men's tailors, from accessories producers to textile companies, exhibited there. A picture of a fashion show held in *Fiera* in 1948 (Figure 5.1) testifies to the way that fashion was presented very soon after the war: this show appeared to be initiated as a promotion of the fiber producer Italviscosa.[22]

In addition to the *Fiera*, from 1957 another international specialized textile fair took place in Milan, the *Mercato Internazionale del Tessile per l'Abbigliamento e l'Arredamento* (MITAM), as discussed in Chapter 3. MITAM represented the most important showcase for the country's textile production, but, like all fairs of this kind, it consisted of a long series of variously sized impersonal stands hosted in anonymous pavilions. However, in 1967 a small group of Como silk industrialists tried out an alternative model, organizing fashion show performances in the stunning setting of the Grand Hotel Villa d'Este in Cernobbio on Lake Como. The

Figure 5.1 High-fashion show in the Italviscosa pavilion at the Milan Trade Fair, 1948. Author Ancilotti and Martinotti. Courtesy Archivio Storico Fondazione Fiera Milano.

innovative idea was to add value to the Como district's textile production.[23] The change of setting, the glamour of the location, and the quality of the materials on show made this event an unmissable annual appointment for textile producers and designers from all over the world. Fashion designer Cleonice Capece recollects how she used to get ideas for her future collection in the Villa d'Este hotel after purchasing fabrics at the fair.[24]

As seen in Chapter 4, during the 1960s Milan was also the headquarters of many of the *carnettisti* and later of the influential *Camera Nazionale della Moda Italiana*.[25] The city was also key for fashion retail: Foot argues that the department store La Rinascente was another important factor that made Milan the international capital of design more generally. Designers in the field of fashion and furniture such as Bruno Munari, Ignazio Gardella, and Giorgio Armani were all located there.[26]

This concentration of industry, trade, and design created the backdrop for a series of events that helped shaped the city into the capital of *prêt-à-porter* around the end of the 1960s and the beginning of the 1970s. In 1967, Fiorucci opened its Milan boutique in Galleria Passerella in San Babila: with its lighting, its imported goods, and its innovative products such as jeans, it was the pioneer among the plethora of spectacular designer shops that would open in Milan in the following decade. In the same year the Missonis organized their fashion show in the Solari swimming pool, featuring inflatable plastic sofas. It was the first of many such avant-garde and spectacular performances created in Milan's most disparate locations to promote fashion.

Milan has been considered the center of the industrial districts. In the immediate vicinity lies Como with its century-old silk production, Legnano and Gallarate, known for their cotton, and Biella, known for fine wool. The further one moves from the Milanese epicenter, the more centers of specialized production can be found, such as knitwear in Carpi, leather in Tuscany, shoes and jeans in Marche, and wool in Prato. It was mainly in Milan, though also to some extent in Florence and some regions of the northeast, that fashion products were designed, programmed, created, and communicated in strict connection with the factories spread around the nearby territory. Milan is intimately connected to the industrial system of the country, a system that in the post-war year was changing drastically, as explained in the next chapter.

The success of Milan, as has been illustrated, happened gradually and did not rely on a singular factor. The concurrence of circumstances such as the presence of specialized press, the vicinity of textile and fabric production, and the historical legacy of the city as a commercial and industrial hub all contributed to the rise of Milan as the capital of Italian ready-to-wear. Finally, the city became the virtual capital of the production clustered around the country in what have been defined as the *distretti produttivi*, as will be analyzed in the next section.

Distretti Industriali (Industrial Districts)

In the period under consideration in this chapter, Italian manufacturing was not uniform. It is complex to unpick the kind of industrial production on which Italian fashion is based. On the one hand, there were larger factories such as Marzotto and Zucchi, based on the American mass-production method, and characterized by vertical integration (or integrated corporations) and a high number of standardized goods.[27] These mass-production factories shared similar characteristics to each other, such as the internalization of all stages of production "from spinning and weaving to garments manufacturing."[28]

On the other hand, a completely opposite structure existed, of small independent firms dispersed in the territory, each producing only a small phase of the final product, all specializing in the same sector, and together almost constituting a virtual factory.

Furthermore, the differentiation between these two models was quite blurred, especially in the 1980s, when it was evident that "many Italian apparel firms combine elements of both the integrated corporation and the network firm."[29] For example, some vertically integrated companies would rely on smaller firms by way of subcontracting orders that could not be fulfilled within their integrated plants. Companies such as GFT encompassed within their boundaries different types of production; and some companies started with one production model and evolved over time.[30]

Regional concentrations of companies working in the same field—specializing in silk, or wool, or leather, but also yarns and the finished products—are known (then and now) as *distretti produttivi* (productive districts) or *distretti industriali* (industrial districts). The firms are usually small to medium-sized and often family-run. They are highly specialized but also very flexible. The regional network system, with its focus on quality and attention to detail, has been considered the backbone of the "Made in Italy" brand.[31] As textile historian Margherita Rosina puts it: "By the 1970s Italian fashion was well established and relied on a solid network of professionals, ranging from pattern-makers and cutters to embroiderers and furriers."[32]

The term "industrial district" is a concept created by the English economist Alfred Marshall, who, according to economist Marco Bellandi, remarks in his definition that:

> The division of labor which characterizes the area is not by individual workers in a single factory but by different highly specialized firms which both compete with each other and complement one another.[33]

Marshall uses this notion in the context of the end of the nineteenth century to describe the production of Lancashire cottons, among others. His concept was later recovered by others such as economists Giacomo Becattini and Sebastiano Brusco to label some Italian regions.[34] What emerges from these economic theories is that there is no universally agreed definition of industrial districts. The nature of the Italian district, during the 1980s, has been the subject of debate.[35] It is not the aim of this study to report on these differences. However, in this chapter I will provide a literature review of the main economic theories that describe the phenomenon of small firms in Italy and highlight how they related to the production of fashion.

The economic literature considers fashion and textile production as a well-stocked field from which to draw examples to describe this phenomenon. For instance, the Marche shoemaking district is described in *Made in Italy: Small-Scale Industrialization and Its Consequences* by anthropologist Michael L. Blim. The Prato district is considered in *The Second Industrial Divide* by economists Michael J. Piore and Charles F. Sabel, and the Como silk-production region is at the core of the study *From Peasant to Entrepreneur: The Survival of the Family Economy in Italy* by Anna Cento Bull and Paul Corner.

Although very insightful, these studies have mainly analyzed fashion and textile production as case studies convenient to illustrate larger economic models and trends that emerged in Italy. As Bull and Corner explain: "The silk industry, and the Como and Brianza region above Milan, have been selected therefore as an industry and a region which exemplify certain aspects of a specifically Italian process of industrialization."[36]

Conversely, in this section I will use economic definitions and analysis to better understand the complex network of small firms of fashion and textile production that have been considered the foundation of the Italian fashion boom between the 1970s and 1980s.

By the first half of the 1980s, Italy was Europe's fastest-growing economy. Edward Goodman stresses how in these years another "economic miracle" occurred, and the country became the fifth, if not the fourth, economy worldwide.[37]

What happened in the decade preceding this phenomenon is key to understanding how Italian industrial production in general, and Italian fashion production in particular, evolved. Piore and Sabel attribute the "radical decentralization of production," very familiar in the Pratese example, as a response to the strike waves of the 1960s. This was meant to be a short-lived ploy until "the worker militancy had passed."[38] However, although initially the conditions of work in the small firms were brutal—these firms insisted on long hours, evaded taxes, and did not pay into the social security system—after a while dependent subcontractors started to federate.[39] According to Piore and Sabel, these changes were visible in terms of rising wages and decreasing unemployment from the mid-1970s. Statistics also suggested that the small firms were by this time selling their products directly to foreign buyers. This transformation was mirrored by changes in the Italian machine-tool industry: for example, Italian shoe machinery began to be marketed in North America because of its flexibility.[40]

By the mid-1970s a global recession caused by the oil crisis of 1973 had hit the clothing industry worldwide. Most countries affected tried to find a way out by reducing production costs. This was carried out by the delocalization of production to places where labor was cheaper and plentiful. For example, the USA relocated production to Central America, France to North Africa, and Germany to East Europe.

The Italian clothing industry was facing the same kind of problem. However, according to Merlo and Polese, in Italy the "delocalization resembled more a decentralization in a domestic scale, as it occurred within the boundaries of the country."[41] After this crisis the Italian textile and clothing industry emerged deeply transformed.[42] Data shows how, between 1971 and 1981, the big companies with more than one hundred employees lost eighty thousands jobs, while smaller companies with fewer than one hundred employees hired more than one hundred thousand people. The data shows that Italy overcame the recession with a process of "deverticalization and decentralization of production."[43] This strategy was aimed at reducing the high cost of labor that had caused the recession. As we will see in this section, along with decentralization, Italian firms also introduced labor-saving technologies, and these made the industry more flexible. Nonetheless, as historians Bull and Corner explain, there is no agreement about the origins of what can be also called "diffused entrepreneurship."[44]

This process of decentralization was not only occurring in the fashion sector but of the whole industrial panorama, and "in 1985 it was estimated that small firms employing fewer than ten workers made up 80 percent of all the Italian manufacturing firms."[45] Furthermore, Blim believes that

The emergence of small-scale industrialization in Italy's central and northeastern region is in many ways the most stunning and interesting facet of the remarkable industrial renaissance that has propelled Italy's economy well past Great Britain and perhaps even France in the Western capital order.[46]

One of the interesting questions Goodman asks himself in the introduction to *Small Firms and Industrial Districts in Italy* is: "[H]ow is it that the Italian Lilliputian firms have stood up to a world of giants?"[47] His answer is that the success of Italian small firms was based on the craft and self-employed workers who relied on values of family and community.[48] Similarly, Piore and Sabel pinpoint four factors as essential to the Italian innovation:

> The Italian extended family, the view of artisan work as a distinct type of economic activity, the existence of merchant traditions connecting the Italian provinces to world market; and the willingness of municipal and regional governments (often allied to the labor movement) to help create the infrastructure that firms required but could not themselves provide.[49]

The central and northeastern economic development of Italy is described in a nutshell by Blim: "spontaneous, small-scale, and flexible in the production method, export-led and niche finding in its marketing, familial in organization, and petty entrepreneurial in character."[50]

As Bull and Corner remind us, though, "the literature on industrial districts has, for some time now, crossed paths with the literature on the Third Italy" [defined below].[51] In their study they compare these two sectors, on one hand the Third Italy industrialization between the 1960s and 1970s and on the other, the region of older industrialization such as northern Lombardy and other sub-Alpine regions.

The 1980s and 90s literature on the Italian industrial system groups Italy into three macro-regions: "the unhappy southern combination of state assistance, Mafia, and rural exodus"; "the northern large-scale industrial expansion"; and the Third Italy (*la Terza Italia*), a concept introduced in 1977 by Italian sociologist Arnaldo Bagnasco in *Tre Italie: La Problematica Territoriale dello Sviluppo Italiano*.[52] His Third Italy consists of the central and northeastern regions of Trentino–Alto Adige, Veneto, Friuli–Venezia Giulia, Emilia Romagna, Toscana, Umbria, and Marche. Blim believes that the economic development of the triangle between Genoa, Milan, and Turin is not distinctive, while the economic progress of the Third Italy "has been extraordinarily successful."[53] In formerly marginal regions, such as Marche, gross domestic product grew at an annual rate of 3.5 percent between the 1970s and 1980s, this is to say 0.4 percent per year more than the national gross domestic product.[54]

Goodman declares that the backbone of the small firms of *la Terza Italia*—especially of the traditional industries such as "fabrics and clothing, shoe-making and leather goods, ceramics, carpentry and furniture"—is the idea of the *artigiano*.[55] The *artigiano* or master craftsman is an independent skillful individual with a passion for details and an eye for relevance. Goodman believes that a good mix of these traits has kept the *artigiano's* firm in business for hundreds of years and such firms became the model for Italian small businesses.[56] At the base of the *artigiano's* economy is the conservative structure of the family which generates a strong sense of commitment among members of the firm. It is also the group that teaches its members to be productive, and that measures the maximum expansion of the firm, which is between five and ten people.[57] The small size of both firm and factory, according to Goodman, encourages dialogue among workers, clients, and entrepreneur and stimulates new ideas. The Italian small firm therefore differentiates itself from other nationalities because "it has family, social and artistic aspects as well as economic."[58]

Goodman's ideas of family and *artigiano* resonate very well with the landscape of fashion and textile production. Most of the Italian fashion and textiles businesses are strongly based on a family network: some, like Missoni and Versace, are still pretty much family-run, although some others have in recent years transformed from family enterprises into international multimillion-euro brands.

In the Italian *Vogue* issue of July–August 1975, an editorial titled "I Clans degli Italiani" (The Italian Clans) was published to report on the various trends of Italian *prêt-à-porter* of that season. Each spread was occupied full bleed by one designer's gang surrounded by either his or her family, such as the Missonis, friends, family, business partners, and their entourage. The copy states how Italians typically have an individualism that tends to separate them into many small groups, each one of them with its precise style code. This article aptly summarizes the essence of what Italian industry and *prêt-à-porter* came to signify: not a national style, but an array of very distinctive styles, each based on their *stilista* (fashion designer) and his or her family or group, as we will see in the next section.[59]

As seen in each picture of this article, the designers are not isolated entities: they are surrounded by their collaborators, workers, and family, all dressed in the brand's clothing and accessories. This visualizes the core attributes of Italian *prêt-à-porter*, a total look that is created in collaboration. The word "clan" not only defines the designer's closed entourage, but also the consumers that buy into the specific style; as for example in the Gianni Versace "clan" picture where among his collaborators and family there are also the countess Cristina Augusta and Anna Falk, followers of his fashion.

Within this landscape of small firms or clans, Goodman believes that "one of the secrets of Italian success has been the ability to revive traditional industries by the careful application of new technologies."[60] This is very true for the Italian fashion and textile industries, many of which, such as Gucci and Prada for example, started as family-run craft industries at the beginning of the twentieth century and evolved into international multimillion-euro brands also quoted on the stock market.[61]

Economic literature around the small firms and industrial districts in Italy has shown how this phenomenon is not static but has evolved through time in the way which has been studied and described. As Sabel declares in *Work and Politics*, the studies carried out in the early 1970s have tended to consider the spread of small firms as an escape for troubled entrepreneurs making fashionable consumer goods for the export market.[62] During the second part of the decade, however, and also due to the fact that this industrial structure reorganized itself, the small workshops came to be seen as a "distinct system of production capable of adapting technology to its own purposes and producing goods, such as sophisticated machine tools, that cannot be dismissed as peripheral to the advanced economies."[63]

Economists agree that, during the 1970s, traditional industries such as textiles, clothing, shoemaking, and leather making showed a special liveliness in the regions where the proliferation of small firms was greater and these companies continued to contribute to overall Italian exports.[64] Blim discusses this liveliness with reference to the Marche region, whose formidable post-war economic development lay in "transformation of preindustrial regional specialties such as shoemaking, clothing, furniture-making, and musical instruments into industrial export goods."[65]

Although the industrial districts were booming between the 1970s and 1980s, nowadays they are still considered an important motor of the Italian economy. Around two hundred thousand manufacturing companies are located in the districts: they employ around two million people, and produce 27.2 percent of the gross domestic product and 46 percent of the exports. Furthermore, 45 percent of the districts are connected to the clothing industry. As Scarpellini notes, in 2001 the ISTAT census recorded for the first time the variegated panorama of the districts. It emerged that around forty-five districts specialized in textile and clothing, and another twenty specialized in leather, hides, and footwear, making the overall fashion sector the employer of seven hundred thousand people.[66]

The *Stilista,* the Link Between Textile and Fashion Production

As previously discussed, there are several different theories about why the industrial structure of Italy changed radically from the 1970s onwards. In this section I analyze how the network of small, flexible, family-run high-tech companies, and the industrial districts in general, have supported the Italian fashion and textile industry.[67] In practice, this interaction required the presence of an intermediary who could work in synergy with the manufacturing landscape.

As demonstrated earlier, the city of Milan offered a context of successful design production, established textile industry, and the fashion press. Within this milieu, a new professional fashion figure took their first steps in the 1970s, a figure who came to define the Italian fashion production of this decade. In Italian they were called *stilisti,* which literally means stylists, but the terminology is confusing. As fashion curator Sonnet Stanfill explains:

> The word *stilista* is more nuanced and multifunctional than either of the English translations "designer" or "stylist" suggests. It came to refer to someone who mediated between the practicalities of industry, the requirements of retail buyers and the needs of the public, while also being aware of the importance of the press.[68]

According to historian Andrea Merlotti, the term *stilista* was first used in studies of Italian literature and described authors that devoted attention to the question of style. In the 1950s the terminology was transported to the industry setting to define someone whose job was to elaborate the design of large-scale goods: in particular, cars.[69] Slowly the terminology moved to fashion. According to Rosina, references to the figure of the fashion *stilista* started to appear in the mid-1960s.[70] This figure is nowadays considered the backbone of the success of the Milanese *prêt-à-porter.* However, writing in 1983, journalist Silvia Giacomoni remembered that this terminology was derogatory in the 1960s, and remarks that it still carried negative connotations in the 1980s.[71] In her opinion, the *stilista* was simply a designer for the clothing industry. Therefore, she finds it useful to compare the differences between the *stilista* and the product designer. She believes that the *stilisti* stood at the crossroads between the designers of the old school and the new ones. Like the old-school designers, they worked toward the simplification and acceleration of the production processes. However, like the new designers, they tried to influence consumers to choose products not only for their qualities, but for their power to define them socially and psychologically.[72]

In her 1983 book, Giacomoni is also very polemical about the *stilisti*. She accuses them of not being deeply rooted in their city of Milan, and of being unable to get together as a group and reflect on their profession. She believes that the *stilisti* were very talented in what they were doing, but they did not have a cultural dimension, probably because they were unable to reflect on their role and unable to connect it to similar professions.[73] Her analysis is based on comparison with designers of the "old generation," such as Marco Zanuso, Gae Aulenti, and Enzo Mari, who were working in the industry but were able to theorize their work.[74] Giacomoni hoped that the idea of having a museum of fashion in Milan could help in this direction.[75] She envisaged a museum that could put together the preservation of historic treasures of the past, an archive of contemporary production, and a school for *stilisti*, photographers, and models. However, such a Milanese museum of fashion has not yet become a reality.[76]

It is important to highlight how in the 1950s, as we saw in Chapter 4, only a very few isolated textile producers programmed production in synergy with the designers. Materials were designed independently of the fashion houses' models. This, therefore, created a divergence between the products and their materials. Conversely, one of the innovations that the *stilista* generated was his/her involvement in textile design in collaboration with textile producers: this would become an important aspect of the *prêt-à-porter* system. Furthermore, with the change of production mode, from couture to ready-to-wear, there was also a shift from the uniqueness of the spectacular dress to the mass-produced dress that could be reproduced in many copies. In this new panorama, the accent was therefore placed on the creativity and centrality of the *stilisti* and their ability to encompass a style.[77]

The *stilista*, together with the fashion designer more generally, has been mythologized in the fashion literature and has been considered the main motor behind the success of Italian *prêt-à-porter*.[78] However, I would like to analyze this phenomenon from a different angle. I see the *stilista* as the result of a changed approach to industrial production; and, as Segre Reinach puts it, the *stilista* "also indicates the assertion of a different fashion culture and underlines the dramatic change that *prêt-à-porter* represents in relation to Italian style."[79]

Walter Albini has been heralded as the prototype of this new professional figure.[80] Trained at the Art Design and Fashion Institute of Turin, he worked for magazines and newspapers making sketches of the fashion shows. After three years under Krizia (a number of his designs are analyzed in Chapter 6), he designed collections for Billy Ballo, Cadette, and Trell.[81] He was the first designer who experimented in Italy with new contractual and aesthetic approaches.[82] In the contractual sphere, he created an equal relationship between producer and designer. Albini did this by opening a small company to produce clothing with his business partner Luciano Papini. The company was called Mister Fox and it had a huge success with its autumn–winter 1970–71 collection, presented at Palazzo Pitti in April 1970 in Florence.[83] In the aesthetic sphere, Albini understood that in the new climate of young fashion, already emerging in Italy in the 1960s (and described in Chapter 3), the fashion creative should not only design singular pieces of clothing. Instead, they created a style, encompassing a complete collection and including accessories that consumers could buy into.

Fashion historians agree that Albini's fashion show at the *Circolo del Giardino* in Milan on April 27, 1971 (for the autumn–winter collection 1971–2) was the point of departure from the old conventions.[84] Albini presented 180 garments produced by five companies. Each company specialized in one sector: Basile for day suits and coats; Escargot for knitwear; Diamant's for shirts; Callaghan for jerseys; and Mister Fox for evening dresses. The collection was unified by the name of Albini, which appeared on each label as "Walter Albini for. . ." followed by the name of the producer.[85]

As Chapter 3 demonstrates, experimental collaborations between industry and couturiers were appearing across the country. Although not always long-lived, they started the dialogue between creative personalities and mass production. In the case of GFT the history of dialogue was uninterrupted, as a collaboration was instituted with *alta moda* and Biki in the 1960s and, in the next decade, the company devised a new method of production in response to the international competition and the shift in consumers' taste. The strategy involved the switch of some of its production from its long-established middle-market products to the one of high-quality ready-to-wear. The typical GFT production was characterized by high-quantity and standardized goods organized in many similar, parallel lines of products. To better exploit the Taylorist production lines a collaboration with the *stilisti* was established. This new relationship started from 1971 with Emanuel Ungaro and continued in 1978 with Giorgio Armani.[86] The GFT/*prêt-à-porter* products signed by the *stilisti* were instead very differentiated, both in the composition of the collections and in the fact that they rapidly followed one another. Furthermore, the quantity was limited to avoid massification and therefore overproduction and the production timing was very strict so as to follow the calendars of events that the *stilista* needed to be part of.[87] As described by political scientist Richard M. Locke, this kind of high-end ready-to-wear was the most specialized and it produced limited quantities, not more than ten or twenty units and using quality, high-cost materials often "especially designed for each model."[88] The *stilista* was authoring lines that the GFT could rapidly and effectively distribute to the domestic and international market. The *stilista* had the freedom to design their products autonomously, and was aided by a team of specialists and collaborators who helped with the textile research and with prototyping the collections for production.

The system of partnership between *stilista* and GFT was radically different from the collaboration between the same company with *alta moda* and Biki in 1957 as seen in Chapter 3. While earlier the couturier was kept out of the production line and only provided drawings, here a whole team was employed to translate in the best possible way the idea of the *stilista*. Locke describes this process as starting with the *stilista*'s sketch. The initial idea on the drawing was interpreted by the *stilista*'s collaborators, the *modellisti*, highly skilled workers who translated the first design into a prototype and then into a manufacturable product. However, this process, instead of being completely taken over by GFT as in the case of Biki, was now a strict collaboration between the whole team. This kind of experimentation between manufacturers and designers was crucial and it showed the way to others around Italy, who devised similar partnerships.

In this period, the *stilisti* were tied to the manufacturing companies that produced their designed goods by consultancy agreements, in the first instance. Subsequently, consultancy agreements were gradually substituted by licensing agreements, which regulated the right to use a design by a manufacturer who was not the original creator. Merlo and Polese pinpoint an evolution of this type of contract that supported the designers and their style, in various ways and through the various stages of their brand development.[89] They believe that this contractual relation between designer and industry was the backbone of Italy's fashion success in this period, as it allowed Italian *stilisti* to "become increasingly independent as far as retailing strategies are concerned."[90] The partnership of Italian fashion designers with industrial clothing companies, such as Armani with GFT or Albini for Zamasport, gave the designers an understanding of the "business world before becoming entrepreneurs themselves," and they were thereby equipped to create their own independent labels at a later date.[91]

Although there were common characteristics, the relationship between *stilisti* and manufacturers could differ greatly. As Giacomoni describes them, partnership models could range from full ownership of the brand name by the manufacturer to a simple consultancy agreement. Therefore in some cases one can speak about turnover, in others about royalties or commissions. In some cases, the *stilista* benefited from forms of shareholding within the company that produced the goods.

One way, as we have seen, was represented by the GFT and *stilista* model, which meant the stylistic qualification of the industrial product in which the GFT had the role of "silent" producer and the *stilista* was promoted as the author. The opposite was also a viable method, as with Max Mara where the designers were employed but their names never emerged, and the only name put forward was that of the brand.[92] Later, Gianni Versace SRL had a different structure: it was much more self-directed, with production given to many companies chosen according to their specialization. These production companies did not have a share in the designer's company.[93] Each *stilista* found their own way of collaborating with the manufacturer to guarantee both maximum flexibility as well as reliability.[94] These agreements provided the *stilisti* with the "financial resources—the royalties paid by industrial firms for license to use the brand and for the promotion of the collections—which made them increasingly independent in matters of business strategy."[95]

The *stilisti*, in their desire to create innovative and distinguished goods, exploited the Italian industrial system very effectively, and in return the manufacturers supported them with creative original products. A *stilista*, either for their brand or for the companies they worked for, would get in touch directly with the producers of raw materials or textiles, and through this interaction they oriented the manufacturers' choice of products, material, and colors. In this way the manufacturers acquired a new sensibility, and got closer to the needs of the market's final products. This is not to say that the vitality of the Italian fashion industry in this period is to be ascribed solely to the intervention of the *stilista*. The *stilisti* in Italy could draw on a lively tradition of artisanal know-how, and instead of just making use of the products available, they always requested goods made with innovative production techniques. In this way the *stilisti* pushed back the boundaries of what manufacturers could achieve. The new relationships between *stilista* and the manufacturers of yarn and textiles created new incentives for manufacturers' innovation, competitiveness, and productivity.[96]

The *Stilista* and Industrial Production

By nature, fashion is not a homogeneous product. It is made of a variety of materials, manufactured in many ways. According to economist Salvo Testa, the Italian fashion supply chain differs from other competitor countries, because it is made up of multiple, distinct parts and at the same time complete as it can satisfy all market levels. Furthermore, because in the fashion business seasonal timing is of the essence, it is a strategic advantage to have business partners and collaborators close by (both logistically and culturally). This advantage is the prerogative mainly of Italian *stilisti* and garment makers. Testa also argues that the ease with which the Italian producers of yarns and textiles interact with clothing manufacturers, knitwear producers, and *stilisti*, favoring the innovation of the product, is linked not only to the geographical and cultural closeness of the players, but also to these companies' smaller dimensions in comparison with the other European producers. This offers Italian suppliers a certain level of flexibility. Finally, in Italy the industries have managed to retain an artisanal culture that, on the contrary, has been lost in other countries such as Germany, France, Great Britain, and the United States.[97]

Italy's fashion industrial districts entail a certain degree of delocalization. As Bianchino explains, this means that the design of *prêt-à-porter* takes place inside the atelier (possibly in Milan) and the production happens somewhere else, probably far away.[98] Conversely, for the *alta moda*, the design project is done externally by professional designers and then the garment is made inside the atelier.[99] This implies that, in the period under consideration, the places of design and realization of the projects were changing drastically. For Milanese *prêt-à-porter*, it was no longer the atelier but the factory where experimentation and research were taking place, as innovative technical solutions were to be found at the factory. Therefore, the Milanese atelier has become the center of design and distribution toward the factories located around Italy, and no longer the place where the garments are made and prototyped.[100] This shift has had implications not only for the location of design, but also for drawing practice, as will be investigated in Chapter 6.

Transition from *Carnettista* to *Stilista*

As explained in Chapter 4, the *carnettista* started to disappear with the decline of the *sartoria* and the contemporary rise of *prêt-à-porter* at the end of 1960s. At this point textile manufacturers such as Faliero Sarti opened commercial departments within their companies and started to contact designers and couturiers by themselves without the aid of the *carnettista*. Roberto Sarti recalls how he oversaw the commercial aspect of his father's company, and how he traveled to Rome with their own sample books and went directly to couturiers such as Irene Galitzine.[101]

In the same period the figure of the *stilista* started to appear, and, as in the example of GFT, anticipated trends in the planning of industrial production.[102] Furthermore, the *stilista* could give directions to the textile producer in matters of taste and style. As Roberto Sarti explains, Giorgio Armani at the beginning of his career would examine Sarti's new seasonal textile production himself and if he did not like something he would tell Roberto Sarti "to sell it to the Germans" and that it was not something he would buy.[103] The textile producer would then take on board the suggestions and produce something that would please a given designer. These requests needed to be balanced as there was the risk of making a collection "too Armani," for example, with a danger of losing other clients with different aesthetics. There had to be a fine balance between following a *stilista's* directions and producing textiles for a wider clientele.[104]

At the end of the 1960s, with the decline of the *sartoria*, some of the *carnettista's* functions were internalized in the textile companies, such as the style office and commercial department. The *carnettista's* function as a barometer of style and taste was taken over by the *stilista*, whose taste was incorporated into their own brand. Just as the *carnettista* was associated with quality and taste for *alta moda*, the *stilista* bestowed an aura of glamour and style to the machine-made garments and collection that bore their name. Although the *stilista* fulfilled a different function than that of the *carnettista*, they both operated as connections between industry and fashion. They linked different producers dispersed in the territory and districts, and with their knowledge of both the fashion industry and textile production they acted as mediators as well as authors by signing their products.

The roles of both *carnettista* and *stilista* make sense in the Italian fashion landscape of small industries, for two reasons. Firstly, they give a unified name in a collection to products coming from different manufacturers. As an example, Walter Albini merged under his name the production of various specialized companies, just as the *carnettisti* would do by collecting under their name the products made by different textile producers.[105] Furthermore, the *stilista* also "helped create specialized companies in different sections of industry, so that they could collaborate to produce a collection with recognizable brand names."[106]

To better understand how the *stilisti* operated in such a panorama, it is important to consider they ways in which they created their own collections and lines. The next chapter will delve into this aspect by examining their design process.

By offering another behind-the-scenes look at textile and fashion production in Italy, this chapter has shown how fashion manufacturing in the country shifted from a verticalized to a more delocalized model, based on the *distretti industriali*. This, together with changes in the social and economic aspects of the country, brought the city of Milan, after years of working at the margins, to move center stage and become synonymous with ready-to-wear fashion.

6

Designing for Mass Production

Designing Fashion

The previous chapter analyzed how *prêt-à-porter* was produced in the *distretti industriali* and coordinated by the *stilisti*. This chapter takes a step back and focuses on how the *stilista*'s creativity is put down on paper, on fashion working drawings, and communicated to the production line. It is argued that these drawings are not merely creative ideas, but they represent a way of communicating between the designers and the intermediary based at the factory. I examine how working fashion drawings, in their complex layering of signs, materials, and authors, offer a lens through which to peek at *prêt-à-porter*'s creation before the final products are commercialized.

During the 1950s, fashion drawings were used mainly for presentation; the designs for *prêt-à-porter* are instead operational drawings. They feature indications of modifications, sizes, models, and order of entry for the fashion show. For these reasons there are cuts in the paper, while additions may be glued, stapled, or attached with adhesive tape. They are working documents. However, these are not only operational drawings; they have also been considered as aesthetic works in their own right. For this reason, traditionally the fashion working drawing has been studied mainly to explain the designer's inspiration and origin of his/her ideas or as a finished fashion illustration.[1] As the field has not been the subject of in-depth academic studies, this section firstly chronicles the ways in which fashion drawings have been approached in previous literature and how the focus has been put on fashion illustration rather than on the more technical drawings.

The second part of the chapter attempts to decode working fashion drawings by unpacking a corpus of 1970s and 1980s works on paper, and highlighting their characteristics such as their materials, style, aesthetics, inscriptions, and the presence of textiles. The analysis of these drawings reveals both creative and productive processes, such as the way the *stilista* visualizes the idea of a product on paper, and how they direct the use of textiles and other materials in the final garment. The drawings can also reveal the way in which the *stilisti* collaborate with various stakeholders. Furthermore, these documents disclose some of the specific mechanisms of the Italian fashion and textile system in the 1970s and 1980s: they underline and expose the behind-the-scenes process of fashion ideation and production. These are very different from the drawings that Italian couturiers used to copy from French designs, as seen in Chapter 2. These are designs for mass-produced, manufactured ready-to-wear clothing, and as such they are new and specific to this period. Working fashion drawings are not pure illustration, they are operational documents and therefore shed light on the process. They thus sit at the intersection between creativity and production and this chapter employs them to scrutinize the creation and production of *prêt-à-porter* fashion.

In the first chapter priority was given to the analysis of garments to understand production. Here the focus is on working fashion drawings used during the creation of ready-to-wear garments. This is because the drawings better show the process behind producing fashion as they incorporate different voices and testify to the ways in which things were made much clearly than the final garment.

Fashion Working Drawings: Literature Review

Fashion working drawings have rarely been the subject of academic investigation, as they have been most often treated as fashion illustrations.[2] These two categories, although very similar and made in the same medium, sit at opposite ends of the fashion production process. Fashion historian Laird Borrelli has written profusely about the subject of fashion drawing without enough distinction between the various types. In her 2008 book *Fashion Illustration by Fashion Designers* she declares that this publication, because it displays the work of fashion designers, differs greatly from her other books on fashion illustration, which showcased the production of professional illustrators. Although she explains in the introduction that most of the drawings in her book were not meant for public view and that these drawings need to be regarded as "working documents to inspire and instruct design," the fact that the book is called *Fashion illustration* makes the distinction between the two categories even less clear.[3]

An exception to the lack of interest in such documents is represented in Italy by the work of Italian fashion historian Gloria Bianchino and historian Arturo Carlo Quintavalle at the *Centro Studi e Archivio della Comunicazone*

(Communication Study Center Archive, CSAC) in Parma. Bianchino and Quintavalle have been collecting and studying the working fashion drawings of Italian *stilisti* together with *croquis* made for couturiers.[4] This rich material has been thematically investigated in a series of exhibitions and publications that have looked at the medium in depth. These include *Brunetta: Moda, Critica Storia* in 1981, *Sorelle Fontana* in 1984, *Italian Fashion Designing* in 1987 and *Walter Albini* in 1988. These publications systematically scrutinize the corpus of fashion drawings with analytical entries and, in the introductory essays, they contextualize them in the historical, national, and international background. These publications offer a helpful framework to better interpret the medium.

In a further publication on fashion drawings, *Moda: Dalla Fiaba al Design*, Bianchino reflects on the lack of scholarship and believes that working drawings in the French fashion ateliers at the beginning of the twentieth century were discarded because they were considered redundant in comparison with the ateliers' beautifully rendered symbolic illustrations in the art nouveau style. Furthermore, she highlights a contradiction within the working fashion drawing itself. Because by nature it refers to a process, and often may not fully represent a finished product, it is usually transformed into fashion illustration. Working fashion drawings have therefore been variously transformed, superseded, or destroyed, leading to a shortage of primary material to investigate, and a consequent paucity of studies in this field.[5]

Although the academic field has not devoted much attention to these objects, there is a proliferation of manuals for fashion students, aimed at teaching them how to draw for the fashion industry. These books offer a better identification of the different types of drawings. Illustrator Patrick John Ireland in his 1982 manual devoted to "students and people in the industry to develop fashion sketching techniques," divides the field into sketches, designs within the fashion industry, presentation drawings, and fashion illustration.[6] These headings help clarify some of the variations within the larger field of fashion drawings. Sketching techniques are mainly taught to students to develop skills when recording fashion shows, reporting on trends, and on a manufactured full collection.[7] The design for the fashion industry is mainly related to designing for a production sheet; it can also be referred to as technical drawing. This type of drawing gives the details of costing and is used to "verify that every aspect is accurate and been accounted for, such as for darts, seams, buttons."[8] Presentation drawings, on the other hand, are used when a designer is showing a collection to potential clients.[9] Finally Ireland gives a very useful definition of fashion illustration, as aimed at promoting designs which are already finished. Therefore the "fashion illustrator does not design, but rather illustrate[s] clothes for promotion."[10] Although these definitions are useful to clarify an otherwise confused field, Ireland does not decode the characteristics of fashion working drawings.

Fashion Working Drawings Decoded

Although the distinction between fashion illustration and designers' working drawings is blurred in Borrelli's book title, she gives a few definitions and designers' opinions that help us to better understand the nature of, as she puts it, "designers' sketches." Borrelli does so by asking some designers what their relationship with the medium is. From their answers, it emerges that drawings can create atmosphere, tactile sensations, and emotions. Furthermore, for some of them the drawing is an immediate way to translate an idea, but, as many designers declare, often the drawing is only the beginning of an idea and does not always correspond to the final objects. In the words of a Central Saint Martin's graduate, Molly Grad, the fashion working drawing "is a way of seeing into a designer's thought process."[11] For others, however, the drawing and the final garment completely correspond.[12] Whatever the singular opinions, it is clear that in its unfinished nature the working drawing encompasses, and results from, a process.

Through the words of many of the designers interviewed by Borrelli, a polyphony of opinions emerges. Often the drawing is disassociated from the final garment because of the process that operates between idea and product. The drawing does not have physical limitations and can carry an atmosphere that is sometimes difficult to translate into the final garment.[13] The creatives behind the British label Boudicca define drawing as "the major printer of the imagination."[14] For some, such as Hervé L. Leroux, the drawing is only a starting point; for others, the drawings are the ideal to which the final garment needs to aspire.[15] In yet another view, James Thomas sees the drawing as a space where accidents can happen, which are important for his design process.[16] For some, drawings are the start, but for others, such as Michael Vollbracht, the fabric is the outset of the process and the drawing comes second.[17] On the contrary, Jens Laugesen believes that the final garment is a better version of the design on paper because it is real and not an "illustration of an idea."[18] The above quotes demonstrate how, whatever value a given designer puts on the working fashion drawings, they are mainly the onset of the creative process. Whether done by hand or using computers, they are the direct contact with the designer's inspirations and visions. In ready-to-wear these initial unique ideas are then multiplied in the making of hundreds of reproducible garments.

However, while working drawings can be positioned at the beginning of the process of making fashion, they are also composite and multilayered testimonies to the complex path of fashion production. If carefully decoded, one can unearth the textile producers, accessory makers, name of the model, order of fashion show entrance, and much more.

As we have seen, these sorts of documents are difficult to study as they do not often survive in designers' archives, as they are considered ephemeral objects not worth preserving. Their working nature is often visible in the poor-quality paper employed, or the different hands (authors) present in the same page. Often words are crossed out, notes are scribbled, and stains of ink, coffee, or glue are scattered around. These documents were never created to be seen in a public setting. However, they are often incredibly detailed and artistic. In this section I analyze working fashion drawings by some Italian *stilisti* of the late 1970s and 1980s, such as Krizia, Gianni Versace, Gianfranco Ferré, and Walter Albini, to understand their function, and thereby to unpick some aspects of the process and production of Italian ready-to-wear.

A seminal exhibition on Versace's work, *L'Abito per Pensare*, was organized in 1989 at the Castello Sforzesco in Milan. On that occasion a thorough examination of the *stilista*'s production was displayed. Among the many objects in the exhibition were working fashion drawings. The editor of the catalog, fashion historian Nicoletta Bocca, unpicks a wealth of information from them, revealing a level of detail only possible because the information was retrieved in collaboration with factory workers, designers, and collaborators for the exhibition. For instance, Bocca states that one ensemble was requested as a prototype, but no indication on the drawing hints at this as the information came from verbal communication.[19]

She differentiates the drawings made for Versace production according to four stages. The first stage is a very stylized drawing by Versace with a wealth of written indications and few garment details. The second is a more detailed drawing (*disegno prepatorio*) made to express the *stilista*'s ideas. The third stage is a drawing of a look, a very detailed drawing with the addition of accessories, a model's face and hairstyle. This is made to communicate to the *modellisti* the total vision and look wanted by Versace. Finally, the fourth stage is a drawing for illustration used by the press office to present the model to journalists.[20] Furthermore, the fashion working drawings had to be translated into a "technical drawing." Most designers do not do this by themselves: it is usually the responsibility of a team of junior designers. The technical drawing includes all the information for the realization of the garments, as well as a photocopy of the drawing and a list of all materials needed for the final piece. The quantities are necessary to measure the cost of production related to the use of materials.[21] Only by analyzing this technical sheet can one work out exactly what textiles were finally employed in the garments included in the final collection. This is because different materials from a variety of producers are tried out in the making of the prototypes.[22] Therefore, it is not necessarily the fabric that is attached to the working fashion drawing that is used in the final product.[23]

Bocca argues that the temptation to realize a beautiful drawing can be damaging to the design project, because it focuses on details that are not essential, that do not respond to the real problems of production, and that slow down the creative process. While a client, the designer, or maybe the press would more appreciate a finished, beautiful drawing, the factory workers preferred Versace's bare preparatory drawings because they were very clear about the proportions that were crucial for the *modellisti*.[24]

This is more of a concern in the ready-to-wear setting, as the fast and accurate production of the garment is the key to its success. In couture, there was the need to illustrate the garment for a client, but now communication with production is paramount, as the two operations are not happening in the same environment. This fashion manufacturing shift leads to the decline of the *figurinista*, the person responsible for visualizing garments for the clients to choose from. With *prêt-à-porter* the *figurinista* and the *stilista* merge into one person who must be able, through drawings, to communicate to the factory floor. The "selling" role previously performed by fashion illustration is then taken over mainly by the photographic image.[25] According to Testa, the changes to the structure of the atelier and to the relationship with the industrial production also change the way in which a garment is created. The sketch, as he calls is, is only a small part of the process that arrives at the production of a dress. The *stilista* constantly intervenes in this process to guarantee the quality and aesthetics.

Bocca also explains that Versace changed many details in the prototyping stage and that his final garments were very different from the initial drawings for this reason. Each designer works in a different way, but there are some general rules that can be extrapolated to better understand these drawings.[26] What follows is an analysis of the working fashion drawing in its various forms: type of paper, drawing, style, aesthetic, and textiles.

Paper, Type of Drawing, and Inscriptions

In the absence of a specific literature on the field, I believe the best approach to understanding working fashion drawings is to use the inside-out method and to unpeel the layers, starting from the type of paper employed. This will reveal how every aspect matters, and that each has a function that can be decoded.

Often the drawings are on thin, white, anonymous photocopy paper, but nicer quality cardboard has also been employed. Sometime the page is stapled on to thicker cardboard with punch holes on the sides. This is probably done to collect and organize the final selected drawings of a collection in a folder, as seen in Plate 12. On this type of material, the *stilista*, or the person who physically make the drawings, designs in pencil, pen, markers, or pastels, his or her idea of a certain model or collection. The drawings on the page can take several forms, for example in Figure 6.1 Walter Albini is experimenting with different types of collars for a blouse and therefore, as he is working out a specific detail, the lines are just sketched. On other occasions, details such as the back, an accessory, or an alternative element may be enlarged and carefully defined to better communicate the final desired effect as seen in Plate 15, where the tie and cuff-links are enlarged. Interpreting the various hands and inscriptions on a fashion working drawing can be a very fiddly and painstaking activity. The handwriting does not always belong to the designer, and often it is hard to decode. The multiplicity of voices, detected on the drawing through the different handwriting, testifies to the collaborative nature of such projects. In this light, the designer is not seen as the lone genius who is producing single-handedly the collection, but each garment is a collaborative effort.

Often the inscriptions describe some aspects of the garment, such as specifying that the hem is meant to be in passementerie, or the color and fabric that is supposed to be used (especially when the drawings are only black-and-white sketches in pencil).[27] Some of the words are inscribed to explain the sketch of the designer, as in Plate 13. Here, the arrow explains how part of the T-shirt should be produced. In this case there are alternating bands of eyelets and chains. The handwriting is not necessarily the *stilista*'s but could possibly be the *modellista* or a collaborator who had worked out what kind of production method is best applied to the initial ideas.

The inscriptions are often in different colors, and this helps us to detect who is writing. Sometimes a dialogue can almost be reconstructed. In one instance an inscription on a Krizia Maglia drawing reads: "Gisella call me before making the model—I am afraid that this textile will roll up."[28] In some cases, questions and answers are indicated on the drawing: such as: "cotton or wool?" "I prefer wool."[29]

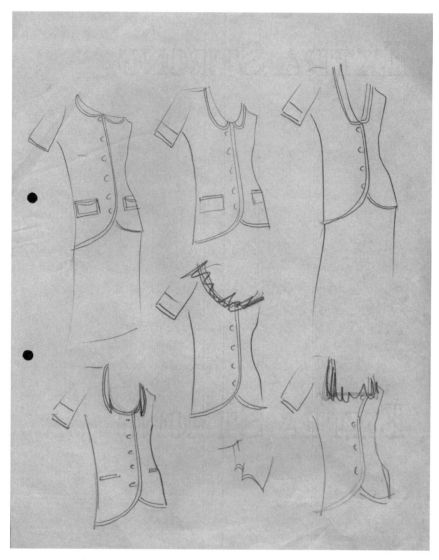

Figure 6.1 Walter Albini for Krizia, working fashion drawing, 1965–70. Courtesy of Centro Studi e Archivio della Comunicazione, Università degli Studi di Parma.

At the factory, more than one trial and prototype would be made to interpret the drawing. As is evident in Plate 13, the modifications, such as shortening the sleeve or centering the plait, are listed precisely under the headings "first trial" and "second trial."

When the drawing is very elaborate and the item represented has probably been selected for production, or is in a much more advanced creative stage, the inscriptions became more prominent. Often, they are extended onto the reverse of the main drawing.[30] These indications are very precise, and they imply that some sorts of prototypes have been already tried out. They refer to the lengths of waistcoat and seams, for example. Also, there are suggestions as to how to try to "make the shoulders more squared" or how to make the pockets. The most precise and refined drawings also tend to have the largest number of written indications. In the case of Plate 15, the drawing is in color and facial features are detailed, the model is smoking a long cigarette, and all the elements of the outfit are carefully drawn, even the little elastic band at the arm. Furthermore, buttons and cufflinks are shown in enlarged detail, the types of fabrics have been finalized, and samples of the wool yarn are attached with tape. According to Bocca a drawing densely surrounded by writing indicates how the *modellista* technically will make the piece. In this specific case, the indications on the verso represent the variations decided during the first trial that must be implemented in the second prototype.[31]

The drawing in Plate 15 was found in a folder together with similar drawings, probably part of a collection that was produced. On drawing number 24 of the same series (Plate 16) there is a picture of an editorial pinned to the paper that shows how the final look was photographed and modeled. The striking difference between the initial drawing and the finalized cardigan shows how the mood or the initial idea of a collection can be modified or even lost when the garment is finally made and styled for press purposes.

Often the drawings are beautifully rendered with plenty of details, such as facial features and hairstyles. Colors are applied carefully and the whole composition is deliberately balanced. If the drawing remains in a pristine status with no corrections and writings, it probably did not pass the idea stage and was never translated into a finished garment. However, the lack of writing or alterations on the drawings could mean that the dialogue between *stilista* and *modellista* happened orally as with Versace.[32] Another explanation, according to Bianchino, could be that the "clean" drawings are executed after the garment was already finished, and so became just an illustration of it. However, the more the initial drawing has been modified and worked on, the more it represents an advanced stage of production. In a 1979 Krizia drawing (Plate 17) the delicate nuance of color and precious details are coarsely superimposed with quick sketches of flowers, and arrows that indicate their planned position. Operational needs are clearly superimposed and gain priority over the aesthetics of the composition.

Style and Aesthetics

As seen in the previous section, every designer has a very personal relationship with fashion designing. Gianfranco Ferré, for example, designed his garments himself, with a very distinctive style.[33] According to the director of the former Fondazione Gianfranco Ferré, Rita Airaghi,

> For Ferré creating an outfit means starting a process of formal constructing through the elaboration of simple geometrical forms into complex structure developed into their three-dimensionality. The first step required in this process of elaboration is the "definition" of the forms themselves by means of a *bozzetto*, a sketch.[34]

In contrast, Krizia's *stilista* and brand owner Mariuccia Mandelli did not design herself; instead a team of designers is in charge of putting her various ideas down on paper. If they propose their own ideas, these need to be verified and approved by the head.[35] According to Quintavalle and Bianchino, Krizia's project planning and designing form an example of the industrialization of fashion even in its ideation phase. These authors believe that the drawings realized for Krizia by different designers all follow the same structure, they are precise and feature details, they are drawings on which one could work, and they are either physically sent to the factory or their photocopy is.[36]

In Italian *prêt-à-porter* the different brands and *stilisti* develop a unique and specific style not only for their garments and accessories, but also for their drawings.[37] This is a significant change from the previous decade, when fashion drawings for the Italian couture houses were commissioned from the same *figurinisti* and they ended up looking very similar one to another. The couture atelier was more concerned to create a typified style that reconnected to French couture, rather than to develop its unique trademark.[38]

Textiles

Working drawings are not exclusively made of paper. Textile samples, and sometimes leather and yarns, are glued, stapled, or attached with adhesive tape to the page.

Although the sample dimensions are small, they are important, as skillful designers can get a wealth of information about the pattern, consistency, touch, and materials. Bigger material samples, however, are employed in other types of documents that are used to record an entire collection. These sheets are sometimes called *schede colori*, and they offer an overview of the materials used within the final collection.

The samples of fabric or other materials such as leather or wool not only indicate the fabric for the main outfit, but also for accessories, such as hosiery and shoes. Such documents remind us that, at this stage of production, the collection is only a prototype, hence the indication of how many pairs of tights and shoes are needed for the setting up of the fashion show.

How these little pieces of material reach this position is the result of a journey from the textile mill to the designer and back. Prato wool textile producer Roberto Sarti remembers how some *stilisti* like Armani would come to his mill to view his textile collection, and they would pair the drawings to the fabrics. Sarti remembers that the *stilisti* would go to him with their drawings and take samples of textiles, saying, "This textile I will use for this drawing; this other textile for this other model . . . It was like playing cards," Sarti said.[39] According to this recollection, the fashion drawing came first and then the *stilisti*, who had deep knowledge of the Italian production panorama, sourced the material they wanted to use. As Sarti admits, sometimes the designers would ask for special textile production or an exclusive color. This was the case with Versace. He liked the houndstooth wool fabric Sarti produced in 1983 (for the autumn/winter collection 1983/4), but he requested a special colorway for himself in black and white to use for the leather and wool ensemble.

Textile historian Chiara Buss writes about the relationship between Gianni Versace and the material he used, that

> When considering direct intervention in the production of the material itself, it is essential to clarify the extent to which a stylist can influence the actual making of the material. In the majority of cases, textile manufacturers present fashion designers with a vast range of textiles each season, and it is the designer who narrows down the selection choosing the textures, patterns and colors best suited to transforming his idea into shapes and volumes. He often introduces only marginal variations so that the resulting material remains in keeping with his own style. Very often these variations aim to neutralize an overly characterful fabric, as too flamboyant a fabric can detract from the designer's formal concept. But Versace intervened in the most fundamental aspects of the fabric itself, involving himself with yarns and their blends, the weave, the pattern and the finish. He asked for the fabrics to be put through unprecedented processes in order to achieve something that had never been done before. Rather than choose any of the samples shown to him, he let them serve as trials for the fabrics he wanted.[40]

She adds that, without the support of the centuries-old Italian artisanal tradition and the constant technical updating of the industry, the creativity of Versace could not have emerged. Although this is a very strong claim, a different industry would have certainly changed the nature of his brand's output. Analyzing the working drawings of one designer, it is evident how a polyphony of producers is involved in the making of the final garment.

However, many drawings remain only on paper and were never developed into three-dimensional garments. In the case of Versace, around one thousand drawings would be made for a collection. This number would be reduced by the *stilista* in consultation with collaborators, including the person responsible for the relationship with the factory. Of these, some would be prototyped after a second selection made inside the factory for reasons of economic rationalization. A further selection would be made to decide what became part of the collection to be sold and still fewer garments were presented in the fashion show, which according to Bocca included around one hundred exits with four hundred pieces combined with each other.

The textile applied to the drawing is often marked with the reference production number of the textile producer. This is a very important little code that identifies a given fabric in its specific colorway, and it allows us to trace the path that a textile travels from production to final use.

For instance, if one looks for this unique number within the Faliero Sarti archive, it is possible to follow the various steps in the production of the fabric. The same code is present on many pieces of fabric. The *tirelle*, big sample pieces of fabric, are used to show to the client the range and variety of the company's production. They are big enough that it is possible to appreciate the pattern repeat, and how they feel when physically touched. They are normally preserved together with their color variations to show alternatives. Hence, they almost work as a record of the company's production through the years.

The same reference production number is present in the *libri tecnici* (technical books). These are books that testify to the technical characteristics of the fabrics, the name of the client, the name of the product, and its code, as well as the method of production.

The same code and textile can be also found as a small textile sample in big books. The purpose of such collections is to give an overview of the whole production of a given year. They are for internal use, a practical reference for workers in the factory. Here the fabric is cut into a small rectangle and gives an idea of what the final product would look like. Furthermore, as it is put into the context of the year of production, the book represents the creativity of the wool producer.

Samples of these fabrics would then leave the textile manufacturing company once the designers came and decided what textile they wanted to use. The type of material attached to the drawings varies depending on the garment produced. In the drawings for Krizia Maglia, the company's knitwear collection, a variety of wool and silk yarns are attached to the drawings, as they are the real foundation material of the garment (such as in Plate 18).[41] In some drawings the yarn is also knitted to show the technique employed to use the yarn, and a knitted sample is added to the drawing as seen in Plate 19. The textile samples are also arranged to visualize how the colors would have looked together in an attempt to translate the *stilista*'s ideas as seen in Plate 20. From my analysis of Krizia, Albini and Versace, it appears that textiles are present when the drawings are more finalized. However, not all the designers would work in the same way.

Investigating the role of textiles in connection with these drawings reveals how they have been used in the production setting. Here textiles are a tangible part of the creative process. Whereas in the previous five chapters I have investigated textiles through their production aspects—their fibers, the production methods, the way in which they were commercialized—here we can see their function as integral to a collaborative creative process. The swatches of fabrics attached to these drawings represent different players. If we look at them from a production perspective, they represent the textile manufacturers. These little squares stapled or simply glued to the page bear witness to the inventiveness and technical knowledge of the textile mills as well as representing the variety of their production. They also, however, exemplify only "the tip of the iceberg," as not all the season's production would be selected by a designer, and only relatively few fabrics would leave the factory floor to be used in the final garment manufacturing.

As we have deduced from the drawings, there is no longer an exclusive relationship between one designer and one textile producer. In the *Sala Bianca*, as seen in Chapter 1, one designer was, for promotional reasons, associated with one textile manufacturer. Now, there is instead an assortment of voices and players involved in the production of fashion. For example, in Krizia's drawings a number of producers emerge.[42] Furthermore, more than one silk or wool supplier is present, and this indicates that a given fashion house would choose a producer according to the specific fabric available in a yearly collection, and not because of a formal pre-arranged agreement. This could also happen before, but in the 1960s, for example, the *carnettista* would work as an intermediary, whereas now the textile mills were equipped with internal departments devoted to the relationships with the *stilisti* and the system was more structured and institutionalized.

We can conclude that these drawings expose how different suppliers and manufacturers collaborated to make a final look. In the 1970s, there was no *stilista*'s unique company that produced the totality of the garments and its accessories from scratch, and all within the same factory floor. The production, however, happens in a system of synergy between small and medium firms. As seen in Chapter 4 in the case of the silk weavers and printers, the production of fashion happens in a diffused territorial system, instead of being under the same unified factory floor of one company.

Gianfranco Ferré: A Case Study

To better understand the delocalized system of fashion and textile production in the 1970s and 1980s, it is useful to take as an example the structure of the Gianfranco Ferré company. Compared to other Italian *stilisti*'s companies, the Ferré structure was simpler, as it was based solely on the collaboration between Gianfranco Ferré and the industrialist Franco Mattioli from Bologna. The two were business partners with fifty percent each of two limited companies: Gianfranco Ferré SRL and Diffusione Ferré. Gianfranco Ferré SRL owned the trademark, and was mainly a stylistic studio based in Milan. It designed the production of the Gianfranco Ferré lines in collaboration with twelve manufacturers: Baila for womenswear made in fabric, Nadini for knitwear, La Matta for leatherwork, Boulevard for men's shirts, Redaelli for menswear made in fabric, Marvel for swimwear, Sir Robert for belts, Dei Mutti for handbags, Harpers for ties, Pasquali for shoes, Gambini for eyewear, and Abbigliamento Abbruzzese for sportwear for both men and women.[43] Furthermore, Abbigliamento Abbruzzese, together with the aforementioned manufacturers, also produced Oaks by Gianfranco Ferré, a second line designed by Ferré himself but very different from his first line, as it was aimed at a younger market, was colorful, and was sold at a lower price.[44] In addition, Ferré was giving anonymous consultancy to the companies Baila, Nadini, La Matta, Boulevard, Redaelli, and Marvel for their production made for different brands.

According to the contracts with the twelve manufacturers, Gianfranco Ferré SRL had the right to choose the types of textiles to use, the manufacturing procedures, and the final prices. The companies for which Ferré worked were all autonomous: for example, Baila was owned 100 percent by Mattioli. It had 140 workers and commissioned a significant part of its work from a third party. Seventy per cent of its turnover was the production for the Ferré lines.[45]

In a 2018 interview with the author, Rita Airaghi, then personal assistant of Gianfranco Ferré, explained how the royalties system worked.[46] Gianfranco Ferré SRL oversaw the creative input into a collection, which included the design process and the final stage of distribution of the finished products. The producers, such as the companies owned by Mattioli, were responsible for paying for raw materials, producing the collection, and their employees' salaries. Gianfranco Ferré SRL would then get a percentage of the items sold and the producers would get another percentage.

In this way, the direction came from the studio in Milan while the production was diffused around the territory, only to be reunited in the final product back at the Milanese studio before being distributed. This system, although quite complicated to describe, provided flexibility to the *stilista's* label, as it made it possible to collaborate directly with smaller companies that specialized in the manufacturing of a given type of garment or accessories. The *stilista* had to maintain the overview of the collection and its unity, while its various parts were being produced in several companies distributed around the territory. To understand how this worked, we can find many clues in the fashion drawings for a garment or collection.

Airaghi explains that Gianfranco Ferré worked with different styles and types of fashion drawing, according to their function: one might be a technical drawing, another a more refined drawing to visualize the fashion show. At the beginning of the creative process, the very sketchy initial idea was laid out as a drawing (an example of which can be seen in Figure 6.2). Although only outlined on the paper with a quick pencil line, this design already contains all the characteristics of the final garments: the oversized jacket, the blouse, the pleated skirt, and the belt. However, this sketch represented just an initial, embryonic stage of the final product. Since the look was subsequently selected to be included in the collection, Gianfranco Ferré then produced more precise working fashion drawings as seen in Plates 21, 22 and 23. Airaghi recalls how these kinds of drawings were never just sent over to the factory to be translated by the *modellista*. There was always a meeting between Gianfranco Ferré and the *modellista*, an occasion for the two to clarify aspects of the garments not included in the drawing. At first, the original drawings were given to the *modellista* at the factory and a photocopy was retained at the *stilista's* Milan office for reference. Later, the company realized the value of such drawings and the opposite was done. The original drawings were all kept in the style office, and they are now conserved in the Gianfranco Ferré Research Center.[47]

Ferré's initial working drawings were almost always sketched on photocopy paper, often A4, but sometimes, for a larger composition, also on A3. The drawing was normally made just in pencil, often with a red number indicating the model code at the top right-hand corner. Sometimes, especially for straightforward

Figure 6.2 Gianfranco Ferré, sketch for look 32, *prêt-à-porter*, spring/summer 1984. Courtesy of Centro di Ricerca Gianfranco Ferré, Politecnico di Milano.

garments, the drawing is the only element on the page, with no further inscriptions. On other occasions, the *stilista* adds indications for the *modellista* to clarify some aspects of line, materials, or constructions.

On the drawing of the jacket (Plate 21) an inscription reads "Giacca come modello 23" (jacket the same as number 23 model). This is a clear message to the *modellista* to make this item the same way as they did for number 23, which they had probably already discussed.[48]

It is evident from Figure 6.2 and Plates 21, 22, and 23 how the outfit that was only drafted in the preparatory sketch is further developed and constructed in the working drawing, where each element of the outfit is designed on a different sheet of paper. In Plate 21 the jacket occupies almost the whole of the page without details of the body which is wearing the garment. In addition, at the bottom right corner a piece of fabric by the Biellese wool mill Fila is attached to the paper together with an indication of the product code. This number, as we have seen in the previous section, is very useful to understand what type of textile the designer wanted to use. According to Airaghi, Ferré, together with his research team, found the fabrics that best worked for a collection, and then passed the information on to the factory that was making the garments. The whole economic burden to acquire the meters necessary to make the collection would fall on the manufacturer and not on Gianfranco Ferré SLR.[49]

Plates 22 and 23 refer to the skirt of the outfit. Plate 22 indicates the fabric to use, its length, and the type of pleating, as well as the belt. However, it was probably not clear what the *stilista* wanted to achieve, and so a second, more detailed drawing was made (Plate 23). In this case both a front and a back view of the skirt are drawn out. A couple more inscriptions clarify the length, the slit, and how the sash was meant to be attached to the skirt. The inscription reads "Fascia attaccata solo nel fianco" (sash attached only on the side). With these few adjustments, the idea of the *stilista* became clearer to the *modellista*, and the garments were later produced. It is interesting to note how the *crêpe de chine* printed silk, produced by the Como-based Stucchi silk mill to be used in the manufacturing of the skirt, is applied on the paper already pleated, probably to show how the *stilista* wanted the final pleat to look.

The photographs of the models on the catwalk wearing the finished garments show the complete look including shoes, accessories such as the tie folded inside the jacket pocket, and hairstyle (Plate 24). Images such as these are important documents to show the overview of the ensemble and how the finished garments would have looked when worn by a model. However, the drawings allow for a deeper investigation into the layers of production, the choice of the garment's material, and the *stilista*'s creative input.

As seen previously, textile samples bear witness to the designer's vision for a garment, and they play an important part in the creation of a collection, as well as representing the myriad of textile mills involved in the fashion production. Yet they are also employed at the end of the creative process to visualize the succession of colors and patterns in a final collection, as shown in the *scheda colori* in Plate 25. Here the fabrics, attached to black cardboard, are grouped to represent the final ensembles. Each sample stands for a component of the final look, such as a jacket, skirt, or shirt, and each group is indicated by a symbol, such as a triangle, a square, or a moon wedge. The same symbols are repeated on the technical drawings to identify the items belonging to the outfit. These groups together give an immediate portrayal of each ensemble, its color, pattern, and material, as well as, when seen together on the page, the overall look of the collection. A working document such as this was most likely made when the collection was in a more final stage of programming. It would offer designers and their team a visual aid to plan the fashion show's catwalk exits of each model, as well as to balance the overall composition of the collection in terms of colors, materials, and patterns.[50]

This case study has shown how Gianfranco Ferré utilized drawings to pin his creative ideas onto paper. It has also shown how these working documents were the medium of communication between the designer's team in Milan and production expertise scattered around Italy.

The detailed investigation into working fashion drawings in this chapter has revealed how a plurality of voices and authors is included in the making of a garment, from the *modellisti* who translate the designer's creative sketches into workable prototypes to the various textile mills who offer their technical know-how to satisfy the requests for innovative materials. This, together with the analysis of the Italian fashion designer, the *stilista*, destabilizes the idea of the fashion design as a one-man process.

However, as this system started to be pinpointed and theorized by economists from all over the world, it started to change once more. The *distretti industriali* were the industrial structure at the core of the success and development of Milanese *prêt-à-porter*. However, at the beginning of the 1980s, at the peak of its success, new directions were taken by designers, such as Giorgio Armani, who started diffusion lines such as Mani and Emporio Armani, leaving at the helm the brand "Giorgio Armani, Via Borgonuovo 21." This system worked like a pyramid. At the top, the first line had the role of maintaining the brand's name and its exclusivity. This production was much more artisanal, and here Armani could experiment with his creativity both in terms of a project and in terms of materials. The second line was aimed at mass sales, and therefore the ideas of the first lines had to be adapted to a much more industrial product that had to appeal to a wider public. The last, younger line had much more provocative ideas, more connected to an advertising image.[51] As Merlo declares, the Armani company provided the blueprint for other Italian fashion companies set up between the 1970s and 1980s.[52] Other designers such as Franco Moschino followed this lead, and in this way, the branded designer products reached a wider, more often international public.[53]

Conversely, in its top lines, Italian *prêt-à-porter*, which started as a way of democratizing exclusive fashion and reconfiguring industrial production for a younger, less elitist public, was now getting closer to the prices and exclusiveness of *alta moda*. *Stilisti* like Gianni Versace, Gianfranco Ferré, and Giorgio Armani, who made their names by designing an industrial product, started their own couture lines.[54] Furthermore, from the start of the 1990s, a new panorama of production and consumption began to appear. According to Segre Reinach, *prêt-à-porter* was hit by a crisis, based on a further delocalization of fashion production, Chinese competition, counterfeits, the "fluctuating meanings of the idea of 'Made in Italy' and the creation in Italy and abroad of large luxury groups that encompassed various brands."[55]

Still later, toward the end of the 1990s, some brands like Armani and Versace decided to go in the opposite direction from delocalization around the country and to take control of the whole supply chain.[56] Armani took over a factory in Settimo Torinese from the GFT group, its main licensee. He also bought Miss Deanna, a knitwear company in Emilia Romagna.[57]

According to Merlo, the fact that major brands like Armani, Versace, and Moschino were based on large textile manufacturing firms and tailoring traditions demonstrates that the role played by the industrial district needs to be revisited.[58] However, this statement is based on how the companies' business strategy has evolved in the 1990s and 2000s. This chapter has exclusively investigated the period between the 1970s and 1980 and has demonstrated that at the beginning of the relationship between industry and designers, the districts played an important role. That situation has inevitably changed as successful brands expanded and internationalized their operation in an attempt to compete with French and American counterparts.

Conclusion

In the introduction of this book I stated, quoting Zeitlin, that the past can be (re) discovered if it is investigated through questions motivated by current developments. For me, this moment of re(discovery) was ignited during field work in 2012, when I was faced by the rich manufacturing know-how and expertise behind Italian fashion products. I started to ask myself questions such as: What were the relationships between design and materials, of final products and production? Were these separated? Or should we look at them together to better understand the success of Italian fashion?

Furthermore, it was obvious to me that Italian ready-to-wear had been acclaimed internationally since the 1980s, but the history that led to that success was unclear. Italian mass-manufactured fashion seemed to have appeared from nowhere. Ready-to-wear Italian fashion was, and is, admired for the quality of its materials, so much so that many French brands today produce their goods, such as shoes and bags, in Italy, and many of their suppliers of textiles and leather are Italian companies.[1] This attitude is so widespread that it passes almost unnoticed. If we look at the soles of shoes that are famous worldwide by the likes of Manolo Blahnik and Christian Louboutin, they clearly state "Made in Italy." Why is this and what does it mean? Is Italy today merely a supplier and producer of products designed elsewhere, or is there a deeper relationship? A possible answer to this is that Italy, although now an industrialized country, still retains an artisanal know-how which is paramount when making complex accessories like shoes and bags that require technical knowledge and hand-made processes. Answering these questions is beyond the scope of this book, but the investigation carried out with my research helps understand better the present by (re)analyzing the past.

The importance of materials is often heralded in the literature as a key aspect of Italian fashion.[2] The mechanisms behind textile and fashion production and how this relationship pushed forward the development of the successful Italian ready-to-wear have, however, not been clear. Today Italian fashion brands such as Gucci, Valentino, Prada, and Fendi are still at the top of the international fashion scene. It is still very relevant today to examine the roots of the Italian fashion system to better understand the present. This volume has investigated exactly this and connected Italian know-how in terms of techniques and materials with the development of ready-to-wear in the country.

In doing so this book has made several original contributions to the field. The initial research question of the project aimed firstly to examine the role that textile manufacturing played in the transformation of the Italian fashion landscape from hand-made and couture garments to mass-produced fashion, and secondly why and how Italian fashion and textile production worked together and influenced each other in developing an integrated fashion system in Italy between 1945 and 1985. The unique point of view and strength of this research is the focus on materials and production as this is the aspect of Italian fashion that has been largely under-researched. By examining how the system worked and what were its mechanisms, I shed light on innovative aspects that have mostly passed unnoticed. The "inside-out" method employed here offers a new directionality to the study of Italian fashion.

The book started with an analysis of the fibers employed in the making of Italian fashion in the 1950s. It continued by looking at how textiles were commercialized in the 1960s by the *carnettisti* and how their role helped Italian textiles manufacturers emerge as strong players behind the success of fashion in the next decade. It closed by examining the design and production of garments in networks of small companies around Italy in 1980s. Throughout these six chapters, the main focus has been on the production of Italian textiles and fashion, and how the two sectors influenced and interacted with each other to build a coherent and integrated system during the forty years following the end of the Second World War. I have navigated the chronology 1945 to 1985 by adopting a case study approach, guided by a focus on materials that highlighted a series of previously unknown aspects that are fundamental to understanding Italian textiles and fashion production and design.

Changes within the system were not immediate, and it often took years for their repercussions to be appreciated. Therefore, examining the Italian textile and fashion industries over a four-decade period allows for a full investigation of the evolution of the fashion system. The analysis of a large chronology also offers the opportunity to examine historical processes not just in their immediate context, but to trace their roots further back toward their origins, and to see their influence on future developments.

By deconstructing the mechanisms and understanding how things were working, this book has systematically addressed a number of myths that have grown up around the aura of Italian fashion. These demythologized aspects include: the genesis of ready-to-wear; how couturiers and designers were not solely responsible for the success and the making of products; how a number of intermediaries were essential cogs in the system; and how "Made in Italy" is a complex and multilayered term that shifts in every decade.

While, in the existing literature, ready-to-wear has mainly been analyzed from the end of the 1960s onwards, this book has continued the work started by Nicola White with *Reconstructing Italian Fashion* and built on this to demonstrate that *moda boutique* incorporated aspects of high-quality mass production much earlier than previously understood, in the 1950s. The Simonetta case study in Chapter 2 and its focus on *moda boutique* has redefined the role of Italian *alta moda* and exposed the mechanisms for how Italian fashion had been, at least from the start of the 1950s, already made in series, as opposed to being made exclusively by hand. Undoubtedly, as was examined in that chapter, *alta moda* played an important role as an ambassador of Italian style, especially with the events organized by Giovanni Battista Giorgini for the American market in the 1950s. These early mass-produced experiments therefore shaped the development of Italian ready-to-wear later in the 1970s and 1980s. The *Gruppo Finanziario Tessile* (GFT) is a key example of the continuity between decades, from the early collaboration between GFT and the couturier Biki at the end of the 1950s to the subsequent success of the relationship with the *stilisti* at the base of the Italian *prêt-à-porter* success. As investigated in this book, the GFT story provides a red thread to follow to understand the origin of Italian ready-to-wear. This investigation has provided historical evidence of the success of the Italian ready-to-wear system in the 1980s as the result of a slow progression from the end of the Second World War rather than the sudden international success of the late 1980s.

This book has clearly demonstrated that it is paramount to investigate two systems in parallel to truly understand the history of Italian fashion. Points of contact need to be investigated in order to appreciate how these two separate realms worked with and communicated to each other. This research has also shown how fashion comes into being thanks to a range of stakeholders, beyond the fashion designer or producer. The in-depth unpicking of stages of production has revealed the importance and position of various players. This is the first study that analyzes in depth the role and history of the *carnettisti*, little-known intermediaries who were fundamental in influencing the type of textile production that could better serve the needs of *alta moda*. This research has also thrown a spotlight onto the *modellisti*, factory workers who were responsible for translating the vision of the *stilisti* into technical drawings and prototypes that could be efficiently mass produced by manufacturers. Including more players reveals a complex system that does not rely exclusively on the designer as "genius," which has been the dominant idea in fashion history.[3]

This type of analysis could only be done by breaking down the system into different moments. I have looked at the fashion system, of which textile manufacturing is a part, as a process and not as a given complete unity. What I have learned by juxtaposing the Italian textiles and fashion systems is that fashion is not the only the driving agency, but also that textiles, on certain occasions, were pushing innovation. The quality of Italian textiles was the aspect that the press and critics were celebrating in the 1950s. This opened opportunities for Italian dressmakers and couturiers. In the 1960s the relationship swapped and *alta moda* was seen as the pinnacle of the fashion system while textile manufacturers were influenced by the demands of fashion through the careful and important work of the *carnettisti*. With the emergence of the *stilisti* in the 1970s, Italian textile manufacturing once more played a key role in defining fashion aesthetic and its allure.

The key innovative angle of this book has been to examine fashion from the perspective of materials and production processes. This has led me to devise a multidisciplinary approach that has encompassed textiles, fashion, and design history. Existing studies had neglected to analyze the close and reciprocal relationship between textile and fashion, production and product, inside and outside. In current literature the focus was mainly placed on the outside, on the style and surface of the finished fashion products and their designers. I have reversed this approach and instead examined the Italian fashion phenomenon through different lenses. This has been achieved through a focus on the rediscovery of primary sources, on examining the inside of objects, such as textiles and their component (fibers), on the unpicking of productive processes, and on the roles played by intermediaries and lesser-known figures in textile and fashion system. I define this as the "inside-out" method because it brings to the fore aspects that had been kept hidden or in the background. This book has demonstrated the richness of the "inside-out" method as a tool to investigate fashion and textile production. With this approach I have shown how the "Made in Italy" label operated behind the clichéd characteristics associated with its brand image. By foregrounding the role of materials and production, this approach has exposed elements that were previously overlooked, such as the use of artificial and synthetic materials in *alta moda*, the existence of proto-mass production as early as the 1950s, and a complex network of players, makers, and intermediaries.

This concluding chapter focuses on the elements that make this book innovative and highlights aspects that this new research has brought to the fore.

Inside Fashion: The Role of Materials and Production

In May 2017, the Victoria and Albert Museum in London staged the exhibition *Balenciaga: Shaping Fashion* on the Spanish couturier Cristóbal Balenciaga, curated by Cassie Davies-Strodder (May 27, 2017—February 18, 2018). One display case in the first part of the exhibition included an analysis of Balenciaga's collaborative relationships with textile manufacturers such as the Swiss company, Abraham Ltd, and London-based Ascher. On display were not only the final garments, but also textile samples, sketches, and collection boards that testified to the working process of couturiers and his rapport with textile manufacturers. The exhibition also mentioned the high-quality copies of couture garments produced by department stores such as Harrods. Although these aspects were just a small part of an exhibition that displayed over a hundred couture pieces, they indicated a shift in how museums display and investigate fashion. The analysis of how Balenciaga designed and produced his revered couture creations played an important part in showing a wider public some behind-the-scenes aspects of fashion manufacturing, which was also my aim with this book. My investigation into the mechanisms of production, and into the use of materials, highlighted a number of aspects that will be relevant not only for the understanding of Italian fashion production, but also for the wider field of fashion history—and I hope that my approach will be part of a broader emerging interest in production. These aspects are the role of fibers and materials, the internationalization of the country's output, and the industrialization and use of machinery in Italian textile and fashion production. I will illustrate them in more details in the subsections that follow.

Fibers and Materials

Focusing on the inside of objects and on the use of materials led me to also investigate the types of fibers employed, an aspect that has been almost completely overlooked in the literature.[4] In Chapter 1 I looked at Italian textile fibers that were used for Italian fashion. I have shown how, as early as the 1950s, artificial and synthetics fibers were also present alongside natural fibers in the making of Italian fashion. This finding transforms the accepted image of Italian *alta moda* as employing solely natural fibers such as wool, cottons, and silks.

I have been able to show how the choice of fibers and raw materials used in fashion production is not only a matter of aesthetics, but also relates to political and economic realms. The Marshall Plan aides, for example, encouraged Italy to import and use American cotton, as the USA had surpluses of the fibers that needed to be sold. Similarly, the use of synthetics in Italian fashion was the result of the long domestic history and success of the Italian synthetics industry alongside Italy's aspiration to modernity. The synthetic producer SNIA Viscosa played an important role in popularizing the use of synthetic fibers in fashion and helped legitimize the new fibers with the public and buyers via the organization of large international fashion shows and exhibitions. Furthermore, my analysis stresses an important point: fibers and textiles, because of their unfinished nature, were difficult to promote. Fashion was therefore used to popularize their use with a wider public. Finished garments were employed in fashion shows and advertisements because they were more familiar and "usable" products that would immediately capture the buyers' and wearers' attention.

Italian fashion has often been praised for the quality of its materials and Italy remains world famous today for the quality of its leather and silk, to name just two, and for some manufacturing specialties such as tanning. However, I was surprised to discover during this research that the formula "Italian materials equal Italian fashion" has not always been valid throughout the period analyzed in this book, as Italian designers did not always exclusively use Italian materials. As early as the 1950s Italian couturiers were collaborating with foreign textile and fiber manufacturers such as Cohama in the USA and employing foreign fabrics in their creations. In the 1960s, it was a widespread practice for the Italian products not to be fully "Made in Italy" as Italian designers were not necessarily using a fully Italian supply chain. This had become a problem that institutions such as CNMI set to rectify through the establishment of special prizes to be given to those designers that were exclusively creating models with Italian materials. In the 1970s and 1980s this trend was reversed and the majority of the *stilisti* relied more and more on the Italian factories and producers based in the territory. This book has demonstrated how the close relationship between producers and designers played a major role in defining the success of the Italian *prêt-à-porter* system that developed in this decade.

Internationalization

As discussed in the Introduction, the field of fashion history has not questioned fashion production in depth. Certain aspects and players have not been analyzed, and therefore our understanding of fashion history is incomplete. In this book I have demonstrated how, for instance, it is important to look beyond national borders in examining fashion history. My analysis of the role played by materials, specifically fibers and textiles, and their sometimes complicated production mechanisms, has revealed a combination of influences from different countries that affected the design of the finished fashion products. Such considerations further problematize the meaning of "Made in Italy." I have shown the fluidity that lies beneath the label, not only by looking at the role played by the USA in Chapter 2, but also with the case of the Italo-Japanese company Lucrezia in Chapter 3. This research has established that the internationalization of Italian fashion happened early and did not only involve a binary relationship with USA. Italy needed other trading partners too. In the 1960s this trend did not diminish, but grew beyond the binary relationship of Italy and America, as brands such as Lucrezia demonstrate. Giorgini was behind such an enterprise which aimed to promote Japanese fibers and textiles through the allure of Italian fashion. This venture was also backed by a Japanese synthetic fiber producer and a department store, and it is a testament to how Giorgini's entrepreneurial abilities were not only put to the service of "purely" "Made in Italy" products. His scope was much wider reaching, and transnational. He saw an opportunity in a new market, such as Japan, and used his marketing ability to promote Italian fashion in the country, at the same time as bringing Japanese products, financial resources, and commercial scope to Italy.

This research has also shown how the influence of the USA was not only confined to the 1950s and Marshall Plan aid, as has been previously understood.[5] It continued into the 1960s and permeated many aspects of manufacturing, design, style, and commerce. Events such as the American-organized *Italy at Work* exhibition promoted Italian textile companies, such as Ravasi, to the American market. The USA as a market and as an industrial pioneer also influenced the ways in which manufacturers were reorganized, as the GFT, Max Mara, and La Rinascente examples have shown. In addition, the USA, as a powerful and wealthy export market, had the economic weight, with its buying power, to influence certain outputs of Italian fashion. This was the case for Italian couture, which transformed some of its output into mass production with the creation of lines of *moda boutique*. This influence continued well into the 1960s, as seen in the Nattier example: the USA became the first market to buy Nattier's products at a moment when French companies rejected them. In this way, the US market was a direct influence on the success of certain companies.

Industrialization

The Italian fashion system experienced a late industrialization. This become evident when, at the end of the Second World War, Italian brands and manufacturers were eager to produce in high numbers, but did not have the know-how and appropriate machinery to do so. They had to look elsewhere for help. This can clearly be seen with the collaboration of Milan-based department store La Rinascente and US ready-to-wear manufacturers Donnybrook and Rosenfeld, which offered American-made machinery to the Italians. This example is just the start of a process that gradually placed *moda boutique* side by side with *alta moda*. This leaning toward high-quality standardized semi-machine-made products continued in the 1960s with experiments by Biki and GFT, Sorelle Fontana, and Brioni, as Chapter 3 has shown. By the 1960s Italian production had adapted to foreign demands and adopted more industrialized manufacturing strategies and machines in order to standardize production and make it more efficient. However, as the Capece story shows, in the 1960s some brands still produced Italian ready-to-wear *a cottimo* (at piece rate) without a fully industrialized plant. This is a recurrent aspect of Italian fashion and very much still a defining characteristic of the country's type of production. Although industrialized, the country has retained pockets of hand-made and almost artisanal production that co-exist with the big manufacturers.

The various attempts to combine industry and fashion became more standardized and efficient in the late 1970s when a new type of player, the *stilista*, came to work across factories and design studios. The *stilista* collaborated organically with the industry to produce high-end *prêt-à-porter*, the output that had come to define Italian style by the 1980s. When industrialization came to Italy it was different as it was based on a system of industrial districts centered on family businesses. The late industrialization also meant that the country retained much artisanal know-how and traditions that were later married up with localized industrialization organized around the industrial districts. Industrialization in Italy was never so widespread as to wipe out the artisanal traditions and more "hand-made" ways of working. Although Italy came late to ready-to-wear, it succeeded in becoming one of the world's fashion centers with the city of Milan at its helm.

My book concludes in 1985, because after the international success of Italian *stilisti* and the high-end *prêt-à-porter* in the 1980s, a new shift occurred in the fashion panorama. The 1990s were a difficult period for Italian fashion for various reasons. According to Segre Reinach, one factor was that many Italian brands lost touch with their "democratic" origins, an important aspect of their initial success.[6] Furthermore, production shifted once more with the introduction of new players such as China. The equilibrium and synergies that had been reached in the previous decade between fashion and textile production changed to become more global and delocalized. New designers and brands also emerged in the new panorama, such as Dolce & Gabbana and Miuccia Prada.

The "inside-out" method which is at the core of this book, with its analysis of textile production when investigating fashion, reveals Italian fashion as a more complex and multilayered system in which agency is not only exercised by fashion designers and consumer demand, but also by fibers, textiles, and intermediaries. This approach is the key contribution that this book has made to the field of textile, fashion, and design history. It has unlocked aspects that were previously under-researched. This method is applicable to other fashion areas outside Italy and could reveal, as it did in this case, a richer understanding of fashion production worldwide. This means that, if the model of my book were to be applied to other fashion centers, this could show a richer panorama and a portrait of other fashion outputs. This book has therefore contributed not only to Italian fashion history, but potentially to transnational and global histories of fashion. It has shown that, by including in the investigation the realms of materials and production previously under-researched and yet vital aspects are revealed, ultimately leading to a more rounded picture of fashion.

Notes

Introduction

1 Jonathan Zeitlin, "Industrial Districts and Regional Clusters," in *The Oxford Handbook of Business History* (Oxford: Oxford University Press, 2008), pp. 219–43 (p. 235).

2 Nicola White, *Reconstructing Italian Fashion: America and the Development of the Italian Fashion Industry* (Oxford: Berg, 2000), p. 35.

3 Ibid., p. 172; Simona Segre Reinach, "The City of Prêt-à-Porter in the World of Fast Fashion," in *Fashion's World Cities*, ed. Christopher Breward and David Gilbert (Oxford: Berg, 2006) pp. 123–34 (p. 123).

4 See note 52, this chapter.

5 Eugenia Paulicelli, *Fashion Under Fascism: Beyond the Black Shirt* (Oxford: Berg, 2004); White, *Reconstructing Italian Fashion;* many monographs have been written on singular designers. For a historical recollection see Sofia Gnoli, *The Origins of Italian Fashion 1900–1945* (London: V&A Publishing, 2014); Sofia Gnoli, *Moda: dalla Nascita della Haute Couture a Oggi* (Rome: Carocci, 2012); Elisabetta Merlo, *Moda Italiana: Storia di un'Industria dall'Ottocento a Oggi* (Venice: Marsilio, 2003); Elisabetta Merlo and Francesca Polese, "Turning Fashion into Business: The Emergence of Milan as an International Fashion Hub," *The Business History Review*, 80 (2006), 415–47; Elisabetta Merlo, "Italian Fashion Business: Achievements and Challenges (1970s–2000s)," *Business History*, 53 (2011), 344; Ivan Paris, "Fashion as a System: Changes in Demand as the Basis for the Establishment of the Italian Fashion System (1960–1970)," *Enterprise & Society*, 11 (2010), 524–59.

6 An exception to this trend are the works and publications of the Fondazione Antonio Ratti such as Margherita Rosina and Francina Chiara, *L'Età dell'Eleganza: Le Filande e Tessiture Costa nella Como degli Anni Cinquanta* (Como: NodoLibri, 2010); Margherita Rosina and Francina Chiara, *Emilio Pucci e Como: 1950–1980* (Como: NodoLibri, 2014).

7 Margherita Rosina, "Textiles: The Foundation of Italian Couture," in *The Glamour of Italian Fashion since 1945*, ed. Sonnet Stanfill (London: V&A Publishing, 2014), pp. 76–93 (76–8); Simona Segre Reinach, "The Italian Fashion Revolution in Milan," in *The Glamour of Italian Fashion since 1945*, ed. Sonnet Stanfill (London: V&A Publishing, 2014), pp. 58–71 (p. 69); note that in this article, although Segre Reinach surveys the twentieth-century history of the Italian textile industry, she omits to mention the artificial and synthetic textile industry.

8   Ivan Paris, *Oggetti Cuciti: L'Abbigliamento Pronto in Italia dal Primo Dopoguerra Agli Anni Settanta* (Milan: Franco Angeli, 2006), p. 21.

9   With the exception of Lesley Ellis Miller, "Perfect Harmony: Textile Manufacturers and Haute Couture, 1947–57," in *The Golden Age of Couture: Paris and London, 1947–57* (London: V&A Publishing, 2007), pp. 113–36 and of Lou Taylor, "De-Coding the Hierarchy of Fashion Textiles," in *Disentangling Textiles: Techniques for the Study of Designed Objects*, ed. Mary Schoeser and Christine Boydell (London: Middlesex University Press, 2002), p. 68.

10 Christopher Breward, *The Culture of Fashion: A New History of Fashionable Dress* (Manchester: Manchester University Press, 1995), p. 1; Peter McNeil, "Conference Report: The Future of Fashion Studies," *Fashion Theory: The Journal of Dress*, 14 (2010), 105–10.

11 Ellen Leopold, "The Manufacture of the Fashion System," in *Chic Thrills: A Fashion Reader*, ed. Juliet Ash and Elizabeth Wilson (London: Pandora, 1992), pp. 101–17.

12 Elizabeth Wilson, *Adorned in Dreams: Fashion and Modernity* (London: Virago, 1985), p. 48.

13 Ibid.

14 Ibid., p. 11.

15 Christopher Breward, "Cultures, Identities, Histories: Fashioning a Cultural Approach to Dress," *Fashion Theory: The Journal of Dress, Body & Culture*, 2 (1998), 301–13 (p. 303).

16 Breward, *The Culture of Fashion*, p. 5.

17 Dominique Veillon, *Fashion Under the Occupation* (Oxford: Berg, 2002).

18 Nancy L. Green, *Ready-to-Wear and Ready-to-Work: A Century of Industry and Immigrants in Paris and New York* (Durham, NC and London: Duke University Press, 1997).

19 Yuniya Kawamura, *Fashion-Ology* (Oxford: Berg, 2004), p. 1.

20 Ibid.

21 Jonathan Faiers, *Tartan* (Oxford: Berg, 2008), p. 3.

22 Textiles that Changed the World, https://www.bloomsbury.com/uk/series/textiles-that-changed-the-world/ [accessed August 10, 2019].

23 Valerie Steele, "A Museum of Fashion is More than a Clothes-Bag," *Fashion Theory*, 2 (1998), 327–35 (p. 327), Lou Taylor, "Doing the Laundry? A Reassessment of Object-Based Dress History," *Fashion Theory: The Journal of Dress, Body & Culture*, 2 (1998), 337–58 (p. 347).

24 Kaori O'Connor, "The Other Half: The Material Culture of New Fibers," in *Clothing as Material Culture*, ed. Kuchler Susanne and Miller Daniel (Oxford: Berg, 2005), pp. 41–60 (p. 44).

25 Gnoli, *La Moda*, pp. 18–22.

26 Sofia Gnoli, *La Donna, L'Eleganza, Il Fascismo: La Moda Italiana dalle Origini all'Ente Nazionale della Moda* (Catania: Edizioni del Prisma, 2000); Paulicelli, *Fashion under Fascism*.

27 Sofia Gnoli, *Un Secolo Di Moda Italiana, 1900–2000* (Rome: Meltemi, 2005) and Gnoli, *La Moda*.

28 Grazietta Butazzi, *1922–1943 Vent'Anni di Moda Italiana: Proposta per un Museo Della Moda a Milano* (Florence: Centro Di, 1980), Natalia Aspesi, *Il Lusso e l'Autarchia: Storia dell'Eleganza Italiana, 1930–1944* (Milan: Rizzoli, 1982); Caterina Chiarelli, *Moda Femminile tra le due Guerre*, Galleria Del Costume (Livorno: Sillabe, 2000).

29 Gloria Bianchino et al., *Italian Fashion: Vol. 1: The Origins of High Fashion and Knitwear* (Milan: Electa, 1987); Grazietta Butazzi et al., *Italian Fashion: Vol. 2: From Anti-Fashion to Stylism* (Milan: Electa, 1987); Gloria Bianchino, ed., *Disegno della Moda Italiana 1945–1980: Italian Fashion Designing 1945–1980* (Parma: CSAC dell'Università di Parma, 1987); Bonizza Giordani-Aragno, *Il Disegno dell'Alta Moda Italiana: 1940–1970* (Rome: De Luca, 1982).

30 Grazietta Butazzi, "Introduction," in Bianchino et al., *Italian Fashion* pp. 7–10 (p. 7).

31 Guido Vergani, *Anche "L'Abito Fa Pensare' Se Lo Firma Il Grande Stilista*, https://ricerca.repubblica.it/repubblica/archivio/repubblica/1989/04/14/anche-abito-fa-pensare-se-lo [accessed January 12, 2019].

32 Simona Segre Reinach, "*Fatto in Italia: La Cultura Made in Italy (1960–2000)* by Paola Colaiacomo (ed.)/ *Oggetti Cuciti: L'Abbigliamento Pronto in Italia Dal Primo Dopoguerra Agli Anni Settanta* by Ivan Paris," *Fashion Theory*, 13 (2009), 121–6 (p. 124).

33 Such as Maria Luisa Frisa, *Italian Eyes: Italian Fashion Photographs from 1951 to Today* (Florence: Fondazione Pitti Discovery, 2005); Maria Luisa Frisa, Anna Mattirolo and Stefano Tonchi, eds., *Bellissima: Italy and High Fashion, 1945–1968* (Milan: Electa, 2014). The exhibition *Bellissima* at the MAXXI museum in Rome (December 2, 2014 to May 3, 2015 and *Italiana: L'Italia vista dalla Moda* 1971–2001, at Palazzo Reale, Milan (February 22 to May 6, 2018).

34 Enrica Morini, *Storia della Moda: XVIII–XXI Secolo* (Milan: Skira, 2010); Adelheid Rasche, ed., *Coats!: Max Mara, 60 Years of Italian Fashion* (Milan: Skira, 2011).

35 Simona Segre Reinach, "China and Italy: Fast Fashion Versus Prêt-à-Porter. Towards a New Culture of Fashion," *Fashion Theory*, 9 (2005), 43–56.

36 Merlo and Polese, "Turning Fashion into Business"; Merlo, "Italian Fashion Business."

37 Segre Reinach, "*Fatto in Italia*," p. 125.

38 Merlo, *Moda Italiana*; Elisabetta Merlo, "'Size Revolution': The Industrial Foundations of the Italian Clothing Business," *Business History*, 57 (2015), 919–41.

39 Emanuela Scarpellini, *La Stoffa dell'Italia: Storia e Cultura della Moda dal 1945 a Oggi* (Rome: Laterza, 2017).

40 An example is Sarah Mower, *Gucci by Gucci: 85 Years of Gucci* (London: Thames & Hudson, 2006).

41 An exception to this is Rasche, ed., *Coats! Max Mara, 60 Years of Italian Fashion*.

42 Nicola White, "The Role of America in the Development of the Italian Fashion Industry 1945–1965" (unpublished MPhil dissertation, Kingston University, London, 1997); White, *Reconstructing Italian Fashion*.

43 White, *Reconstructing Italian Fashion*, p. 1.

44 Claire Wilcox, ed., *The Art and Craft of Gianni Versace* (London: V&A Publications, 2002). The exhibition *Versace at the V&A*, at the V&A from October 17 to January 12, 2003. Salvatore Ferragamo, *The Art of the Shoe 1927–1960* (exhibition at the V&A from October 31, 1987 to February 7, 1988). *Anna Piaggi Fashion-ology*, V&A from February 2 to April 23, 2006.

45 *Gianni Versace* (Met Museum, New York December 11, 1997– March 22, 1998 and *Schiaparelli and Prada: Impossible Conversations* (Met Museum New York, May 10–August 19, 2012).

46 Dilys Blum, *Roberto Capucci: Art into Fashion* (New Haven: Philadelphia Museum of Art in association with Yale University Press, 2011). The exhibition ran from March 16, 2011 to June 5, 2011.

47 Valerie Steele, ed., *Fashion, Italian Style* (New York: The Museum at FIT, 2003). One exception was played by the retrospective on the Sala Bianca at the Musée des Arts de la Mode et du Textile in Paris with *La Renaissance de la Mode Italienne: Florence, La Sala Bianca 1952–1973* (The Renaissance of Italian Fashion: Florence, La Sala Bianca 1952–1973) which ran from March 19 to August 1, 1993.

48 Grace Lees-Maffei and Kjetil Fallan, eds., *Made in Italy: Rethinking a Century of Italian Design* (London: Bloomsbury Academic, 2014); Eugenia Paulicelli, "Fashion: The Cultural Economy of Made in Italy," *Fashion Practice-the Journal of Design Creative Process & the Fashion Industry*, 6 (2014), 155–74.

49 Lees-Maffei and Fallan, *Made in Italy.*

50 As seen in the widespread monographs on individual designers and exhibitions in the previous section; for business history see the work of Paris, Merlo, and Polese.

51 Neri Fadigati, "Giovanni Battista Giorgini, La Famiglia, Il Contributo alla Nascita del made in Italy, Le Fonti Archivistiche," *ZoneModa Journal*, 8 (2018), 1–15.

52 Monica Gallai, "Il riordinamento e l'inventariazione dell'Archivio della Moda Italiana di Giovan Battista Giorgini: resoconto del primo anno di lavoro," http://www.archiviodistato.firenze.it/asfi/fileadmin/risorse/allegati_materiali_di_studio/archivio_moda_giorgini.pdf [accessed June 22, 2019]. According to Neri Fadigati, there are 72 boxes with around 60.000 documents and around 100 photographs dated between 1951 and 2002: Fadigati, "Giovanni Battista Giorgini," p. 15.

53 These materials are organized chronologically, and each album is dedicated to one of the events.

54 Fadigati, "Giovanni Battista Giorgini," p. 13.

55 I am grateful to Sonnet Stanfill for pointing out the existence of this material to me.

56 In 2018 Sonnet Stanfill highlighted that she was not able to find evidence of the details of Giorgini's fee. Stanfill Sonnet, "American Buyers and the Italian Fashion Industry, 1950–55," in Lee Blaszczyk Regina and Pouillard Véronique, eds., *European Fashion: The Creation of a Global Industry* (Manchester: Manchester University Press, 2018), pp. 146–69. For further details on the fee see p.59 of this book.

57 The little-known archive of this organization was in the process of being cataloged at the time of my research and the inventory has now been published in Elisabetta Merlo and Maria Natalina Trevisano, *Lo Stile Italiano nelle Carte: Inventario dell'Archivio Storico della Camera Nazionale della Moda Italiana (1958–1989)*, Pubblicazioni Degli Archivi Di Stato Strumenti CCII (Rome: Ministero per i Beni Culturali Direzione Generale Archivi, 2018).

58 For more information on Italian fashion magazines see Monti Gabriele, "Through a Paper Looking Glass," in *Bellissima: Italy and High Fashion, 1945–1968* (Milan: Electa, 2014); Paris, *Oggetti Cuciti*, p. 40. In this instance I am using the magazines as sources and not themselves as objects.

59 Tim Ingold, *Making: Anthropology, Archaeology, Art and Architecture* (London: Routledge, 2013), p. 7.

60 Grace Lees-Maffei, "The Production–Consumption–Mediation Paradigm," *Journal of Design History*, 22 (2009), 351–76.

61 Carlo Marco Belfanti, "History as an Intangible Asset for the Italian Fashion Business (1950–1954)," *Journal of Historical Research in Marketing*, 7 (2015), 74–90.

62 O'Connor, "The Other Half," pp. 44–5. O'Connor also explains that the conventional material culture studies have taken into account as the main object of interest the physical and social processes of transformation and not the materiality of fibers.

63 Kaori O'Connor, "Lycra, Babyboomers and the Immaterial Culture of the New Midlife: A Study of Commerce and Culture" (unpublished PhD dissertation, University College London, 2004).

64 For example, the label inside the Emilio Pucci Bikini (V&A: T.237a, b -1998) "Exclusively for Saks Fifth Avenue."

65 Helen Alexandra Palmer, "The Myth and Reality of Haute Couture. Consumption. Social Function and Taste in Toronto. 1945–1963' (unpublished PhD dissertation, Brighton University, 1994), p. 297; Alexandra Palmer, *Couture and Commerce: The Transatlantic Fashion Trade in the 1950s* (Vancouver, BC: UBC Press, 2001).

66 Regina Lee Blaszczyk, "Styling Synthetics: DuPont's Marketing of Fabrics and Fashions in Postwar America," *The Business History Review*, 80 (2006), 485–528.

67 Irene Brin, "La moda si prepara all'inverno" in *La Settimana Incom Illustrata* 30 (July 23, 1955), quoted in Cinzia Capalbo, "In the Capital: Institutions in Support of Fashion," in *Bellissima: Italy and High Fashion, 1945–1968* (Milan: Electa, 2014), pp. 350–53. Also on Irene Brin see Vittoria Caterina Caratozzolo, *Irene Brin: Italian Style in Fashion* (Venice: Marsilio, 2006).

68 Giuliana Chesne Dauphine Griffo, "G.B. Giorgini: The Rise of Italian Fashion," in Butazzi et al., *Italian Fashion*, pp. 66–71; Sofia Gnoli, *Un Secolo Di Moda Italiana, 1900–2000* (Rome: Meltemi, 2005), pp. 139–76; Roberta Orsi Landini, "The Sala Bianca," in *Bellissima: Italy and High Fashion, 1945–1968* (Milan: Electa, 2014), pp. 324–27; Guido Vergani, *La Sala Bianca: Nascita Della Moda Italiana* (Milan: Electa, 1992); Giorgini Archive in Florence State archive; Neri Fadigati, "Giovanni

Battista Giorgini, La Famiglia, Il Contributo Alla Nascita Del made in Italy, Le Fonti
Archivistiche," *ZoneModa Journal*, 8 (2018), 1–15.

69 Jay Cocks, "Giorgio Armani: Suiting Up for Easy Street," *Time*, April 5, 1982.

1 Fibers and the Making of Italian Textiles in the Post-War Period

1 One notable exception is the work of Nicola White, *Reconstructing Italian Fashion*.

2 The only publication devoted to the subject merely gives a historical overview of synthetics and artificial fibers without assessing their significance: Maura Garofoli and Bonizza Giordani-Aragno, *Le Fibre Intelligenti: Un Secolo di Storia e Cinquant'Anni di Moda* (Milan: Electa, 1991).

3 Despite the size of the Italian artificial and synthetic textile manufacturing industry, its impact on fashion has only been investigated in the interwar period and in the context of the Fascist regime's autarchy. See Merlo, *Moda Italiana*, pp. 65–6 and Paulicelli, *Fashion under Fascism*, p. 102. Studies such as Rosina and Chiara, *Età dell'Eleganza* have highlighted the role played by silk in the development of Italian fashion, but no studies have been devoted to the role of artificial and synthetic fabrics in the post-war period.

4 "High Praise Given to Italian Fabrics," *New York Times*, July 1951, p. 18.

5 Gloria Braggiotti Etting, "Florence in Fashion," *Town & Country*, September 1951, p. 138.

6 *Italian-American Business* 2, no. 2 (1952), pp. 5–7 quoted in Merlo and Polese, "Turning Fashion into Business, p. 441.

7 Maria Cacioppo, "Condizione Di Vita Familiare Negli Anni Cinquanta," *Memoria*, 6 (1982), 88 quoted in Paul Ginsborg, *A History of Contemporary Italy: Society and Politics, 1943–1988* (London: Penguin, 1990), p. 210.

8 Before the Marshall Plan entered full operation, the US government offered $176 million of "Interim Aid" to Italy at the beginning of 1948: Ginsborg, *A History of Contemporary Italy*, p. 115.

9 For further information on the importance of the Communist Party during that period, see Christopher Duggan, "Italy in the Cold War and the Legacy of Fascism" in Christopher Duggan and Christopher Wagstaff, eds., *Italy in the Cold War: Politics, Culture and Society, 1948–1958* (Oxford and Washington DC: Berg, 1995), pp. 1–24 (p. 13).

10 Penny Sparke, "The Straw Donkey: Tourist Kitsch or Proto-Design? Craft and Design in Italy, 1945–1960," *Journal of Design History*, 11 (1998), 59–70 (p. 62).

11 Rasche, ed., *Coats! Max Mara, 60 Years of Italian Fashion*; Nicola White, "Max Mara and the Origins of Ready-to-Wear," *Modern Italy*, 1 (1996), 63–88 (p. 67).

12 White, "Max Mara," p. 64; Guido Vergani, *The Fashion Dictionary* (New York: Baldini Castoldi, 2006), p. 820.

13 Penny Sparke, *Italian Design: 1870 to the Present* (London: Thames and Hudson, 1988), pp. 81–2.

14 Vergani, *The Fashion Dictionary*, p. 719

15 Merlo and Polese, "Turning Fashion into Business," pp. 441–2.

16 Advertisement for La Rinascente Donnybrook and Henry, *Novità*, December 1950, p. 2.

17 White, *Reconstructing Italian Fashion*, pp. 169 and 171.

18 For more on the kinds of machines that Italian cotton mills bought from the USA through this scheme, see Merlo, *Moda Italiana*, pp. 80–2.

19 Ibid., p. 82.

20 Ibid., p. 83; on the American impact on the Italian textile industry see also Paris, *Oggetti Cuciti*, pp. 89–91.

21 White, "Max Mara," p. 68.

22 Ibid.

23 Sofia Gnoli, *Moda: dalla Nascita della Haute Couture a Oggi*, pp. 18–22. Eugenia Paulicelli, *Rosa Genoni, La Moda è Una Cosa Seria: Milano, Expo 1906 E La Grande Guerra* (Monza: Deleyva editore, 2015); Elisa Tosi Brandi, *Artisti Del Quotidiano: Sarti E Sartorie Storiche in Emilia-Romagna* (Bologna: CLUEB, 2009), p. 82.

24 Gnoli, *Moda*, p. 81.

25 Cinzia Capalbo, *Storia Della Moda a Roma: Sarti, Culture E Stili Di Una Capitale Dal 1871 a Oggi* (Rome: Donzelli, 2012), p. 102. Quoted in Lucia Floriana Savi, "Italy's Autarky: Fashion and Textiles during the Fascist Regime," *Proceedings of the 2014 Annual Meeting of the ICOM Costume Committee*, "Endymatologika" (Costume Studies), Nafplion and Athens, Greece, 5 vols. (Athens: KIKPE, 2015), p. 179.

26 On this see Savi, *Italy's Autarky*; Gnoli, *La Donna, L'Eleganza, Il Fascismo*; Butazzi, *1922–1943 Vent'Anni Di Moda Italiana*; Natalia Aspesi, *Il Lusso e l'Autarchia: Storia dell'Eleganza Italiana, 1930–1944* (Milan: Rizzoli, 1982); Chiarelli, *Moda Femminile tra le due Guerre*.

27 Butazzi et al., *Italian Fashion*, p. 7 and Tosi Brandi, *Artisti del Quotidiano*, p. 88. For more on translation of French models into Italian ones through toile see White, *Reconstructing Italian Fashion*, p. 75.

28 Savi, *Italy's Autarky*.

29 White, *Reconstructing Italian Fashion*, p. 38.

30 Ibid., p. 41 quoting fashion journalist Elisa Massai and the Italian Central Statistical Institute.

31 White, "Max Mara," p. 68; Rosina "Textiles," p. 76; Ed M. Rosina, *Taroni: The Fabric That Dreams are Made of* (Milan: Rizzoli, 2017), p. 74.

32 Ginsborg, *A History of Contemporary Italy*, p. 471, note 6.

33 Paris, *Oggetti Cuciti*, pp. 88–9.

34 Ibid., p. 88.

35 Wool production grew from 115,000 tons of produce in 1938 to 166,000 in 1950 and cotton from 320,000 tons in 1938 to 363,000 in 1950 (Paris, *Oggetti Cuciti*, p. 89).

36 "Fabrics: Italian Silk Producer Aims at Developing U.S. Market," *Women's Wear Daily*, January 22, 1947, p. 18.

37 Auroria Fiorentini Capitani, *Moda Italiana Anni Cinquanta e Sessanta* (Florence: Cantini, 1991), p. 7.

38 Penny Sparke, "Industrial Design or Industrial Aesthetics? American Influence on the Emergence of the Italian Modern Design Movement, 1948–58," in Duggan and Wagstaff, eds., *Italy in the Cold War*, pp. 159–65 (p. 162).

39 Paris, "Fashion as a System."

40 Giovanna Lazzi, "Light and Shadows in the Sala Bianca: Florence, Fashion and the Press," in Bianchino et al, *Italian Fashion*, pp. 72–7 (p. 77).

41 White describes some of the ways in which the USA, through the Marshall Plan and other initiatives, used the supply of raw materials as a political tool. White, *Reconstructing Italian Fashion*, pp. 10–17.

42 "Sblocco Dei Tessuti E Prossimo Arrivi Di Cotone Sodo," *Il Sole*, 1 August 1945, p. 1.

43 "Italian Fashion Designers Helped by Marshall Plan," *New York Herald Tribune*, August 113, 951. Florence, Archivio di Stato (ASF), GB Giorgini, album 1, code 42.

44 "Industrie Tessili E Esportazioni," *Il Sole*, 21 September 1945, p. 1.

45 "Exchange Makes Retail Prices Lower than Wholesale in Italy," *Women's Wear Daily*, May 12, 1947, p. 11.

46 *Novità*, April 1953, p. 17.

47 International Wool Secretariat advertisement, *Harper's Bazaar UK*, March 1946, p. 89.

48 Several articles in *Novità* such as the ones in the December 1951 issue and in January 1952 bear this slogan.

49 "Sfilate D'autunno. Eco Delle Manifestazioni Organizzate Dal Segretariato Internazionale Della Lana," *Novità*, November 1953, p. 29.

50 "La Moda Nasce Dai Tessuti," *Novità*, February 1953, pp. 16–30; "The Fabric Comes First," *Harper's Bazaar UK*, January 1957, p. 25.

51 "Appuntamento Con La Moda," *Settimana Incom*, 00972, 29/07/1953, https://patrimonio.archivioluce.com/luce-web/detail/IL5000027785/2/palazzo-pitti-sfilata-alta-moda-presentazione-modelli-della-stagione-autunno-inverno.html?startPage=0&jsonVal={%22jsonVal%22:{%22query%22:[%22Appuntamento%20Con%20La%20Moda22],%22fieldDate%22:%22dataNormal%22,%22_perPage%22:20}} [accessed August 23, 2022].

52 Important to mention here is the autarkic legitimation of the casein's fiber, Lanital through a campaign that also included a poem written by Marinetti: "The Poem of the Milk Dress" (1938–9). For more on this see Savi, *Italy's Autarky*; Jeffrey T. Schnapp, "The Fabric of Modern Times," *Critical Inquiry*, 24 (1997), 191–245, JSTOR http://www.jstor.org/stable/1344164 [accessed January 6, 2019].

53 *La Settimana Incom* was one of the most important Italian newsreels of the post-war period. It started in 1946 and mainly reported on football, fashion, and film, but also politics and current affairs. "Moda Italiana a Firenze," *Settimana Incom*, 00902,

06/02/1953, https://patrimonio.archivioluce.com/luce-web/detail/ IL5000023833/2/v-mostra-alta-moda-italiana-palazzo-pitti-altri-sfilano-modelli-antonelli-emilio-luisa-spagnoli.html?startPage=0&jsonVal={%22jsonVal%22:{%22q uery%22:[%22moda%20italiana%20a%20firenze%201953%22],%22fieldDate%22:% 22dataNormal%22,%22_perPage%22:20 [accessed August 23, 2022].

54 Advertisement probably in *Women's Wear Daily*, FAS, G.B. Giorgini, Album 8.

55 "Italy's Textile Industry, Designers Aim for Leading Role in World Fashion," *Sunday World Herald*, May 24, 1953, p. n/a.

56 "Esportazione Di Seta Naturale," *Il Sole*, October 30, 1945, p. 1.

57 "La Mostra Internazionale Della Tessitura Serica Comasca," Il Sole, 18 December 1945, p. 1.

58 No sample books pre-dating 1951 have survived in the archive. The sample books analyzed date from 1951 to 1953.

59 Each sample is also identified with the city of provenance, probably meaning that each city and country had its own added cost. A drawback for the precise analysis of the blends of fibers used in fashion is the fact that garments before 1972 in Italy do not bear a composition label. Before this date only an expert eye would be able to identify the exact composition of a fabric, and only laboratory analyses would allow the precise composition of a fabric to be determined. In order to understand whether and how artificial and synthetic blends were present in Italian fashion in this period, it is necessary to go back to the source of production, namely the textile producers, and to the clients that bought them, such as Harrods in this case.

60 *Novità*, January 1953, p. 7.

61 In March of the same year *Novità* was also featuring a full-page Rhodiatoce advertisement sponsoring the use of the brand for underwear.

62 Italviscosa was a 1939 initiative by SNIA Viscosa, Cisa Viscosa, and Chantillon. This consortium aimed at using the industrial plants of three companies in a more rationalized and efficient way by coordinating the programs of production and sales in accordance with the necessity of the demand markets. Italviscosa also aimed at unifying and therefore saving capital in terms of propaganda and administration in order to stabilize prices for the internal market. In terms of foreign business, Italviscosa presented a unique trade name under which to unite Italian man-made fibers. *Mezzo Secolo Di Snia Viscosa* (Milan: Pan, 1970), p. 38.

63 Legler, Line e Lane, Italviscosa, FAS, G.B. Giorgini, album 8, codes AB A8, 113 and code 119 A.8.

64 In the post-war period (no specific date is indicated), SNIA tried to verticalize its structure and took financial control of cotton mills such as Cotonificio Vittorio Olcese and Cotonificio Veneziano in order to secure a constant use of its production and to offer models for a rationalized use of chemical fibers in *Mezzo Secolo Di Snia Viscosa*, p. 44.

---

65 Established in 1802, DuPont started as a gunpowder producer. In the 1910s the company started to diversify production and in 1930 it discovered nylon. "History," https://www.dupont.com/about/our-history.html [accessed August 22, 2019].

66 Roberto Sarti, interview with the author, July 18, 2017.

67 It is outside the premise of this book to define what can be defined as natural, artificial, or synthetic. While others, such as Ezio Manzini and Jean Baudrillard, have challenged these notions, I am interested here in understanding the cultural status of artificial and synthetic materials within Italian fashion (Jean Baudrillard, *The System of Objects*, trans. James Benedict (London; New York: Verso, 1996) and Ezio Manzini, *The Material of Invention: Materials and Design* (London: Design Council, 1986)).

68 Blaszczyk, "Styling Synthetics."

69 SNIA was founded in Turin in 1917 by Riccardo Gualino and did not have anything to do with production of chemical fibers at first. SNIA stood for *Società Navale Italo Americana* (Italo American Naval Society) and only in 1919, alongside the production of ships and cement, began to produce chemical fibers to face the economic difficulties after the first World War. The following year SNIA acquired the majority share of Viscosa Pavia, the second Italian producer of chemical fibers, and it quickly changed its name permanently to SNIA Viscosa. For a complete history of SNIA Viscosa see *Mezzo Secolo di Snia Viscosa*, pp. 15–20.

70 Grazietta Butazzi, "Gli Anni Trenta: La Moda si Mette a Confronto, tra Autarchia e Nuove Prospettive," in Caterina Chiarelli, ed., *Moda Femminile Tra Le due Guerre* (Livorno: Sillabe, 2000), pp. 12–19. 18; Savi, "Italy's Autarky," p. 177.

71 Schnapp, "The Fabric of Modern Times," p. 191.

72 The important role played by SNIA Viscosa in Italy and the scale of its pre-war business has been mainly studied in relation to the Fascist regime's artificial autarkic fibers policy. For this, see Butazzi, "Gli Anni Trenta; Gnoli, *La Donna, L'Eleganza, Il Fascismo*; Schnapp, "The Fabrics of Modern Times," pp. 203–4. Marinetti also wrote in conjunction with the "Poem of the Milk Dress" another poem, "Il Poema di Torre Viscosa" (The Poem of Viscose Tower) (1938). As soon as the war finished and the Fascist regime was overturned, American Allies came to Italy and the production of Lanital ceased immediately. Although SNIA Viscosa stopped making Lanital, it carried on a similar production with an improved formula and a new name: Merinova. SNIA continued to be a leader in the Italian textiles sector, and its chairman after 1939, Franco Marinotti, was a fervent believer in the successful connection between fashion, textiles, and art.

73 Schnapp, "The Fabric of Modern Times," p. 215.

74 *Sette Canne ed un Vestito*, https://www.dailymotion.com/video/x2omuu [accessed September 1, 2018]. Paulicelli speaks about this documentary in connection with another Antonioni film. Euenia Paulicelli, "Cronaca di un Amore: Fashion and Italian Cinema in Michelangelo Antonioni's Films (1949–1955)," in Graziella Parati,

ed., *New Perspectives in Italian Cultural Studies. Volume 2* (Madison NJ: Fairleigh Dickinson University Press, 2013), pp. 107–29 (pp. 108–9). Rayon is a fiber that is developed from the cellulose of the canna gentile (*Arundo donax*). During the Fascist regime, local forestation programs were encouraged to produce giant cane that could provide Italy with a home source of cellulose, the main material for rayon production.

75 Alfred Gell, "The Technology of Enchantment and the Enchantment of Technology," in Jeremy Coote and Anthony Shelton, eds., *Anthropology, Art and Aesthetics* (Oxford: Clarendon, 1992), pp. 40–63. More work can be done in the future to analyze the relationship between the ways in which synthetic fibers have been represented in the arts and the reactions of consumers.

76 Schnapp, "The Fabric of Modern Times."

77 For more information on Marinotti see "Biografia," http://www.imprese.san. beniculturali.it/web/imprese/protagonisti/scheda-protagonista?p_p_id=56_INSTAN CE_6uZ0&articleId=60603&p_p_lifecycle=1&p_p_state=normal&viewMode=norm al&ambito=protagonisti&groupId=18701 [accessed 23 August, 2022]; Maura Garofoli and Bonizza Giordani-Aragno, *Le Fibre Intelligenti: Un Secolo di Storia e Cinquant'Anni di Moda* (Milan: Electa, 1991), p. 129. This is the only publication devoted to the subject, but it gives only a historical overview of synthetics and artificial fibers without assessing their significance. On CIM see also Ivan Paris, *Oggetti Cuciti*, pp. 188 and 190. Paris believes that CIM was the first organization of its kind in Italy with missions abroad, such as those to Zurich in April 1950 and to Austria in 1952, which involved different dressmakers and couturiers from around Italy similarly to what Giorgini would do in Florence from 1951. Paris also states in a recent essay (Paris Ivan, "Italian Fashion Centre," in *Bellissima: Italy and High Fashion, 1945–1968* (Milan: Electa, 2014), pp. 260–3) that CIM was ex-Fascist Edoardo Alfieri's idea. Jane Cianfarra, "Old, New Blended in Italian Style," *New York Times*, September 10, 1951. FAS, G.B. Giorgini, album 1, code 94.

78 Further information on Marinotti and his son and activities of the International Fashion Center for the Arts and Costume in Elsa Danese, "The High Fashion Shoes at the International Center for the Arts and Costume," in *Bellissima: Italy and High Fashion, 1945–1968* (Milan: Electa, 2014), pp. 302–5.

79 *Snia Dal Filo Allo Spazio* (Milan: Arti Grafiche Occhipinti, n.d.). Andrea Merlotti believes that the most important Italian art historians were called to write for this magazine. Andrea Merlotti, "I Percorsi Della Moda Made in Italy (1951–2010)," in F. Profumo and V. Marchis, eds., *Enciclopedia Italiana Di Scienze, Lettere E Arti, Appendice VIII, Il Contributo Italiano Alla Storia Del Pensiero*, Vol. 3, Technica vols (Rome: Istituto dell' Enciclopedia Italiana, 2013), pp. 630–40 (p. 631).

80 For more information on Paolo Marinotti and CIAC see Stefano Collicelli Cagol, *Venezia e la Vitalità del Contemporaneo: Paolo Marinotti a Palazzo Grassi* (Padua: Il Poligrafo, 2008).

81 Collicelli Cagol, *Venezia e la Vitalità del Contemporaneo*, p. 34.

82 *"Il Centro Internazionale Delle Arti E Del Costume Di Venezia," Il Ticino*, September 10, 1951.

83 *Storia della Bachicoltura dalle Origini ai Giorni Nostri in una Mostra a Venezia*, https://patrimonio.archivioluce.com/luce-web/detail/IL5000042223/2/storia-della-bachicoltura-dalle-origini-ai-giorni-nostri-mostra-veneziana.html [accessed September 1, 2018].

84 Franco Marinotti quoted in "La Mostra dei Tessili dell'Avvenire," *Linea*, Summer 1954, p. 87. This exhibition was organized by the Comitato Italiano del Congresso Internazionale dei Tessili Artificiali e Sintetici and supported by the CIAC.

85 *La Mostra dei Tessili dell'Avvenire*, https://patrimonio.archivioluce.com/luce-web/detail/IL5000042219/2/mostra-del-tessile-avvenire.html?startPage=0&jsonVal={%22jsonVal%22:{%22query%22:[%22tessuti%20dell%27avvenire%22],%22fieldDate%22:%22dataNormal%22,%22_perPage%22:20}} [accessed August 23, 2022]. From this newsreel it is also evident how the textile exhibition *I Tessuti dell'avvenire* was supported by the parade of models on mannequins. Here once more the synthetic and artificial fibers are described as within the reach of everybody.

86 Butazzi, *1922–1943 Vent'Anni Di Moda Italiana*; Caterina Chiarelli, *Moda Femminile tra le Due Guerre*; Mario Lupano and Alessandra Vaccari, *Fashion at the Time of Fascism: Italian Modernist Lifestyle 1922–1943* (Bologna: Damiani, 2009). Paulicelli, *Fashion under Fascism*.

2 The American Export Market and its Influence on Italian Design

1 Because of its undeniable international importance, Italian fashion accounts have often been based on the role and relevance of the *Sala Bianca*, and investigations have rarely looked beyond the borders of the Florence event.

2 Paris, "Fashion as a System," p. 526. Paris acknowledges the role the USA played in the 1950s as it "supplied technology and organizational models for the emergent ready-to-wear industry and provided a market outlet for high-end products. It facilitated emancipation from the French model of fashion in favor of the 'made in Italy' brand" (p. 527). However, he believes that the American connection to Italian fashion had no consequences for the organization of the Italian fashion industry. As this chapter will demonstrate, the US interest, both through encouraging the use of synthetics and artificial fibers and through the business of copies, had a significant influence on how some of the Italian sectors were reorganized after the war.

3 Palmer, *Couture and Commerce*.

4   Other terminologies used in the press at the time were "letter-perfect copy" and "identical twin copies both custom-made and ready-to-wear."

5   White, *Reconstructing Italian Fashion*, pp. 47–8.

6   Simona Segre Reinach, "Italian Fashion: The Metamorphosis of a Cultural Industry," in Lees-Maffei and Fallan, eds., *Made in Italy*, pp. 239–50 (p. 241).

7   For *Italy at Work* see Catharine Rossi, *Crafting Design in Italy: From Post-War to Postmodernism* (Manchester: Manchester University Press, 2015), p. 10. After opening at the Brooklyn Museum, the exhibition travelled to the Art Institute of Chicago; the De Young Museum, San Francisco; the Portland Art Museum; the Minneapolis Institute of Arts; the Museum of Fine Arts in Houston, Texas; the City Art Museum, St. Louis; the Toledo Art Museum; the Albright Art Gallery in Buffalo, New York; the Carnegie Art Museum, Pittsburgh; the Baltimore Museum of Art; and finally the Museum of Art at the Rhode Island School of Design. "Institutional Sponsors," Italy at Work: Her Renaissance in Design Today," *The Brooklyn Museum Bulletin* (Fall 1950), 1, p. 7.

8   Sparke, *The Straw Donkey*; Rossi, *Crafting Design in Italy*, p. 21.

9   Rossi, *Crafting Design in Italy*, p. 10.

10 Merlo and Polese, "Turning Fashion into Business," p. 440.

11 Orsi Landini, "The Sala Bianca," pp. 324–7, Guido Vergani, *La Sala Bianca*. Apart from some authors like Nicola White mentioning the tie-ups (White, *Reconstructing Italian Fashion*, pp. 25–2), no further research has been devoted to the effects that textiles might have had.

12 "Italy at Work. Her Renaissance in Design Today," p. 1.

13 Ratti Foundation former curator Francina Chiara confirmed that the Chariot textile is a printed textile by the company Guido Ravasi printed for the first time in 1949. Email correspondence with the author, September 5, 2016.

14 Murphy, letter to Alice Perkins, August 4, 1950, Brooklyn Museum Archive (BMA), Italy at Work: Her Renaissance in Design Today. [11/30/1950–01/31/1951]. [01]. (1950–1951).

15 Perkins, letter to Michelle Murphy, 10 August 1950, BMA, "Italy at Work: Her Renaissance in Design Today." [11/30/1950–01/31/1951]. [01]. (1950–1951). Murphy, Michelle.

16 Ibid.

17 Meyric R. Rogers, letter, to G. B. Giorgini, August 24, 1950, FAS, G. B. Giorgini Archive, album 2 – February 12–14, 1951. Also on *Italy at Work* see Carlo Marco Belfanti, "Renaissance and 'Made in Italy': Marketing Italian Fashion through History (1949–1952)," *Journal of Modern Italian Studies*, 20 (2015), 53–66; Rossi, *Crafting Design in Italy*; Sparke, "The Straw Donkey'; Vergani, *Fashion Dictionary*.

18 Letter from G. B. Giorgini to M. R. Rogers, September 15, 1950, FAS, G. B. Giorgini Archive, album 2.

19 Ibid.

20 Letter from M. R. Rogers to G. B. Giorgini, September 20, 1950, BMA, Exhibitions: Italy at Work (8): fashion show. Principal respondent: Giorgini, G. B. Corresp re proposal for show to be sponsored by Altman's. (1950/09–1950/10). Records of the office of the director: D|50–51|CN.

21 Letter from Altman to G. B. Giorgini, October 11, 1950, FAS, G. B. Giorgini Archive, Album 2.

22 Murphy, Memorandum to Mr. Nagel regarding the Italian Fashion Show, 13 October 1950, BMA, Exhibitions: Italy at Work (8): fashion show. Principal respondent: Giorgini, G. B. Corresp re proposal for show to be sponsored by Altman's. (1950/09–1950/10). Records of the office the director: D|50–51|CN.

23 Ibid.

24 Ibid.

25 Letter from Sakowitz to G. B. Giorgini, 22 February 1952, FAS, G. B. Giorgini, album 1, code 224.

26 More on "originals" and "copies" in the Simonetta case study in this chapter.

27 Vergani, *La Sala Bianca*, p. 42. Many publications have talked about this Giorgini's first fashion show, including Sonnet Stanfill, *The Glamour of Italian Fashion since 1945* (London: V&A Publishing, 2014).

28 Stanfill, *The Glamour of Italian Fashion*, p. 12.

29 Meyric Reynold Rogers, *Italy at Work: Her Renaissance in Design Today* (Baltimore: Baltimore Museum of Art, 1950), p. 15.

30 Rogers, *Italy at Work*, p. 15.

31 Ibid., p. 43.

32 Brooklyn Museum of Art Library Collections, BMA, institutional files, Italy at Work, Her Renaissance in Design Today, 11/30/1950-1/31/1951.

33 Catharine Rossi, "Crafting Modern Design in Italy, from Post-War to Postmodernism" (PhD dissertation, Royal College of Art, 2011), p. 85.

34 Rossi, *Crafting Design*, p. 17.

35 "Ravasi Silks Selected for Forthcoming Travelling Exhibit of Italian Goods," *Women's Wear Daily*, July 31, 1950, p. 12.

36 Although the name of the exhibition was not directly reported, the textiles described in the *WWD* article were evidently the ones selected from the boutique opened by Ravasi to be shown in the *Italy at Work* exhibition. This can be proved by the presence of the name of Ravasi in the catalogue of *Italy at Work*, and the fact that the exhibition opened in Brooklyn on November 30, 1950 while the article mentions an opening in the fall of the same year. *WWD* further refers to a jury in Italy selecting fabrics for the exhibition, and it is well documented that Rogers travelled to Italy with Amy Alexandre, the American Vice President of CAN, and two other CAN representatives in June 1950. The article was written in July of the same year. For more information on CAN see Rossi, *Crafting Design in Italy*, pp. 12–18.

37 They were identified in collaboration with former Ratti curator Francina Chiara during the research for my PhD thesis.

38 Fondazione Antonio Ratti FAR/C.P.4–2214, 1949.

39 Fondazione Antonio Ratti/FAR cat.LC 1220. The *WWD* article concludes that, apart from the prints, the Ravasi firm was not strongly influenced by fashion trends. However, Rosina and Chiara demonstrate that Ravasi was indeed involved in fashion, as it was the collaborator and producer of the famous Emilio Pucci silk design. For a comprehensive overview of this relationship see Margherita Rosina and Francina Chiara, Emilio Pucci e Como: 1950–1980 (Como: NodoLibri, 2014). More information on Ravasi: Margherita Rosina and Francina Chiara, eds., *Guido Ravasi: Il Signore della Seta* (Como: NodoLibri, 2008).

40 Brooklyn Museum Collection number 54.63.2.

41 See for example Gianluca Bauzano, "The High Notes of High Fashion," in *Bellissima: Italy and High Fashion, 1945–1968* (Milan: Electa, 2014) pp. 268–71 (p. 268). Virtually every article, publication and monograph on Italian fashion mentions the Sala Bianca.

42 Maria Canella, "Elisa Massai," in *Bellissima: Italy and High Fashion, 1945–1968* (Milan: Electa, 2014), pp. 276–9 (p. 277); Vergani, *Fashion Dictionary*, p. 814.

43 Rosina, "Textiles," p. 76.

44 "Italy Gets Dressed Up," *Life*, August 20, 1951, pp. 104–12 (p. 107).

45 Walter Lucas, "Florence Has Designs on Fashion," *The Christian Science Monitor*, n.d., FSA, G. B. Giorgini Archive, album 1, code 23.

46 Carmel Snow, "Italian Designers' Grand Entrance," *New York Journal-American*, August 26, 1951. FSA, G. B. Giorgini Archive, album 1, code 50.

47 White, *Reconstructing Italian Fashion*, p. 48.

48 "What's Going on in Italy?," *Women's Wear Daily,* 22 August 1951, p. 16.

49 Gian Carlo Fusco, "Dietro Tante Donne c'e' Quest'Uomo," *L'Europeo*, February 5, 1953. FSA, G. B. Giorgini Archive, album 6.

50 Carmel Snow, "Dresses Show Originality of Style and Fabric," *New York Journal-American*, February 16, 1953. FSA, G. B. Giorgini Archive, album 6.

51 Letter from Fibrafil to Centro di Firenze per la Moda, June 8, 1961, FSA, G. B. Giorgini Archive, uncatalogued, folder Ex 107.

52 Advertisement for Dralon promoting the collaboration with Italian couturier Cesare Guidi and Italian wool mill Lanificio Figli di Pietro Bertotto, *Novità*, November 1961, p. XXV.

53 "G. B. Giorgini/Moda/XVIII/4 Manifaestazioni Luglio 1959," July 1959, FSA, G. B. Giorgini Archive, uncatalogued folder Ex 92.

54 Letter from Carpenter to G. B. Giorgini, September 26, 1952, 1959," FSA, G. B. Giorgini Archive, album 5.

55 The "neutral ground' refers to the fact that Italy had many fashion cities, such as Rome and Turin, but also Venice. This had caused many polemics and Carpenter thought that Florence was a good compromise amongst them all.

56 White, *Reconstructing Italian Fashion*.

57 Virginia Drane McCallon, "Italy's Bid for Fashion Fame was Started by Houston Visitor," *Houston Post*, n.d., n.p. FSA, G.B. Giorgini Archive, album 1.

58 Merlo, *La Moda Italiana*, p. 75.

59 Ibid.

60 Elizabeth Hawes, *Fashion in Spinach: Experiences of a Dress Designer in France and the United States of America* (New York: Random House, 1938), p. 3.

61 Scarpellini, *La Stoffa dell'Italia*, pp. 42–4.

62 Elizabeth Wilson, *Adorned in Dreams: Fashion and Modernity* (London: University of California, 1992), p.113–115.

63 A paper pattern for a Jole Veneziani skirt cost 150 lire, as seen in *Novità*, December 1950.

64 "La Moda in Svizzera," *Novità*, February 1952, p. 12.

65 McCallon, "Italy's Bid for Fashion Fame was Started by Houston Visitor."

66 Ivan Paris, "Associazioni Italiana Industriali dell'Abbigliamento. L'Autonomia del Settore Industriale da Quello Artigianale e i Primi Tentantivi per un Controllo Instituzionale della Moda," *Università Degli Studi Di Brescia—Dipartimento Di Studi Sociali.Paper* (2005), p. 7.

67 White, *Reconstructing Italian Fashion*, p. 101.

68 Gianni Ghini in White, *Reconstructing Italian Fashion*, p. 100.

69 Paris, "Fashion as a System," p. 534.

70 Paris, *Oggetti Cuciti*, pp. 114–17.

71 Rebecca Arnold, *The American Look: Sportswear, Fashion and the Image of Women in 1930s and 1940s New York* (London: I.B. Tauris, 2008), p. 16.

72 Arnold describes how American sportswear was mass produced and inexpensive: Arnold, *The American Look*, p. 17.

73 Enrica Morini, *Storia Della Moda: XVIII–XXI Secolo* (Milan: Skira, 2010), p. 315.

74 "Jole Veneziani Apre la Serie Veneziani-Sport," *Novità*, December 1951, p. 22.

75 "Metallic Sweaters to Raincoats in New Boutique at Veneziani-Sport," *Women's Wear Daily*, December 11, 1951, p. 3.

76 Ibid.

77 Letter from Bernard Sakowitz's company to G. B. Giorgini, January 5, 1952, FSA, G. B. Giorgini Archive, uncatalogued, folder 11.

78 Letter from Bernard Sakowitz's auditor to G. B. Giorgini, March 30, 1953, FSA, G. B. Giorgini Archive, uncatalogued, folder 11.

79 Merlo, *Moda Italiana*, p. 71.

80 Eugenia Paulicelli, "Italian Fashion: Yesterday, Today and Tomorrow," *Journal of Modern Italian Studies*, 20 (2015), 3–7 (p. 5).

81 "La Bombe De Florence a E 'Branle' Les Salons De La Haute Couture Parisienne," n.t., n.d. FSA, G. B. Giorgini, album 1. The same news was also reported in an article by

Edna McKenna, "Italy Views for Fashion Lead," n.t., n.d.: "In Italy a suit can be bought for $68 and an evening dress for around $120. Labour in Italy is cheap, and Anny Blatt finds it worthwhile to have all her work done in Italy and then imported to France. (She is a famous name in woolen designs)." FSA, G. B. Giorgini, album 1, code 47.

82 Segre Reinach, "*Fatto in Italia*," p. 122.

83 The difference between export goods and goods available for domestic consumption is evident in the English system. Several fashion and trade magazines openly speak about the export effort that Britain was putting up after the war to win the export market, while in the country raw materials and fashion were still being rationed. On this see "British Fashions Go Abroad," *Harper's Bazaar UK*, July 1948, p. 24; "Editorial," *Fashions and Fabrics Overseas*, July–August 1946, p. 51.

84 Short evening dress (1950), wool and silk, gift of Janet A. Sloane 1982, Metropolitan Museum of Art New York, 1982.427.6a, b.

85 These are: "Fashion" in unknown magazine in Simonetta Visconti press clipping archive, Volume 2, p. 15, Galleria del costume di Palazzo Pitti Florence; Matilda Taylor, "Fashion Significance of Italian Dressmaker Showings: Empire Coats, Rich Dress Fabrics," *Women's Wear Daily*, July 27, 1951; "Italian Formal for Men's Shop Show evening dress," *Women's Wear Daily*, May 15, 1953; "Florence in Fashion," *Town & Country*, September 1951; "Italy Shows a New Strength in her Fashion Trade," *Vogue UK*, September 1951, p. 103. The dress is sometimes also referred to as a "cheese basket" dress.

86 White mentions this in *Reconstructing Italian Fashion*, pp. 47–8.

87 "Janet A. Sloane, 82, a Millinery Stylist," *New York* Times, May 6, 1996, http://www.nytimes.com/1996/05/06/nyregion/janet-a-sloane-82-a-millinery-stylist.html [accessed 10 April 2016].

88 "Fashion: What it Takes to be the New Young Fashion Whiz", *Vogue US*, August 15, 1958, Condé Nast, New York, *ProQuest* [accessed 10 April 2016]. Janet Sloane donated other pieces to the Met alongside the Simonetta, including garments by Dior and other French designers. For more, see "Search the Collection" on the Met's website, https://www.metmuseum.org/art/collection/search [accessed April 10, 2016].

89 "Black on the Beach," *Vogue UK*, November 1948, p. 60. Simonetta founded her fashion house in 1946 in Rome. Her first legendary collection was realized by using the only materials available in the aftermath of the Second World War, such as dishcloths, aprons, uniforms, and ribbons. Simonetta quickly became well known to the American press and market and her dresses were worn by American actresses such as Lauren Bacall and Audrey Hepburn (Vergani, *Fashion Dictionary*, p. 1157 and Gnoli, *Un Secolo di Moda Italiana*, pp. 129–30).

90 "Italy Shows a New Trend in Her Fashion Trade," *Vogue UK*, September 1951, p. 102.

91 The Simonetta press clipping books in Galleria del Costume, Palazzo Pitti, contain several articles and advertisements showing the various products Simonetta endorsed.

92 Braggiotti Etting, "Florence in Fashion," p. 176.

93 Giuliana Chesne Dauphine Griffo, "G. B. Giorgini," p. 66; Sonnet Stanfill, "The Role of the *Sartoria* in post-war Italy," *Journal of Modern Italian Studies*, 20 (2015), 83–91; Neri Fadigati, "Giovanni Battista Giorgini, La Famiglia, Il Contributo Alla Nascita Del made in Italy, Le Fonti Archivistiche," *ZoneModa Journal*, 8 (2018), 1–15.

94 In 1953 the percentage was 7 percent, as seen in a letter from G. B. Giorgini to Bernard Sakowitz, April 20, 1953, FAS, G. B. Giorgini Archive, uncatalogued, folder 11, file 3.

95 M. Sargiacomo, "Institutional Pressures and Isomorphic Change in a High-Fashion Company: The Case of Brioni Roman Style, 1945–89," *Accounting, Business and Financial History*, 18 (2008), 215–41 (p. 224).

96 Enzo Picone, *La Moda Italiana in America*, Congresso Internazionale Della Moda Del Tessile E Dell' Abbigliamento (Naples, September 2–4, 1954), (Naples: E Pironti e Figli Editori, 1954), p. 69. CIAC, Venice.

97 McCallon, "Italy's Bid for Fashion Fame Was Started by Houston Visitor."

98 Andrew Bolton, "Response," in Christopher Breward and Caroline Evans, eds., *Fashion and Modernity* (Oxford: Berg, 2005), pp. 147–50 (p. 147).

99 Ibid.

100 Giorgini, Letter to Bernard Sakowitz, March 21, 1953, FAS, G. B. Giorgini Archive, uncatalogued folder 11, file 3. He also says that he had offered the same deal to others of his accounts such as I. Magnin and B. Altman.

101 Ibid.

102 No evidence of rights to couturiers have been found yet.

103 The reproduction of the dress changed in nature depending on whether it was used for an advertisement, an editorial, or a quick report. The use of photography or illustration raises issues of costs, market, and readers. Some magazines and newspapers, for example, had limitations in image reproduction, and in such cases illustrations would have been easier to use to render the dress. Sketches of the dress appear in the articles "I primi modelli dell'inverno sono apparsi," "Fashion," and "Fashion Significances of Italian dressmaker showings," while photographs appeared in "Florence in Fashion" and "Italy shows a new Strength in her Fashion Trade' (details in note 85 in this chapter).

104 Braggiotti Etting, "Florence in Fashion," *Town and Country*, 1951, pp. 138 and 176; Galleria del Costume di Palazzo Pitti, Simonetta Visconti Archive, volume 2, p. 12.

105 Article "Fashion" from unknown magazine, GCPP, Simonetta Visconti Archive, volume 2, p. 15.

106 Eugenia Sheppard, "Imported Fashions Here: Bergdorf Goodman shows 88. Around 50 at Henri Bendel," *New York Herald Tribune*, September 14, 1951.

107 Guido Vergani, *La Sala Bianca*, p. 99, note 18. Evidence found in the FIT archive (Bergdorf Goodman folders) indicates that Bergdorf Goodman continued importing Simonetta designs until at least 1969. FIT Archive, folder US.NNFIT.SC.201.193.

108 "Visconti Collection shown by Begdorf's for Custom Order," *Women's Wear Daily*, November 14, 1951, p. 3.

109 "Italian Designers Visiting New York," *Vogue US*, February 15, 1952, p. 70. GCPP, Simonetta Visconti Archive Album 2, p. 24.

110 Fashion Institute of Technology, US.NNFIT.SC.20/192. The back of the drawing is inscribed: "Fall '52 evening dresses imports."

111 Extensive research was undertaken in the CSCA Parma archive, which holds more than 2,000 drawings from the Schuberth atelier.

112 A letter from the company Gimbel-Saks Purchasing S.A. to Saks Fifth Avenue refers to sketches sent alongside reports on the 1950 autumn–winter French couture shows. FIT archive, Gimbel Sophie, Box 3, Folder 2. This was confirmed by April Calahan, Curator of Manuscripts Collections, FIT Library Special Collections, who explained that this is a sketch of one of the Schuberth designs by one of Bergdorf Goodman's sketch artists (correspondence with the author November 29, 2021).

113 *Evening Ensemble*, http://www.metmuseum.org/art/collection/search/87361?sortBy=Relevance&ft=emilio+schuberth&offset=0&rpp=20&pos=3 [accessed June 4, 2017].

114 "Micol Fontana, Rome Fashion Designer, Here," *New York Herald Tribune*, September 2, 1951. FAS, G. B. Giorgini Archive, album 1, code 148.

115 Article "Fashion" from unknown magazine, GCPP, Simonetta Visconti Archive, volume 2, p. 15.

116 "Visconti Collection Shown by Bergdorf's for Custom Order," *Women's Wear Daily*, November 14, 1951.

117 Palmer, *Couture and Commerce*, pp. 106–7.

118 White, *Reconstructing Italian Fashion*, p. 48.

119 "Italy Gets Dressed Up," p. 104.

120 Advertisement for Russeks Designer Shop, FAS, G. B. Giorgini Archive, album 1, code 140.

121 Fay Hammond, "Europe Styles, U.S. Copies Draw 750 to Orbach Show," n.t., n.d., GCPP, Simonetta Visconti Archive, volume 2, p. 6.

122 Advertisement for Macy's in *New York Herald Tribune*, March 9, 1952, GCPP, Simonetta Visconti Archive, volume 2, p. 26.

123 White, *Reconstructing Italian Fashion*, p. 48.

124 "Large Italian textile companies were known to send representatives to the USA to search for new markets": White, "Max Mara," p. 68. Similar arrangements between couturiers, *carnettisti* and textile producers continued in the 1960s, as seen in Chapter 4 of this book.

125 Letter from Bernard Sakowitz to G. B. Giorgini, June 13, 1952, FAS, G. B. Giorgini Archive, uncatalogued, folder 11.

126 Taylor, "Fashion Significances of Italian Dressmaker Showings."

127 "Italian Formal for Men's Shop Show," *Women's Wear Daily*, May 15, 1953.

128 Article in *WWD* titled "High Fashion Stores and Volume Retailers at Italian Show" with pictures showing representatives from US volume retailers and Italian couturiers such as Simonetta and Fontana Sisters, *Women's Wear Daily*, July 25, 1951, p. 18.

129 "Italian Designer Caters to Home Seamstresses," *Oregonian*, March 8, 1953. FAS, G. B. Giorgini Archive, album 9.

130 Although the practice of going to Paris was forbidden it continued illegally. For more on this see Sofia Gnoli, *La Moda*; Paulicelli, *Fashion under Fascism*. Also see Irene Brin, "Dirottati in Italia i Buyers Americani," n.t., n.d, GCPP, Simonetta Archive, album 2, p. 28, in which the journalist states how until the 1940s Italians went twice a year to Paris where they would officially buy a number of models, and unofficially also buy a number of toiles provided illegally by "secret pirates" of the French ateliers.

131 Letter from Sorelle Fontana to Giorgini, January 13, 1951, FAS, G. B. Giorgini Archive, album 2.

132 Robiola Elsa, "Collezioni Italiane in Anticipo E in Orario," Il Tempo, 31 March 1951.

133 In Italy in the 1950s the silk industry was one of the few in the country that could draw raw material from the homeland and export a final product. Other European centers had to import silk yarns to feed their looms. For a picture of the Made in Italy label see MET search the collection database: https://www.metmuseum.org/art/collection/search/98031?searchField=All&sortBy=Relevance&ft=Simonetta&offset=0&rpp=40&pos=5 [accessed August 24, 2022]

134 For more information on the original fashion shows see Palmer, *Couture and Commerce*, p. 133.

3 The 1960s, a Decade of Metamorphosis in Italian Fashion

1 "Forever Italy," Vogue US, 1 October 1967, pp. 98–9.

2 Italian heritage was already being used as a promotional tool as early as the immediate post-war period; see Lucia Floriana Savi, "La Moda in Vogue," in Sonnet Stanfill, ed., *The Glamour of Italian Fashion Since 1945* (London: V&A Publishing, 2014), pp. 248–53. See also the Simonetta case study in Chapter 2 of this book.

3 Scarpellini, *La Stoffa Dell'Italia*, p. 49.

4 Elisabetta Merlo, "Le Origini del Sistema Moda," in Carlo Marco Belfanti and Fabio Giusberti, eds., *Storia d'Italia*, 19 vols. (Turin: G. Einaudi, 2003), p. 667; Paris, "Fashion as a System." p. 525.

5   Ginsborg, *A History of Contemporary Italy*, p. 216.

6   Michele Salvati, *Economia e Politica in Italia Dal Dopoguerra a Oggi* (Milano: Garzanti, 1984), pp. 60–1.

7   Emanuela Scarpellini, *Material Nation: A Consumer's History of Modern Italy* (Oxford: Oxford University Press, 2011), p. 134.

8   Silvio Lanaro, *Storia Dell'Italia Repubblicana: Dalla Fine Della Guerra Agli Anni Novanta* (Venice: Marsilio, 1992), p. 223.

9   Scarpellini, *Material Nation*, p. 133.

10 Paris, "Fashion as a System," p. 524.

11 Ibid.

12 Merlo, "Size Revolution," p. 920.

13 Messina, "Italian Woman's Wear: A Successful Industrial Product ", in Butazzi et al., *Italian Fashion*, pp. 26 and 28.

14 "Italy Needs US Technicians to Lead the Way From the Cottage," *Women's Wear Daily*, March 1962 quoted in Merlo, "Size Revolution," p. 929.

15 Ginsborg, *A History of Contemporary Italy*, p. 213.

16 Ibid., p. 214.

17 Germani, "L'esportazione Italiana nel settore della moda" in *L'Abbigliamento Italiano*, 1961, quoted in Paris, "Fashion as a System," p. 535.

18 Camera Nazionale Moda Italiana, [n.d.], p. 5, CNMI, folder 2, file 1.

19 Merlo, "Le Origini del Sistema Moda," p. 692. For a good summary of the partnership developed by Camera Nazionale della Moda between textile manufactures and couturiers see Elisabetta Merlo, *Moda Italiana*, pp. 94–101.

20 "Camera Nazionale Moda Italiana," n.d., p. 5, CNMI, folder 2, file 1.

21 Ibid.

22 "Rapporti industrie tessili moda Italiana," n.d., p. 2, CNMI, folder 2, file 1.

23 Ibid.

24 "Collaborazione tra l'industria tessile e l'alta moda," March 12, 1964, p. 1 and "Premi ed incentivi per elevare la qualità della produzione tessile e potenziare l'alta moda," CNMI, folder 4, file 2.

25 "Attuazione dell'accordo tessile alta moda," December 3, 1966. This document refers to the prize of 1967, but a previous prize of the same type had been in place since 1964: CNMI, folder 4, file 2.

26 "Relazione del consiglio direttivo," October 29, 1964, p. 28, Italy, CNMI, folder 3, file 1.

27 Messina, "Italian Woman's Wear," p. 26.

28 Paris, "Fashion as a System," p. 525.

29 Ibid, p. 526. The first will be analyzed in their first experimentations in this chapter and later in Chapter 5. The second element has been the subject of investigation in Chapter 2.

30 Nicola White, "The Role of America in the Development of the Italian Fashion Industry," p. 37.

31 White, "Max Mara," p. 68.

32 Confederazione Generale dell'Industria Italiana, Annuario 1958, pp. 131–5, Comitato Italiano per il cotone. Abitudini e Preferenze as quoted in Paris, *Fashion as a System*, p. 533.

33 Paris, "Fashion as a System," p. 533; Margherita Rosina, "Como Printed Silk for Women's Wear: A Century of Tradition and Innovation," in *Silk: The 1900's in Como* (Cinisello Balsamo: Silvana Editoriale, 2001), pp. 70–81 (p. 74).

34 Gnoli, *Un Secolo di Moda Italiana*, p. 177.

35 Rosina, "Como Printed Silk," p. 72, and Rosina, "Textiles," p. 83.

36 "La Moda a Palazzo Grassi," *La Ruota Diorama*, n.d., p. 77.

37 "Incontro Nazionale tra la Moda e l'Industria dell'Abbigliamento," October 13, 1962, CNMI, folder 2, file 1.

38 Vergani, *Fashion Dictionary*, p. 908.

39 Paris, "Fashion as a System," p. 540.

40 Ibid., p. 526.

41 Ginsborg, *A History of Contemporary Italy,* pp. 211, 212 and 219.

42 Ibid., p. 239.

43 Paris, "Fashion as a System," p. 539.

44 (No title), pp. 3 and 5, CNMI, folder 2, file 1.

45 This is still nowadays the way in which the sector is named in the economic and export realms.

46 Scarpellini, *La Stoffa Dell'Italia*, pp. 96–104.

47 Simona Segre Reinach, "La Moda nella Cultura Italiana Dai Primi Del Novecento a Oggi," in Carlo Petrini and Ugo Volli, eds., *La Cultura Italiana*, Vol. 4 (Turin: Utet, 2009), pp. 603–61 (p. 629) and Gnoli, *Un Secolo di Moda Italiana*, p. 185; Pierre Restany, "Breve Storia Dello Stile Yéyé," *Domus*, January 1967, p. 34.

48 Schuberth with Delia Biagiotti exported "ready-made" haute couture items. Capucci created boutique clothes distributed by Krizia; in Bianchino, *Disegno della Moda Italiana*, p. 44.

49 Elisabetta Merlo, "When Fashion Met Industry: Biki and Gruppo Finanziario Tessile (1957–72)," *Journal of Modern Italian Studies*, 20 (2015), 92–110 (p. 92).

50 Fiorentini Capitani, *Moda Italiana Anni Cinquanta e Sessanta*, p. 16.

51 Merlo, "When Fashion Met Industry," pp. 98–9.

52 Merlo, "When Fashion Met Industry," p. 102.

53 Paris, "Fashion as a System," p. 530.

54 Merlo, "When Fashion Met Industry," p. 105.

55 Ibid., p. 106.

56 Editorial photograph showing a Cori–Biki coat, *Amica*, October 1967, p. 47.

57 Merlo, "When Fashion Met Industry," p. 107.

58 Paris, "Fashion as a System," p. 530 and Capalbo, *Storia Della Moda a Roma*, p. 153. In 1972 the workers at Sorelle Fontana numbered around three hundred.

59 *Linea Contro linea 1967/ 68: Le Sorelle Fontana - Rai Teche*, https://www.youtube. com/watch?v=HfpZPWdLc7E [accessed November 24, 2018].

60 In 1954 only 88,000 TV licenses were requested in Italy, while by 1960 there were over two million TV sets in the country. John Foot, "Television and the City: The Impact of Television in Milan, 1954–1960," *Contemporary European History*, 8 (1999), 379–94 (pp. 381 and 383).

61 Capalbo, *Storia Della Moda a Roma*, p. 153.

62 Michael J. Piore and Charles F. Sabel, eds., *The Second Industrial Divide: Possibilities for Prosperity* (New York: Basic Books, 1984), p. 155.

63 The workers' demand for higher pay also caused Cleonice Capece to close her atelier and workshop in Via Gregoriana and to move to the UK: Cleonice Capece, interview with the author, May 18, 2017 and *Fashion by Chance: A Visual Autobiography 1960-1974* (Woodbridge: Antique Collectors Club, 2014), p. 220. For more information on this aspect, see also Edward Goodman, Julia Bamford, and Peter Saynor, eds., *Small Firms and Industrial Districts in Italy* (London: Routledge, 1989), p. 18.

64 Sargiacomo, "Institutional Pressures," pp. 226–7.

65 Ibid., pp. 223, 230–1.

66 Ibid., p. 228.

67 Ibid., p. 230.

68 Ibid., p. 229.

69 "The Fashions: European Rtw: The Challengers," *Women's Wear Daily*, March 30, 1967, p. 10.

70 Ibid.

71 "Alta Moda Pronta in Advance," *Women's Wear Daily*, October 17, 1967, p. 5.

72 Ibid.

73 Capece, *Fashion by Chance*, p. 25.

74 Ibid., p. 27.

75 Cleonice Capece, interview with the author, May 18, 2017.

76 Cleonice Capece's list of export invoices, (1965), CNMI, Folder 4, File 7, p. 1.

77 According to *WWD*, Isetan was one of Tokyo's largest department stores: J. W. Cohn, "Japan Reveals Plans for Couture Deal with Italy," *Women's Wear Daily*, June 24, 1963, p. 16. Isetan is still open and Dolce and Gabbana had a show there in September 2017.

78 Isetan Company Ltd *Fascicolo Italian Fashion Show Summer '65*, FAS, G.B. Giorgini Archive, album 61, code 14.

79 Cohn, "Japan Reveals Plans for Couture Deal with Italy."

80 Ibid.

81 Ibid.

82 Capece, *Fashion by Chance*, pp. 108–9.

83 "Relazione," CNMI, folder 4, file 7. In 1972 the application was finally accepted: n.t. September 7, 1972, CNMI, folder 4, file 7.

84 Paris, "Fashion as a System," p. 538.

85 Ibid.

86 Merlo, "When Fashion Met Industry," p. 102.

87 Ibid., p. 96.

88 "Alta Moda Pronta in Advance," p. 9

89 Gnoli, *Un Secolo di Moda Italiana*, p. 200.

4 Fashion Meets Industry: The Role of *Carnettisti* in Domestic and International Markets

1 Recent works that emerged from the research project "The Enterprise of Culture: International Structures and Connections in the Fashion Industry since 1945" have focused on, as Regina Lee Blaszczyk and Véronique Pouillard highlight, "the work of fashion professionals who worked behind-the-scenes as intermediaries." Regina Lee Blaszczyk Regina and Véronique Pouillard, eds., *European Fashion: The Creation of a Global Industry* (Manchester: Manchester University Press, 2018), p. 5.

2 Carolyn Sargentson, "The Manufacture and Marketing of Luxury Goods: The Marchands Merciers of Late 17th and 18th Century Paris," in Anthony Turner and Robert Fox, eds., *Luxury Trades and Consumerism in Ancien Régime Paris: Studies in the History* (Aldershot: Ashgate, 1998), pp. 99–137 (p. 99).

3 Ibid., p. 104.

4 Chiara Buss, ed., *Silk: The 1900s in Como* (Cinisello Balsamo: Silvana Editoriale, 2001), p. 11.

5 Interview with the author, May 31, 2017.

6 Pierre Besson, Givenchy and Tessuti Corisia Advertisment, *Vogue Italia*, April 1969, p. 16.

7 Franco De Felice, interview with the author, May 25, 2016; Brenda Azario, interview with the author, May 31, 2017.

8 Buss, *Silk*, p. 12.

9 Buss, *Silk*, p. 12, footnote 8, copied here: "The Lucchini firm was already active in Milan in 1831 in the sale of fabrics and garments made according to pattern. Since 1950 it has been a converter, supplying fabrics for the Italian and French high-fashion industries. The Gandini firm, after successfully working as *carnettisti* in Milan from 1925, became a firm of converters in 1962. They supply fabrics for the French, Italian and U.S. high fashion industries."

10 Buss, *Silk*, p. 12.

11 Ibid.

12 Rosina, "Como Printed Silk," p. 77; the name of the *carnettista* Lucchini, for example, was already present in 1947 in the magazine *Bellezza*: Relazione della XVIII

presentazione di Moda 20–24 Luglio 1959, G. B. Giorgini/Moda/XVIII/4
Manifestazioni Luglio 1959, FSA, G. B. Giorgini Archive, uncatalogued folder ex 92.

13 "Camera Nazionale della Moda," [n.d.], p. 3, CNMI, folder 2, file 1.

14 Francina Chiara, "An Outlining of Index of Companies," in *Silk: The 1900's in Como* (Cinisello Balsamo: Silvana Editoriale, 2001) pp. 332–341 (p. 338). Franco De Felice, interview with author, May 25, 2016.

15 Franco De Felice, interview with author, May 25, 2016.

16 De Felice highlights that the engravers were always external, because no weaver was equipped with this type of internal department. Franco De Felice, interview with author, May 25, 2016.

17 Merlo, *Moda Italiana*, p. 102.

18 Brenda Azario, interview with the author, May 31, 2017.

19 Roberto Sarti, interview with the author, July 18, 2017.

20 Franco De Felice, interview with author, May 25, 2016.

21 Brenda Azario, interview with the author, May 31, 2017.

22 Roberto Sarti, interview with the author, July 18, 2017.

23 Rosina, "Como Printed Silk," p. 77.

24 Ibid.

25 By 1965 the *Assortitori Tessuti Novità* were fourteen in total and they were mainly based in Milan, with a few in Turin and one in Rome. "Elenco assortitori tessuti novità," September 23, 1965, CNMI, Folder 5, file 2.

26 The *carnettisti* who started this group were the following: Satam, Sassi, Sanet, Gandini, Start, Lucchini, Poggio, and Chiri; Letter "Inserimento in seno alla Camera Nazionale della Moda Italiana quale Gruppo qualificato," May 13, 1965, CNMI, folder 13, file 10.

27 Letter, May 15, 1965, CNMI, folder 13, file 10.

28 Letter from Walter Pession to Ferdinando Chiri, May 31. 1965, CNMI, folder 31, file 4.

29 "Verbale della riunione per la costituzione del gruppo "Assortitori tessuti novità," October 9, 1965, CNMI, folder 10, file 3 and advertisement "Assortitori Tessuti Novità," in *Linea Italiana*, Spring–Summer, 1969, [n.p.].

30 *Vogue Italia*, the new Condé Nast magazine, was launched in November 1965 with a first issue titled both *Novità* and *Vogue*, priced at 500 lire. It featured the model Benedetta Barzini, photographed by Gianpaolo Barbieri, adorned only with Bulgari jewels.

31 Bruno Sassi and Lancetti advertisement, *Vogue Italia*, March 1967, p. 66.

32 Andrew Bolton in "Response," in Breward and Evans, eds., *Fashion and Modernity*, pp. 147–50 (p. 147), describes how couturiers in France used signatures to attest themselves at the beginning of twentieth century.

33 Fabiani and Gandini advertisement, *Vogue Italia*, March 1969, p. 189; Bruno Sassi advertisement, *Vogue Italia*, March 1968, p. 117, SISAN advertisement, *Vogue Italia*, March 1969, p. 192; Sanet and Antonelli Advertisement, *Vogue Italia*, September 1966, p. 27.

34 Brenda Azario, interview with the author, May 31, 2017.

35 Letter from Pietro Parizio to the associates, November 30, 1967, CNMI, folder 4, file 2.

36 Roberto Sarti, in his interview with the author, July 18, 2017, stated his belief that the textile alone was nothing and that it needed the couturiers for the textile to come alive.

37 Marie Christine Martin Guyot, "Spring Fabrics in Paris," *Womens' Wear Daily*, February 6, 1963, p. 48.

38 Unpublished notes from a lecture given by Brenda Azario titled "Fashion 1900 to 1982" at the Victoria and Albert Museum, March 29, 1982, p. 1.

39 Brenda Tandy and Vittorio Azario married in 1960.

40 Brenda Azario, interviews with Margherita Rosina January 18, 2013 and with Lucia Savi July 5, 2013.

41 Ibid.

42 Azario, "Fashion 1900 to 1982," p. 5 and interviews with Margherita Rosina January 18, 2013 and with Lucia Savi July 5, 2013.

43 Margherita Rosina and Lucia F. Savi, "Nattier: Textile Innovators," in Sonnet Stanfill, ed., *The Glamour of Italian Fashion since 1945* (London: V&A Publishing, 2014), p. 257.

44 Azario, "Fashion 1900 to 1982," p. 3.

45 Brenda Azario interview with the author, May 31, 2017.

46 Azario, "Fashion 1900 to 1982," p. 1.

47 "Design Trendsetters. Azario Architect of Fabric," *Trends Fabrics and Fashion*, June 1966, number 1, p. 29.

48 Brenda Azario, interviews with Margherita Rosina January 18, 2013 and with Lucia Savi July 5, 2013.

49 Azario, "Fashion 1900 to 1982," p. 6.

50 Ibid., p. 4.

51 Savi, "Nattier," p. 257.

52 Azario, "Fashion 1900 to 1982," p.3 and interviews with Margherita Rosina January 18, 2013 and with Lucia Savi July 5, 2013.

53 Azario, "Fashion 1900 to 1982," p. 6.

54 Savi, "Nattier," p. 257.

55 "Design Trendsetters. Azario Architect of Fabric."

56 *The Ambassador*, March 1967.

57 *Vogue US*, cover, August 1963.

58 Advertisement Neiman Marcus', *Vogue US*, 1 October 1960, p. 45.

59 *Vogue US*, 1 October 1960.

60 "Advertisement Neiman Marcus," *Vogue US*, 1 October 1960, p. 45.

61 Ibid.

62 Brenda Azario, interviews with Margherita Rosina January 18, 2013 and with Lucia Savi July 5, 2013.

63 *Amica*, Spring/Summer issue 1967, n.p.

64 The term *modellista* in this period is different from the modellista working in clothing production companies in the 1980s as seen in Chapter 6. Nicola White defines the toile as "a cotton reproduction of the original model, bearing the crucial details of cut and finish, but sold at a substantially lower price": White, "Max Mara," p. 76.

65 In Palmer, *Couture and Commerce*, p. 45, the author reproduces this quote from Christian Dior, *Talking About Fashion: Christian Dior as told to Elie Rabourdin and Alice Chavane*, trans. Eugenia Sheppard (New York: G.P. Putnam's Sons, 1954), pp. 106–7. Palmer, however, has never been able to find the original files.

66 White, "Max Mara," p. 76.

67 "L'Albero e i Frutti," *Bellezza*, February 1952, pp. 14–19.

68 Guido Vergani and Maria Pezzi, *Maria Pezzi: Una Vita Dentro La Moda* (Milan: Skira, 1998), p. 10.

69 According to Butazzi this was started by the Americans, who after the crisis of 1929 and after the introduction of high costume duty for foreign imported goods started to acquire patterns and the right to reproduce them from the French couturiers. Grazietta Butazzi, "Gli Anni Trenta", p. 12.

70 Bianchino, *Italian Fashion Designing*, p. 17.

71 Ibid., p. 23.

72 Vergani and Pezzi, *Maria Pezzi*, p. 10.

73 Tosi Brandi, *Artisti del Quotidiano*, p. 88.

74 Vergani, *Fashion Dictionary*, p. 1066.

75 Brenda Azario, interview with the author, May 31, 2017.

76 The same sample appears in the pages for Lapidus and Ektor in the Nattier book 1968 consulted at Bauman Rare Books New York in 2016. https://www.baumanrarebooks.com/rare-books/nattier/textile-sample-archive/89099.aspx [accessed August 25, 2022]

77 "Technology in Fashion: Nattier's Triumph," *Women's Wear Daily*, August 8, 1966, p. 25.

78 Feathers and Flowers textile Nattier exclusive to Valentino, "Modern Jazz," *Women's Wear Daily*, February 14, 1967, p. 16.

79 Rosina, "Textiles," p. 88.

80 Scarpellini, *La Stoffa Dell'Italia*, p. 43.

81 Rosina, "Textiles," p. 268, n. 40.

82 De Felice, interview with the author, May 25, 2016.

83 Ibid.

84 The striped Fabiani Vogue Pattern 1798 is visible here: https://vintagepatterns.fandom.com/wiki/Vogue_1798_A [accessed 25 August, 2022].

85 *Vogue US*, September 15, 1968, p. 114; Brenda Azario, interview with the author, May 31, 2017 and "WWdeadline," *Women's Wear Daily*, May 11, 1967, p. 12: "The success of Ungaro rtw—always the slight flare, lifted waistline, and those splendid Nattier fabrics—is spreading like oil. And yet no one has seen the delivered goods . . . Bonwitt Teller, which has New York exclusivity, is now up to 50 to 60 pieces."

86 Letter from Amos Ciabattoni to Serica Bini, February 11, 1967, CNMI, folder 4, file 4.

87 Letter from Serica Bini to Patrick de Barentzen, February 13, 1967, CNMI, folder 4, file 4.

88 Brenda Azario, interview with the author, May 31, 2017.

89 Letter from Serica Bini to Amos Ciabattoni, February 15, 1967, CNMI, folder 4, file 2.

90 As we have seen, the *carnettisti* had a number of possible buyers for the meters not taken by designers and dressmakers, such as department stores, fabric stores, and even *Vogue* magazine readers who bought the paper patterns.

91 Letter from Serica Bini to Amos Ciabattoni, February 15, 1967, Italia, CNMI, folder, 4, file 2.

92 "Premi e incentive per elevare la qualità della produzione tessile e potenziare l'alta moda Italiana," n.d., CNMI, folder 4, file 2.

93 Laura B. Piccoli, "I Carnettisti 2," *L'Abbigliamento Italiano*, 1970, p. 5.

94 Ibid.

95 Brenda Azario, interview with the author, May 31, 2017.

96 Cleonice Capece, interview with the author, May 18, 2017.

97 In *Vogue Italia* March 1985 an article described how Susy Gandini and Pietro Lucchini worked as interpreters and mediators between designers and textile producers.

98 Prudence Glynn, "Brenda Azario: Not Really Crippled, Just Someone Who Sits Down a Lot," *The Times*, September 23, 1976), 12.

99 Letter from Amos Ciabattoni to Serica Bini, February 21, 1967 CNMI, folder 4, file 2.

100 Ibid. With the exception of a percentage of exclusive textiles that could be indicated only with the *carnettista*'s name.

101 Advertisement Seletex, *Linea Italiana*, Spring/ Summer 1966, n.p., Roberto Sarti disclosed that the advertisements which published the names of textile producer, *carnettista*, and couturier were paid for jointly by the *carnettista* and the textile producer. The *carnettista*, the producer and the couturier decided together what piece to photograph. As a result, the textile producer had an advertisement, the *carnettista* sold some meters, and the *alta moda* atelier was satisfied because their name was circulating. This system meant that everybody was happy. Sarti, interview with the author, July 18, 2017.

102 Nicola White, "The Role of America in the Development of the Italian Fashion Industry," p. 33.

103 Monti Gabriele, "Through a Paper Looking Glass," in *Bellissima: Italy and High Fashion, 1945–1968* (Milan: Electa, 2014), p. 35.

104 Rosina, "Textiles," p. 85.

105 Ibid., p. 88.

106 Ibid.

107 Ibid.

5 Milan and the *Stilisti*

1 Christopher Duggan, *A Concise History of Italy*, second edition (New York: Cambridge University Press, 2014) pp. 272–87.

2 Richard M. Locke, "Unity in Diversity: Strategy and Structure of the Italian Apparel Industry in the 1980s," in *Per Una Storia Della Moda Pronta: Problemi E Ricerche: Atti Del V Convegno Internazionale Del CISST, Milano, 26–28 Febbraio 1990* (Florence: EDIFIR edizioni, 1991), pp. 251–69 (p. 256).

3 However, Bull and Corner believe that certain characteristics found in the "third Italy" can be found elsewhere in Italy and in an earlier period. They demonstrate this through the Como Silk industry case study. Anna Cento Bull and Paul Corner, *From Peasant to Entrepreneur: The Survival of the Family Economy in Italy* (Oxford: Berg, 1993), pp. 131–53.

4 Segre Reinach, "The City of Prêt-à-Porter in the World of Fast Fashion."

5 Paris, "Fashion as a System," p. 525; John Foot, *Milan Since the Miracle: City, Culture and Identity* (Oxford: Berg, 2001), p. 125; Simona Segre Reinach, "Milan as a Fashion City," in Joanne Eicher, ed., *Berg Encyclopedia of World Dress and Fashion* (Oxford: Berg, 2010), pp. 259–63 (p. 259).

6 Messina, "Italian Woman's Wear," p. 29

7 Guido Vergani, *Dizionario Della Moda* (New York: Baldini Castoldi, 2004), p. 834.

8 Segre Reinach, "The City of Prêt-à-Porter in the World of Fast Fashion," p. 124.

9 *Dagli Anni '50 a Oggi*, http://www.pittimmagine.com/corporate/about.html [accessed April 4, 2017].

10 Paola Iannace, "La Moda, Macchina Economica E Laboratorio Di modernità," in *Moda a Milano: Stile e Impresa nella Città Che Cambia* (Milan: Abitare Segesta Cataloghi, 2002), p. 12.

11 Segre Reinach, "The City of Prêt-À-Porter in the World of Fast Fashion," p. 124.

12 Segre Reinach, "Milan as a Fashion City," p. 259.

13 Ibid.

14 Merlo and Polese, "Turning Fashion into Business," p. 431.

15 Susie Hopkins, "Milliners," in *The Berg Companion to Fashion*, ed. Valerie Steele (Oxford: Berg, 2010), pp. 508–12.

16 Merlo and Polese, "Turning Fashion into Business," p. 432.

17 Such as *Lidel* (1919–35), *Grandi firme* (1924–39), *Annabella* (1933), and *Grazia* (1938) in Merlotti, "I percorsi della moda Made in Italy (1951–2010)," p. 636.

18 Furthermore, from 1945 onwards, publishers such as Mondadori and Rizzoli all had their own fashion magazines. Mondadori continued to publish *Grazia*, flanked in 1957 by *Arianna*, which from 1973 became the Italian version of *Cosmopolitan*. Rizzoli published *Annabella* and *La Donna*, and Rusconi *Gioia* and *Rakam*. Also, the newspaper *Corriere della Sera* in 1962 started its fashion magazine *Amica* in Milan. See Merlotti, "I Percorsi Della Moda Made in Italy (1951–2010)," pp. 636–7.

19 The first few editions of the magazine were still published under the title *Novità*, from October 1964 to November 1965. Then the name was changed into *Vogue and Novità* and finally in May 1966 to *Vogue Italia*. Thereafter, a concentration of fashion journalists and photographers, such as Ugo Mulas, Alfa Castaldi, Adriana Mulassano, and Maria Pezzi lived in the city; see Segre Reinach, "Milan as a Fashion City," p. 260.

20 Foot, *Milan Since the Miracle*, p. 121.

21 Ibid., pp. 121–2.

22 Picture number 1948_096, Italy, Milan, Archivio Storico Fondazione Fiera Milano.

23 Margherita Rosina (ed), *Taroni: The Fabric That Dreams are Made of* (Milan: Rizzoli, 2017), pp. 140–1, from IdeaComo, more trading and commercial shows were also springing up in the city and its vicinity, such as Mipel *Mercato Italiano della Pelletteria* (Italian Fur Market) 1962.

24 Interview with the author, May 18, 2017.

25 Half of the *carnettisti* registered in 1969 were based in Milan and these were: Lucchini, Etoile, Gandini, Sassi, Satam, Scotlaine and Star: *Assortitori Tessuti Novità*, in *Linea Italiana*, Spring–Summer, 1969, n.p. The *Camera Nazionale della moda Italiana* was established in Rome in 1958 (see Chapter 2) and it definitely moved to Milan in 1988 (personal email correspondence with Dr Tiziana Dassi at Bocconi University, Milan, August 28, 2018).

26 Foot, *Milan Since the Miracle*, p. 122.

27 Locke, "Unity in Diversity," p. 256.

28 For a more in-depth description of the integrated corporation see Locke, "Unity in Diversity," pp. 256–7.

29 Locke, "Unity in Diversity," p. 257.

30 Ibid.

31 Emanuela Scarpellini, "The Business of Fashion," in Sonnet Stanfill, ed., *The Glamour of Italian Fashion since 1945* (London: V&A Publishing, 2014), pp. 226–39.

32 Margherita Rosina, "'The Thousand-Carat Dresses,'" in Enrico Quinto and Paolo Tinarelli, eds., (Milan: Skira, 2013), p. 195.

33 Marco Bellandi, "The Role of Small Firms in the Development of Italian Manufacturing Industry," in Goodman, Bamford, and Saynor, eds., *Small Firms and Industrial Districts in Italy*, pp. 31–52 (pp. 20–1). For more information on Marshall's definition of industrial districts see Fiorenza Belussi and Katia Caldari, "At the Origin of the Industrial District: Alfred Marshall and the Cambridge School," *Cambridge Journal of Economics*, Volume 33 (1 March 2009), 335–55.

34 Zeitlin, "Industrial Districts and Regional Clusters," pp. 219–20.

35 According to Bellandi, some such as Becattini define a territorial system of small and medium firms "producing a group of commodities whose products are processes which can be split into different phases." Others refer to it as "a system of firms rather than as an exact geographical concentration": Bellandi, "The Role of Small Firms in the Development of Italian Manufacturing Industry," p. 21. For more information on

the debate also outside Italy, see Zeitlin, "Industrial Districts and Regional Clusters," pp. 222–4 and also Bull and Corner, *From Peasant to Entrepreneur*, pp. 131–53.

36 Bull and Corner, *From Peasant to Entrepreneur*, p. 1.

37 Goodman, Bamford, and Saynor, *Small Firms and Industrial Districts in Italy*, p. 1.

38 Piore and Sabel, *The Second Industrial Divide*, p. 226.

39 Ibid., pp. 226–7.

40 Ibid., p. 227 and note 13.

41 Elisabetta Merlo and Francesca Polese, "Italy," in *Berg Encyclopedia of World Dress and Fashion* (Oxford: Berg, 2010), pp. 217–58 (p. 255).

42 Ibid.

43 Ibid.

44 Bull and Corner, *From Peasant to Entrepreneur*, pp. 139 and 142.

45 Goodman, Bamford, and Saynor, *Small Firms and Industrial Districts in Italy*, p. 10.

46 Michael L. Blim, *Made in Italy: Small-Scale Industrialization and its Consequences* (New York and London: Praeger, 1990), p. 1.

47 Goodman, Bamford, and Saynor, *Small Firms and Industrial Districts in Italy*, p. 3.

48 Ibid., pp. 3–4.

49 Piore and Sabel, *The Second Industrial Divide*, p. 227.

50 Blim, *Made in Italy*, p. 3.

51 Bull and Corner, *From Peasant to Entrepreneur*, p. 138.

52 Blim, *Made in Italy*, pp. 1–2. Sabel divides Italy in the same way in Charles F. Sabel, *Work and Politics: The Division of Labour in Industry* (Cambridge: Cambridge University Press, 1982, 1982), p. 220.

53 According to Blim, *Made in Italy*, pp. 1–2.

54 Ibid., p. 2.

55 Goodman, Bamford, and Saynor, *Small Firms and Industrial Districts in Italy*, p. 29 footnote: "The term *Terza Italia*, the third Italy, distinguishes the area of north-central and north-east Italy from the south of the country and from the area of heavy industry of the north-west' and p. 9.

56 Ibid., p. 6.

57 Ibid., pp. 7–8.

58 Ibid., p. 9.

59 "I Clans degli Italiani," *Vogue Italia*, July–August 1975, pp. 50–1.

60 Goodman, Bamford, and Saynor, *Small Firms and Industrial Districts in Italy*, p. 8.

61 Furthermore, the *stilista* often designs the machinery for the realization of new forms, therefore he/she intervenes directly in how the garments are produced. Bianchino, *Disegno della Moda Italiana*, p. 47.

62 Piore and Sabel, *The Second Industrial Divide*, p. 220, note 63.

63 Sabel, *Work and Politics*, p. 26, note 63.

64 Bellandi, "The Role of Small Firms in the Development of Italian Manufacturing Industry," p. 31.

65 Blim, *Made in Italy*, p. 6.

66 Scarpellini, "The Business of Fashion," p. 232 (Since 2001, another census was taken in 2011 and the results on the districts can be found at https://www.istat.it/it/.)

67 Piore and Sabel, *The Second Industrial Divide*, pp. 222–3.

68 Stanfill, *The Glamour of Italian Fashion since 1945*, pp. 23–4.

69 Merlotti, *I Percorsi Della Moda made in Italy (1951–2010)*, p. 637.

70 Rosina, "Textiles," p. 88.

71 Silvia Giacomoni, *L'Italia Della Moda* (Milan: Mazzotta, 1984), p. 59.

72 Ibid., p. 62.

73 Ibid., p. 64.

74 Ibid., p. 62.

75 This is a battle that the director of the Civiche Raccolte di Arte Applicate del Castello Sforzesco, Clelia Alberici, had been fighting since 1976.

76 Since 2010 Palazzo Morando in Milan has been allocated as the museum to exhibit the Milanese historic textile collection and the collections of dresses, accessories, and uniforms from Raccolte d'Arti Applicate del Castello Sforzesco. *Costume Moda Immagine Palazzo Morando*, http://www.costumemodaimmagine.mi.it/ edn [accessed September 4, 2018]. However, this museum does not yet respond to the need for an institution that could preserve and promote contemporary Italian fashion. More on this aspect in the Introduction of this book.

77 Bianchino, *Disegno Della Moda Italiana*, p. 46.

78 Gnoli, *Un Secolo di Moda Italiana*, pp. 189–96; Segre Reinach, "The City of Prêt-à-Porter in the World of Fast Fashion," p. 124.

79 Segre Reinach, "The City of Prêt-À-Porter in the World of Fast Fashion," p. 124.

80 Morini, *Storia Della Moda*, p. 326 and Simona Segre Reinach, "Albini, Walter," in Valerie Steele, ed., *The Berg Companion to Fashion* (Oxford: Berg, 2010), pp. 19–20. Merlo and Polese, *Italy*, p. 256.

81 Vergani, *The Fashion Dictionary*, p. 27

82 Morini, *Storia Della Moda*, p. 326.

83 Ibid., pp. 326–7.

84 Gnoli, *Un Secolo di Moda Italiana*, p. 192, Enrica Morini and Nicoletta Bocca, "Stylism in Women's Fashion," in Grazietta Butazzi, ed., *Italian Fashion: From Anti-Fashion to Stylism*, 2 vols. (Milan: Electa, 1987), pp. 64–101.

85 Morini, *Storia Della Moda*, pp. 330–1.

86 These collaborations continued with Valentino (1979), Louis Féraud (1982), Massimo Osti (1984), Chiara Boni (1985), and Claude Montana and Jimmy Taverniti of Dior (1987); as detailed in Giulia Caccia and Sara Micheletta, *Gruppo Finanziario Tessile Inventario* (Turin: 2014), p. xi.

87 Caccia and Micheletta, *Gruppo Finanziario Tessile*, p. xi.

88 Locke, "Unity in Diversity," pp. 260–1.

89 These included an emerging stage, a style extension, production of related articles, such as accessories and cosmetics, and the final stage of internationalization. Merlo and Polese, "Italy," p. 257.

90 Ibid.

91 Ibid.

92 Morini, *Storia Della Moda*, p. 336.

93 Ibid.

94 Giacomoni, *L'Italia Della Moda*, p. 77.

95 Merlo, "Italian Fashion Business," p. 351.

96 Giacomoni, *L'Italia Della Moda*, p. 13.

97 Salvo Testa, "La Specificità Della Filiera Italiana Della Moda," in *Storia d'Italia: La Moda* (Turin: Giulio Einaudi, 2003), pp. 699–734 (p. 711).

98 Maria Giuseppina Muzzarelli, *Breve Storia Della Moda in Italia* (Bologna: Il Mulino, 2014), p. 183. She describes how in the industrial district of Carpi, knitwear was produced and designed, but signed somewhere else.

99 Bianchino, *Disegno Della Moda Italiana*, p. 47.

100 Gloria Bianchino and Arturo Carlo Quintavalle, *Moda: Dalla Fiaba al Design. Italia, 1951–1989* (Novara: DeAgostini, 1989), p. 132.

101 Roberto Sarti, interview with the author, July 18, 2017.

102 Merlo and Polese, "Italy," p. 256.

103 Roberto Sarti, interview with the author, July 18, 2017.

104 Ibid.

105 On the other hand, some *stilisti* such as Armani for GFT worked for a bigger company directing the production.

106 Segre Reinach, "Albini, Walter," p. 19.

6 Designing for Mass Production

1 For example, in fashion exhibitions such as *The Glamour of Italian Fashion*, the sketches by Mila Schon and Jole Veneziani were used to accompany the display of their respective garments. Furthermore, recently Maison Valentino, for their haute couture high-profile garments worn by celebrities at the Festival of Cinema of Venice, shared on Instagram what they call a sketch of their creation. This, however, is not a working drawing or sketch where the idea is tested and worked out, but a very finalized drawing (Instagram Maison Valentino on September 2, 2018).

2 No academic books in English have been specifically written on the subject. Fashion illustration has been analyzed in more detail, but there has not been much critical work. For an overview of fashion illustration history see Laird Borrelli, "Fashion

Illustration," in Valerie Steele, ed., *The Berg Companion to Fashion* (Oxford: Berg, 2010), pp. 288–90. There have been few Italian books written on the subject.

3   Laird Borrelli, *Fashion Illustration by Fashion Designers* (London: Thames & Hudson, 2008), p. 7.

4   The CSAC collection preserves around 70,000 fashion drawings from the 1940s to 1980s by Italian fashion designers: see *Moda*, https://www.csacparma.it/portfolio/moda/ [accessed September 2, 2018].

5   Bianchino and Quintavalle, *Moda: Dalla Fiaba al Design*, pp. 140–1.

6   Patrick J. Ireland, *Fashion Design: Drawing and Presentation* (London: Batsford Academic and Educational, 1982), p. 6.

7   Ibid.

8   Ibid., p. 56.

9   Ibid., p. 95.

10 Ibid., p. 6.

11 Borrelli, *Fashion Illustration by Fashion Designers*, p. 7.

12 Ibid., pp. 8–9.

13 Ibid., p. 34.

14 Ibid., p. 42.

15 Ibid., p. 108 and p. 91.

16 Ibid., p. 114.

17 Ibid., p. 124.

18 Ireland, *Fashion Design*, p. 118.

19 Nicoletta Bocca, "La Forma Del Processo Creativo," in Nicoletta Bocca and Chiara Buss, eds., *Gianni Versace: L'Abito Per Pensare* (Milan: Arnoldo Mondadori Editore Arte, 1989), pp. 194–204 (p. 202).

20 Ibid., p. 199.

21 Ibid., p. 202.

22 Ibid., p. 203, drawing 162 d.

23 In the case of the Versace exhibition, many of the technical drawings were conserved in the factory in Novara. It is important to highlight this because the rest of the drawings preserved by the CSAC center in Parma were normally kept in the style office of the designer. The significance of provenance is important to highlight who the end users of these objects were.

24 Bocca, "La Forma del Processo Creativo," p. 198, drawing 160a.

25 Ibid.

26 Ibid., p. 202.

27 Walter Albini drawing for Krizia 1965–70, Archivio Moda, CSAC, Università di Parma.

28 Krizia, drawing 117, 1979, Archivio Moda, CSAC, Università di Parma.

29 Krizia Maglia, drawing 2, Estate 1981, Archivio Moda, CSAC, Università di Parma.

30 Krizia, working fashion drawing, no. 3, 1971, Archivio Moda, CSCA, Università di Parma.

31 Bocca, "La Forma del Processo Creativo," p. 202.

32 Ibid.

33 Bianchino and Quintavalle, *Moda: Dalla Fiaba al Design*, p. 153.

34 Rita Airaghi, *Disegni* (Milan: Skira, 2010), p. 5. The former Fondazione Gianfranco Ferré has now become the Centro di Ricerca Gianfranco Ferré at the Politecnico of Milan https://www.centroricercagianfrancoferre.it/home/intro.php [Accessed September 21, 2022]

35 Bianchino and Quintavalle, *Moda: Dalla Fiaba al Design*, p. 209.

36 Ibid., pp. 209–10.

37 Gloria Bianchino, in *Italian Fashion Designing*, pp. 44–53, defines genres of Italian fashion drawing and finds artistic references for some of them (e.g., Ferré connected with Russian constructivists; Armani was more influenced by the 1930s). She compares the design inside the atelier of *prêt-à-porter* to the one in an architectural studio: the *stilista* is similar to the architect who designs the project. However, its development, layout, and execution are done by another designer within the team.

38 Bianchino, *Italian Fashion Designing*, p. 20.

39 Roberto Sarti, interview with the author, July 18, 2017.

40 Claire Wilcox, Valerie Mendes, and Chiara Buss, *The Art and Craft of Gianni Versace* (London: V&A Publications, 2002), pp. 122–3.

41 It is interesting to note that the yarn could come from a supplier, while the sample knitted would come from the knitwear mill.

42 List of producers detected on Krizia's drawings: Galtrucco, Mantero, Faliero Sarti, Curi, Bevilacqua, Canepa, Bini, Ricceri, Borgomaneri.

43 Giacomoni, *L'Italia Della Moda*, pp. 80–1.

44 Rita Airaghi, interview with the author, June 18, 2018.

45 Giacomoni, *L'Italia Della Moda*, pp. 80–1.

46 Ibid.

47 Except for a donation of several drawings that was made to the CSAC Parma archive.

48 The relationship between *stilista* and *modellista* or the specialist worker in a manufacturer could last for years, and they came to know each other's needs very quickly. This is the case, for example, of the relationship between Gianni Versace and the company which specialized in embroidery, Vichi Ricami, with which he collaborated for most of his very elaborate pieces. Cristina Vichi recalls how her mother Olga Bolognesi would meet Versace and he would show her some reference photos of the theme he had in mind, together with the working drawing. She would then start the research on the materials, on the types of manufacturing and the design.

She would then make a sample. Versace trusted the creativity of Mrs. Bolognesi, but he would not hesitate to admonish her if he did not like the samples (conversation via Facebook Messenger between Cristina Vichi and the author, September 2, 2018).

49 Rita Airaghi, interview with the author, June 18, 2018.

50 Each group is identified with a symbol, such as a square or a wedge; this is also reproduced on the *stilista*'s drawings so that the two sets of documents can be reconnected.

51 Morini, *Storia Della Moda*, p. 343.

52 Merlo, "Italian Fashion Business," p. 355.

53 Ibid.

54 Rosina, "Textiles," pp. 89–91; Morini, *Storia Della Moda*, pp. 341–3.

55 Segre Reinach, "The City of Prêt-à-Porter," p. 128; Segre Reinach, "Italian Fashion," p. 244.

56 Merlo, "Italian Fashion Business," p. 356.

57 Ibid., p. 352.

58 Ibid., p. 359.

Conclusion

1   Michael Specter, "High-Heel Heaven: A Visit to the Madcap World of Manolo Blahnik," *The New Yorker*, March 12, 2000, https://www.newyorker.com/magazine/2000/03/20/high-heel-heaven-2 [accessed August 26, 2022]; and Rita Airaghi, interview with the author, June 18, 2018.

2   Rosina, "Textiles," pp. 76–8; Segre Reinach, "The Italian Fashion Revolution in Milan," p. 69.

3   Kawamura, *Fashion-ology*, p. 45.

4   The only exception is a very technical book: Maura Garofoli and Bonizza Giordani-Aragno, *Le Fibre Intelligenti: Un Secolo di Storia e Cinquant'Anni di Moda* (Milan: Electa, 1991).

5   White, *Reconstructing Italian Fashion*.

6   Segre Reinach, "Milan as a Fashion City."

Bibliography

Primary Sources

Archival Material

Como, Fondazione Antonio Ratti, Ravasi Archive

Como, Clerici Tessuto, Historical Textiles Sample Books

Florence, Florence State Archive, Fondo Giorgini Giovanni Battista, Albums 1, 2, 5, 6, 61, non-catalog materials folders 11, ex. 107, and ex. 92

Florence, Galleria del Costume di Palazzo Pitti, Simonetta Visconti Archive, Volume 1, 2 and 3

London, Harrods Archive, Cloth Sample Book 1951–1953

Milan, Università Commerciale L. Bocconi, Biblioteca e Archivi, Camera Nazionale della Moda Italiana (CNMI), folders 1, 2, 3, 4, 5, 13, 10, 31

Milan, Archivio Storico Fondazione Fiera Milano, Photographic Archive

Milan, Archivio della Fondazione Gianfranco Ferré, spring/summer 1984

New York, Brooklyn Museum Archives (BMA):
— "Italy at Work: Her Renaissance in Design Today." [11/30/1950–01/31/1951]. [01]. (1950–1951). Murphy, Michelle
— Records of the office the director: D|50–51|CN

New York, FIT archive, Begdorf Goodman, folder US.NNFIT.SC.201.193; Gimble Sophie Box 3, folder 2

New York, Nattier Archive

Parma, Centro Studi e Archivio della Comunicazione (CSAC), Archivio Moda, Walter Albini, Krizia and Schuberth folders

Prato, Faliero Sarti Archive, Internal Sample Book Archive

Reggio Emilia, Max Mara Archive, Magazine Archive

Venice, Centro Studi di Storia del Tessuto e del Costume Palazzo Mocenigo, SNIA Viscosa

Fashion Collections

Fashion Museum Bath

Fashion Institute of Technology

Museum Galleria del Costume, Palazzo Pitti

Max Mara

Philadelphia Museum of Modern Art

Philadelphia, Robert and Penny Fox Historic Costume Collection
The Victoria and Albert Museum

Articles

"Gli Accordi Commerciali Con La Danimarca," *Il Sole* (March 22, 1946), 1

"Advertisement for La Rinascente/ Donnybrooke and Henry Rosendelf," *Novità* (December 1950), 2

"Advertisement Neiman Marcus," *Vogue US* (October 1, 1960), 45–52

"L'Albero e i Frutti," *Bellezza* (February 1952), 14–19

"Alta Moda Pronta in Advance," *Women's Wear Daily* (October 17, 1967), 4–5

"Black on the Beach," *Vogue UK* (November 1948), 60–61

"La Bombe De Florence a e 'Branle' Les Salons De La Haute Couture Parisienne," n.t. (n.d.), n.p.

"British Fashions Go Abroad," *Harper's Bazaar UK* (July 1948), 24–6

"Il Centro Internazionale delle Arti e del Costume di Venezia," *Il Ticino* (September 10, 1951)

"I Clans Degli Italiani," *Vogue Italia* (July–August 1975), 50–75

"Countess Visconti here with Collection for Bergdorf Goodman," *New York Herald Tribune* (November 14, 1951)

"Design Trendsetters. Azario Architect of Fabric," *Trends Fabrics and Fashion* (June 1966, number 1), 29–30

"Donnybrook Licenses Coat Styles for Italian Firm," *Women's Wear Daily* (June 28, 1950), 14

"Editorial," *Fashions and Fabrics Overseas* (July–August 1946), 51

"Esportazione di Seta Naturale," *Il Sole* (October 30, 1945), 1

"Un Evidente Certezza," *Ripresa delle Fiere* (August 12, 1946), 1

"Exchange Makes Retail Prices Lower than Wholesale in Italy," *Women's Wear Daily* (May 12, 1947), 11

"The Fabric Comes First," *Harper's Bazaar UK* (January 1957), 25

"Fabrics: Italian Silk Producer Aims at Developing U.S. Market," *Women's Wear Daily* (January 22, 1947), 18

"Fashion: Italy the Spring Collections," *Vogue US* (March 1963), 122–8

"The Fashions: European Rtw: The Challenges," *Women's Wear Daily* (March 30, 1967), 10–11

"Gandini. Qui Sotto c'è' Una Donna," *Vogue Italia* (March 1985), 291

"High Fashion Stores and Volume Retailers at Italian Show," *Women's Wear Daily* (July 25, 1951), 18

"High Praise Given to Italian Fabrics," *New York Times* (July 1951), 18

"Industrie Tessili e Esportazioni," *Il Sole* (September 21, 1945), 1

"Interest is Urged in Italian Goods," *Women's Wear Daily* (January 9, 1951), 63

"Italian Designer Caters to Home Seamstresses," *Oregonian* (March 8, 1953) (n.p)

"Italian Designers Visiting New York," *Vogue US* (February 15, 1952), 70–71

"Italian Evenings," *Harper's Bazaar UK* (November 1952), 55

"Italian Fashion Designers Helped by Marshall Plan," *New York Herald Tribune* (August 13, 1951)

"Italy at Work: Her Renaissance in Design Today," *The Brooklyn Museum Bulletin* (Fall 1950), 1

"Italy Gets Dressed Up," *Life* (August 20, 1951), 104–12

"Italy Shows a New Trend in Her Fashion Trade," *Vogue UK* (September 1951), 102–3

"Italy's Textile Industry, Designers Aim for Leading Role in World Fashion," *Sunday World Herald* (May 24, 1953), n/a

"Jole Veneziani Apre La Serie Veneziani-Sport," *Novità* (December 1951), 22–3

"Lucchini. Un Grande Interprete del Tessuto," *Vogue Italia* (March 1985), 291

"Metallic Sweaters to Raincoats in New Boutique at Veneziani-Sport," *Women's Wear Daily* (December 11, 1951), 3

"Micol Fontana, Rome Fashion Designer, Here," *New York Herald Tribune* (September 2, 1951) n.p.

"La Moda a Palazzo Grassi," *La Ruota Diorama* (n.d) 77–9

"La Moda in Svizzera," *Novità* (February 1952), 12

"La Moda Nasce dai Tessuti," *Novità* (February 1953), 16–30

"Modern Jazz," *Women's Wear Daily* (February 14, 1967), 16

"La Mostra dei Tessili dell'Avvenire," *Linea* (Summer 1954), 87

"La Mostra Internazionale della Tessitura Serica Comasca," *Il Sole* (December 18, 1945), 1

"Sfilate d'autunno. Eco delle Manifestazioni Organizzate Dal Segretariato Internazionale della Lana," *Novità* (November 1953), 29

"Prestigioso Panorama nell'Abbigliamento," *Ripresa delle Fiere* (December 1946), 2

"Problemi dell'Economia Mondiale dei Tessuti," *Ripresa delle Fiere* (August 12, 1946), 2

"Ravasi Silks Selected for Forthcoming Travelling Exhibit of Italian Goods," *Women's Wear Daily* (July 31, 1950), 12

"Sblocco dei Tessuti e Prossimo Arrivi di Cotone Sodo," *Il Sole,* (August 1, 1945), 1

"Gli Scambi Con l'Estero," *Il Sole* (March 23, 1946), 2

"Technology in Fashion: Nattier's Triumph," *Women's Wear Daily* (August 8, 1966), 25

"Textile Exposition: Italy Regaining Cloth Output," *Women's Wear Daily* (May 14, 1947), 14

"Visconti Collection Shown by Begdorf's for Custom Order," *Women's Wear Daily* (November 14, 1951), 3

"What's Going on in Italy?", *Women's Wear Daily* (August 22, 1951), 16–17

"Wwdeadline," *Women's Wear Daily* (May 11, 1967), 12

Brin, Irene, "Dirottati in Italia i Buyers Americani," n.t. (n.d.), n.p.

Cacioppo, Maria, "Condizione di Vita Familiare negli Anni Cinquanta," *Memoria,* 6 (1982), 88

Carter, Ernestine, "The People Page," *The Sunday Times* (August 16, 1964), 34

Cianfarra, Jane, "Old, New Blended in Italian Style," *New York Times* (September 10, 1951)

Cocks, Jay, "Giorgio Armani: Suiting Up for Easy Street," *Time* (April 5, 1982)

Cohn, J. W., "Japan Reveals Plans for Couture Deal with Italy," *Women's Wear Daily* (June 24, 1963), 16

Drane Mc Callon, Virginia, "Italy's Bid for Fashion Fame was Started by Houston Visitor," *Houston Post* (n.d.), n.p.

Etting, Gloria Braggiotti, "Florence in Fashion," *Town and Country* (September 1951), 138–76

Fadigati, Neri, "Giovanni Battista Giorgini, La Famiglia, Il Contributo alla Nascita del made in Italy, le Fonti Archivistiche," *ZoneModa Journal*, 8 (2018), 1–15

Fusco, Gian Carlo, "Dietro Tante Donne c'e' Quest'Uomo," *L'Europeo* (February 5, 1953)

Glynn, Prudence, "Brenda Azario: Not Really Crippled, Just Someone Who Sits Down a Lot," *The Times* (September 23, 1976), 12

Hammond, Fay, "Europe Styles, U.S. Copies Draw 750 to Orbach Show," n.t. (n.d.)

Kennedy, Fraser, "Fashion: The Valentina Vision," *Vogue US* (1995)

Lucas, Walter, "Florence Has Designs on Fashion," *The Christian Science Monitor* (n.d.)

Martin Guyot, Marie C., "Spring Fabrics in Paris," *Women's Wear Daily* (February 6, 1963), 48

McKenna, Edna, "Italy Views for Fashion Lead," n.t. (n.d.)

Piccoli, Laura B., "I Carnettisti 2," *L'Abbigliamento Italiano*, 1970 (month is missing).

Restany, Pierre, "Breve Storia dello Stile Yéyé," *Domus* (January 1967), 34–41

Robiola, Elsa, "Collezioni Italiane in Anticipo e in Orario," *Il Tempo* (March 31, 1951)

Rykwert, J., "The Italian Metamorphosis 1943–1968," *Domus* (1995)

Sheppard, Eugenia, "Imported Fashions Here: Bergdorf Goodman Shows 88. Around 50 at Henri Bendel," *New York Herald Tribune* (September 14, 1951)

Snow, Carmel, "Dresses Show Originality of Style and Fabric," *New York Journal-American* (February 16, 1953)

Snow, Carmel, "Italian Designers' Grand Entrance," *New York Journal-American* (August 26, 1951)

Taylor, Matilda, "Fashion Significances of Italian Dressmaker Showings: Empire Coats, Rich Dress Fabrics," *Women's Wear Daily* (July 27, 1951), 3

Turba, Umberto, "Sulla Necessità di Razionalizzare l'Industria delle Confezioni Femminili e Per Bambini," *Il Sole* (April 7, 1945), 1

Secondary Sources

Mezzo Secolo di Snia Viscosa (Milan: Pan, 1970)

Per Una Storia della Moda Pronta: Problemi e Ricerche. Atti del V Convegno Internazionale del CISST, Milano, 26–28 Febbraio 1990. (Florence: Edifir, 1991)

Snia Dal Filo allo Spazio (Milan: Arti Grafiche Occhipinti, n.d.)

Airaghi, Rita, *Disegni* (Milan: Skira, 2010)

Arnold, Rebecca, *The American Look: Sportswear, Fashion and the Image of Women in 1930s and 1940s New York* (London: I.B. Tauris, 2008)

Ash, Juliet and Elizabeth Wilson, eds., *Chic Thrills: Fashion Reader* (Pandora, 1992)

Aspesi, Natalia, *Il Lusso e l'Autarchia: Storia dell'Eleganza Italiana, 1930–1944* (Milan: Rizzoli, 1982)

Baudrillard, Jean, *The System of Objects,* trans. James Benedict (London; New York: Verso, 1996)

Bauzano, Gianluca, "The High Notes of High Fashion," in *Bellissima: Italy and High Fashion, 1945–1968* (Milan: Electa, 2014), pp. 268–71

Belfanti, Carlo M. and Fabio Giusberti, *Storia d'Italia: La Moda*, 19 vols (Turin: Giulio Einaudi, 2003)

Belfanti, Carlo M. and Fabio Giusberti, "History as an Intangible Asset for the Italian Fashion Business (1950–1954)," *Journal of Historical Research in Marketing,* 7 (2015), 74–90

Belfanti, Carlo M. and Fabio Giusberti, "Renaissance and 'Made in Italy': Marketing Italian Fashion through History (1949–1952)," *Journal of Modern Italian Studies,* 20 (2015), 53–66

Bellandi, Marco, "The Role of Small Firms in the Development of Italian Manufacturing Industry," in *Small Firms and Industrial Districts in Italy*, ed. Edward Goodman, Julia Bamford, and Peter Saynor (London: Routledge, 1989), pp. 31–52

Belussi, Fiorenza and Katia Caldari, "At the Origin of the Industrial District: Alfred Marshall and the Cambridge School," *Cambridge Journal of Economics,* 33 (March 1, 2009), 335–55

Bianchino, Gloria, ed., *Disegno della Moda Italiana 1945–1980 (Italian Fashion Designing 1945–1980)* (Parma: CSAC dell'Università di Parma, 1987)

Bianchino, Gloria et al, *Italian Fashion: Vol. 1: The Origins of High Fashion and Knitwear* (Milan: Electa, 1987)

Bianchino, Gloria and Arturo Quintavalle, *Sorelle Fontana* (Parma: Università di Parma, Centro studi e archivio della comunicazione, 1984)

Bianchino, Gloria and Arturo Carlo Quintavalle, *Moda: dalla Fiaba al Design. Italia, 1951–1989* (Novara: DeAgostini, 1989)

Blaszczyk, Regina Lee, "Styling Synthetics: DuPont's Marketing of Fabrics and Fashions in Postwar America," *The Business History Review,* 80 (2006), 485–528

Blaszczyk, Regina Lee and Pouillard Véronique, *European Fashion: The Creation of a Global Industry*, p. 5

Blim, Michael L., *Made in Italy: Small-Scale Industrialization and its Consequences* (New York and London: Praeger, 1990)

Blum, Dilys, *Roberto Capucci: Art into Fashion* (New Haven: Philadelphia Museum of Art in association with Yale University Press, 2011)

Bocca, Nicoletta, "La Forma del Processo Creativo," in *Gianni Versace: L'Abito Per Pensare*, ed. Nicoletta Bocca and Chiara Buss (Milan: Arnoldo Mondadori Editore Arte, 1989), pp. 194–204

Bocca, Nicoletta and Chiara Buss, eds., *Gianni Versace: L'Abito Per Pensare* (Milan: Arnoldo Mondadori Editore Arte, 1989)

Bolton, Andrew, "Response," in *Fashion and Modernity*, ed. by Christopher Breward and Caroline Evans (Oxford: Berg, 2005), pp. 147–50

Borrelli, Laird, "Fashion Illustration," in *The Berg Companion to Fashion*, ed. Valerie Steele (Oxford: Berg, 2010), pp. 288–90

Borrelli, Laird, *Fashion Illustration by Fashion Designers* (London: Thames & Hudson, 2008)

Boselli, Mario, "La Leadership Internazionale di Milano Nella Moda," in *Moda a Milano: Stile e Impresa Nella Città che Cambia* (Milan: Abitare Segesta Cataloghi, 2002), pp. 28–35

Bottelli, Paola, "Lo Stilista Imprenditore: Un Fenomeno Milanese," in *Moda a Milano: Stile e Impresa Nella Città Che Cambia*, ed. Ampelio Bucci (Milan: Abitare Segesta Cataloghi, 2002), pp. 50–3

Bottero, Amelia, *Nostra Signora La Moda* (Milan: Mursia, 1979)

Bourdieu, Pierre, *Distinction: A Social Critique of the Judgement of Taste* (London: Routledge, 2010)

Breward, Christopher, *The Culture of Fashion: A New History of Fashionable Dress* (Manchester: Manchester University Press, 1995)

Breward, Christopher, "Cultures, Identities, Histories: Fashioning a Cultural Approach to Dress," *Fashion Theory: The Journal of Dress, Body & Culture,* 2 (1998), 301–13

Breward, Christopher and David Gilbert, *Fashion's World Cities* (Oxford: Berg, 2006)

Breward, Christopher and Caroline Evans, *Fashion and Modernity* (Oxford: Berg, 2005)

Brown, Bill, "Thing Theory," *Critical Inquiry,* 28 (2001), 1–22

Bucci, Ampelio, ed., *Moda a Milano: Stile e Impresa Nella Città Che Cambia* (Milan: Abitare Segesta Cataloghi, 2002)

Bucci, Ampelio, ed., "Il Sistema Italiano della Moda: Un Nuovo Modello Industriale e dei Consumi," in *Moda a Milano: Stile e Impresa Nella Città Che Cambia* (Milan: Abitare Segesta Cataloghi, 2002), pp. 14–25

Bull, Anna Cento and Paul Corner, *From Peasant to Entrepreneur: The Survival of the Family Economy in Italy* (Oxford: Berg, 1993)

Buss, Chiara, "The Craft of Gianni Versace," in *The Art and Craft of Gianni Versace* (London: V&A Publications, 2002), pp. 122–59

Buss, Chiara, "La Re-Invenzione della Materia," in *Gianni Versace: L'Abito Per Pensare*, ed. Nicoletta Bocca and Chiara Buss (Milan: Arnoldo Mondadori Editore Arte, 1989), pp. 152–91

Buss, Chiara, *Silk: The 1900s in Como* (Cinisello Balsamo: Silvana Editoriale, 2001)

Butazzi, Grazietta, *1922–1943: Vent'Anni di Moda Italiana: Proposta Per Un Museo della Moda a Milano* (Florence: Centro di, 1980)

Butazzi, Grazietta, "Gli Anni Trenta: La Moda Italiana si Mette a Confronto, tra Autarchia e Nuove Prospettive," in *Moda Femminile tra le due Guerre*, ed. Caterina Chiarelli (Livorno: Sillabe, 2000), pp. 12–19

Butazzi, Grazietta et al., *Italian Fashion: Vol. 2: From Anti-Fashion to Stylism* (Milan: Electa, 1987)

Caccia, Giulia and Sara Micheletta, *Gruppo Finanziario Tessile Inventario* (Turin: 2014)

Capalbo, Cinzia, "In the Capital: Institutions in Support of Fashion," in *Bellissima: Italy and High Fashion, 1945–1968* (Milan: Electa, 2014), pp. 350–3

Capalbo, Cinzia, *Storia della Moda a Roma: Sarti, Culture e Stili di Una Capitale Dal 1871 a Oggi* (Rome: Donzelli, 2012)

Capece, Cleonice, *Fashion by Chance: A Visual Autobiography 1960–1974* (Woodbridge: Antique Collectors Club, 2014)

Caratozzolo, Vittoria C., *Irene Brin: Italian Style in Fashion* (Venice: Marsilio, 2006)

Chiara, Francina, "An Outlining of Index of Companies," in *Silk: The 1900's in Como* (Cinisello Balsamo: Silvana Editoriale, 2001), pp. 332–41

Chiarelli, Caterina, *Moda Femminile tra le due Guerre* (Livorno: Sillabe, 2000)

Collicelli Cagol, Stefano, *Venezia e La Vitalità del Contemporaneo: Paolo Marinotti a Palazzo Grassi* (Padua: Il Poligrafo, 2008)

Corner, Paul Richard and Anna Cento Bull, *From Peasant to Entrepreneur: Survival of the Family Economy in Italy* (Oxford: Berg, 1994)

Danese, Elsa, "The High Fashion Shoes at the International Center for the Arts and Costume," in *Bellissima: Italy and High Fashion, 1945–1968* (Milan: Electa, 2014), pp. 302–5

Dauphine Griffo, Giuliana Chesne, "G. B. Giorgini: The Rise of Italian Fashion," in *Italian Fashion: The Origins of High Fashion and Knitwear*, ed. Grazietta Butazzi (Milan: Electa, 1987), pp. 66–71

De Pietri, Stephen and Melissa Leventon, eds., *New Look to Now: French Haute Couture, 1947–1987* (New York: Rizzoli, 1989)

Duggan, Christopher, *A Concise History of Italy*, second edition (New York: Cambridge University Press, 2014)

Duggan, Christopher and Christopher Wagstaff, eds., *Italy in the Cold War: Politics, Culture, and Society, 1948–1958* (Washington, DC: Berg Publishers, 1995)

Eicher, Joanne B., *Berg Encyclopedia of World Dress and Fashion* (Oxford: Berg, 2010)

Entwistle, Joanne, "Bruno Latour: Actor-Network-Theory and Fashion," in *Thinking through Fashion: A Guide to Key Theorists*, ed. Agnès Rocamora and Anneke Smelik (London: I.B. Tauris, 2016), pp. 269–84

Faiers, Jonathan, *Tartan* (Oxford: Berg, 2008)

Fiorentini Capitani, Aurora, *Moda Italiana Anni Cinquanta e Sessanta* (Florence: Cantini, 1991)

Foot, John, *Milan Since the Miracle: City, Culture and Identity* (Oxford: Berg, 2001)

Forgacs, David and Stephen Gundle, *Mass Culture and Italian Society from Fascism to the Cold War* (Bloomington: Indiana University Press, 2008)

Frisa, Maria L., *Italian Eyes: Italian Fashion Photographs from 1951 to Today* (Florence: Fondazione Pitti Immagine Discovery, 2005)

Frisa, Maria L., Anna Mattirolo, and Stefano Tonchi, eds., *Bellissima: Italy and High Fashion, 1945–1968* (Milan: Electa, 2014)

Gabriele, Monti, "Through a Paper Looking Glass," in *Bellissima: Italy and High Fashion, 1945–1968* (Milan: Electa, 2014)

Galleria del Costume di Palazzo Pitti, *Moda Femminile tra le due Guerre* (Livorno: Sillabe, 2000)

Garofoli, Maura and Bonizza Giordani-Aragno, *le Fibre Intelligenti: Un Secolo di Storia e Cinquant'Anni di Moda* (Milan: Electa, 1991)

Geczy, Adam and Vicky Karaminas, "Walter Benjamin: Fashion Modernity and the City Street," in *Thinking through Fashion: A Guide to Key Theorists*, ed. Agnès Rocamora and Anneke Smelik (London: I.B. Tauris, 2016), pp. 81–96

Gell, Alfred, "The Technology of Enchantment and the Enchantment of Technology," in *Anthropology, Art and Aesthetics*, ed. Jeremy Coote and Anthony Shelton (Oxford: Clarendon, 1992), pp. 40–63

Giacomoni, Silvia, *L'Italia della Moda* (Milan: Mazzotta, 1984)

Gianola, Rinaldo, "Design and Fashion: Driving Forces of Italy," in *Made in Italy? 1951–2001*, ed. Luigi Settembrini (Milan: Skira Editore, 2001), pp. 100–3

Ginsborg, Paul, *A History of Contemporary Italy: Society and Politics, 1943–1988* (London: Penguin, 1990)

Giordani-Aragno, Bonizza, *Il Disegno dell'Alta Moda Italiana: 1940–1970* (Rome: De Luca, 1982)

Giordani-Aragno, Bonizza, ed., *Moda Italia: Creativity and Technology in the Italian Fashion System* (Milan: Editoriale Domus, 1988)

Giordani-Aragno, Bonizza, *Callaghan 1966: The Birth of Italian Prêt-à-Porter* (Milan: Mazzotta, 1997)

Giordani-Aragno, Bonizza, Francesca Zaltieri, and Gloria Bianchino, *Walter Albini* (Parma: Università di Parma, Centro studi e archivio della comunicazione, 1988)

Gnoli, Sofia, *La Donna, l'Eleganza, Il Fascismo: La Moda Italiana Dalle Origini all'Ente Nazionale della Moda* (Catania: Edizioni del Prisma, 2000)

Gnoli, Sofia, *Un Secolo di Moda Italiana, 1900–2000* (Rome: Meltemi, 2005)

Gnoli, Sofia, *Moda: dalla Nascita della Haute Couture a Oggi* (Rome: Carocci, 2012)

Gnoli, Sofia, *The Origins of Italian Fashion 1900–1945* (London: V&A Publishing, 2014)

Gnoli, Sofia, "Great Dressmakers of Italian Fashion," in *The Glamour of Italian Fashion since 1945*, ed. Sonnet Stanfill (London: V&A Publishing, 2014), pp. 32–45

Goodman, Edward, Julia Bamford, and Peter Saynor, eds., *Small Firms and Industrial Districts in Italy* (London: Routledge, 1989)

Granata, Francesca, "Fashion Studies In-Between: A Methodological Case Study and Inquiry into the State of Fashion Studies," *Fashion Theory*, 16 (March 2012), 67–82

Graves-Brown, Paul, *Matter, Materiality and Modern Culture* (London: Routledge, 2000)

Green, Nancy L., *Ready-to-Wear and Ready-to-Work: A Century of Industry and Immigrants in Paris and New York* (Durham, NC and London: Duke University Press, 1997)

Gundle, Stephen, "Feminine Beauty, National Identity and Political Conflict in Postwar Italy, 1945–1954," *Contemporary European History*, 8 (1999), 359–78

Gundle, Stephen, "Hollywood Glamour and Mass Consumption in Postwar Italy," in *Fashion: Critical and Primary Sources: The Twentieth Century to Today*, ed. Peter McNeil, 4 vols. (Oxford: Berg, 2009), pp. 261–82

Hawes, Elizabeth, *Fashion in Spinach: Experiences of a Dress Designer in France and the United States of America* (New York: Random House, 1938)

Hopkins, Susie, "Milliners," in *The Berg Companion to Fashion*, ed. Valerie Steele (Oxford: Berg, 2010), pp. 508–12

Iannace, Paola, "La Moda, Macchina Economica e Laboratorio di modernità," in *Moda a Milano: Stile e Impresa Nella Città Che Cambia* (Milan: Abitare Segesta Cataloghi, 2002), p. 12

Ingold, Tim, *Making: Anthropology, Archaeology, Art and Architecture* (London: Routledge, 2013)

Inguanotto, Irina, "Elda Cecchele and the Italian Fashion World: From Salvatore Ferragamo to Roberta di Camerino (1950–1970)," *Textile History*, 43 (2012), 223–49

Ireland, Patrick J., *Fashion Design: Drawing and Presentation* (London: Batsford Academic and Educational, 1982)

Ivan, Paris, "Italian Fashion Centre," in *Bellissima: Italy and High Fashion, 1945–1968* (Milan: Electa, 2014), pp. 260–3

Jolly, Anna and Corinna Kienzler, *Villa Abegg: From Private Residence to Museum J, Rome, Italy, 23–26 March, 2010,* Multidisciplinary Conservation: A Holistic View for Historic Interiors. Joint Interim-Meeting of Five ICOM-CC Working Groups, Rome edn (2010)

Jones, Geoffrey and Jonathan Zeitlin, *The Oxford Handbook of Business History* (Oxford: Oxford University Press, 2008)

Kawamura, Yuniya, *Fashion-ology* (Oxford: Berg, 2004)

Kawamura, Yuniya, *The Japanese Revolution in Paris Fashion* (Oxford: Berg, 2004)

Kawamura, Yuniya, "Social and Technical Differences among Haute Couture, Demi-Couture and Prêt-à-Porter," in *The Japanese Revolution in Paris Fashion: Dress, Body, Culture* (Oxford: Berg, 2004), pp. 73–88

Kawamura, Yuniya, *Doing Research in Fashion and Dress: An Introduction to Qualitative Methods* (Oxford: Berg, 2011)

Kopytoff, Igor, "The Cultural Biography of Things," in *the Social Life of Things: Commodities in Cultural Perspective*, ed. Arjun Appadurai (Cambridge: Cambridge University Press, 1986), pp. 64–9

Küchler, Susanne and Daniel Miller, *Clothing as Material Culture* (Oxford: Berg, 2005)

Lanaro, Silvio, *Storia dell'Italia Repubblicana: Dalla Fine della Guerra Agli Anni Novanta* (Venice: Marsilio, 1992)

Lazzi, Giovanna, "Light and Shadows in the Sala Bianca: Florence, Fashion and the Press," in *Italian Fashion: The Origins of High Fashion and Knitwear*, ed. Gloria Bianchino et al. (Milan: Electa, 1987), pp. 72–7

Lees-Maffei, Grace, "The Production–Consumption–Mediation Paradigm," *Journal of Design History*, 22 (2009), 351–76

Lees-Maffei, Grace and Kjetil Fallan, eds., *Made in Italy: Rethinking a Century of Italian Design* (London: Bloomsbury Academic, 2014)

Lehmann, Ulrich, *Tigersprung: Fashion in Modernity* (Cambridge, Mass.: MIT Press, 2000)

Leopold, Ellen, "The Manufacture of the Fashion System," in *Chic Thrills: A Fashion Reader*, ed. Juliet Ash and Elizabeth Wilson (London: Pandora, 1992), pp. 101–17

Leventon, Melissa, "Shopping for Style: Couture in America," in *New Look to Now: French Haute Couture, 1947–1987*, ed. Stephen de Pietri and Melissa Leventon (New York: Rizzoli, 1989), pp. 23–7

Levi Pisetzky, Rosita, *Il Costume e La Moda Nella Società Italiana* (Turin: Einaudi, 1978)

Locke, Richard M., "Unity in Diversity: Strategy and Structure of the Italian Apparel Industry in the 1980s," in *Per Una Storia della Moda Pronta: Problemi e Ricerche: Atti del V Convegno Internazionale del CISST, Milano, 26–28 Febbraio 1990* (Florence: EDIFIR edizioni, 1991), pp. 251–69

Lupano, Mario and Alessandra Vaccari, *Fashion at the Time of Fascism: Italian Modernist Lifestyle 1922–1943* (Bologna: Damiani, 2009)

Macchion, Laura, Pamela Danese, and Andrea Vinelli, "Redefining Supply Network Strategies to Face Changing Environments: A Study from the Fashion and Luxury Industry," *Operations Management Research*, 8 (2015), 15–31

Macchion, Laura et al., "Production and Supply Network Strategies within the Fashion Industry," *International Journal of Production Economics*, 163 (2015), 173–88

Manzini, Ezio, *The Material of Invention: Materials and Design* (London: Design Council, 1986)

Marshall, Alfred, *Principles of Economics, Vol. 1* (London: Macmillan & Co., 1890)

Martin, Richard H., *Fashion and Surrealism* (London: Thames and Hudson, 1988)

McNeil, Peter, "Conference Report: The Future of Fashion Studies," *Fashion Theory: The Journal of Dress*, 14 (2010), 105–10

McNeil, Peter, *Fashion: Critical and Primary Sources, The Twentieth Century to Today*, 4 vols. (Oxford: Berg, 2009)

Merlo, Elisabetta, *Moda Italiana: Storia di un'Industria dall'Ottocento a Oggi* (Venice: Marsilio, 2003)

Merlo, Elisabetta, "Le Origini del Sistema Moda," in *Storia d'Italia*, ed. Carlo Marco Belfanti and Fabio Giusberti, 19 vols. (Turin: G. Einaudi, 2003), pp. 667–97

Merlo, Elisabetta, "Italian Fashion Business: Achievements and Challenges (1970s–2000s)," *Business History*, 53 (June 2011), 344–62

Merlo, Elisabetta, "'Size Revolution': The Industrial Foundations of the Italian Clothing Business," *Business History*, 57 (2015), 919–41

Merlo, Elisabetta, "When Fashion Met Industry: Biki and Gruppo Finanziario Tessile (1957–72)," *Journal of Modern Italian Studies*, 20 (2015), 92–110

Merlo, Elisabetta and Francesca Polese, "Turning Fashion into Business: The Emergence of Milan as an International Fashion Hub," *The Business History Review,* 80 (2006), 415–47

Merlo, Elisabetta and Francesca Polese, "Italy," in *Berg Encyclopedia of World Dress and Fashion* (Oxford: Berg, 2010), pp. 217–58

Merlo, Elisabetta and Maria Natalina Trevisano, *Lo Stile Italiano Nelle Carte: Inventario dell'Archivio Storico della Camera Nazionale della Moda Italiana (1958–1989),* Pubblicazioni Degli Archivi di Stato Strumenti CCII (Rome: Ministero per i Beni Culturali Direzione Generale Archivi, 2018)

Merlotti, Andrea, "I Percorsi della Moda Made in Italy (1951–2010)," in *Enciclopedia Italiana di Scienze, Lettere e Arti, Appendice VIII, Il Contributo Italiano alla Storia del Pensiero,* ed. F. Profumo and V. Marchis, Vol. 3, Technica vols (Rome: Istituto dell' Enciclopedia Italiana, 2013), pp. 630–40

Messina, Rietta, "Italian Woman's Wear: A Successful Industrial Product," in *Italian Fashion: From Anti-Fashion to Stylism,* ed. Grazietta Butazzi, 2 vols. (Milan: Electa, 1987), pp. 26–31

Mida, Ingrid and Kim Alexandra, *The Dress Detective: A Practical Guide to Object-Based Research in Fashion* (London: Bloomsbury, 2015)

Miller, Daniel, *Stuff* (Cambridge: Polity, 2010)

Miller, Lesley E., *Cristóbal Balenciaga* (London: Batsford, 1993)

Miller, Lesley E., *Cristóbal Balenciaga (1895–1972): The Couturiers' Couturier* (London: V&A Publishing, 2007)

Miller, Lesley E., "Perfect Harmony: Textile Manufacturers and Haute Couture, 1947–57," in *The Golden Age of Couture: Paris and London, 1947–57* (London: V&A Publishing, 2007), pp. 113–36

Mitchell, Katharine, "Beauty Italian Style: Gendered Imaginings of, and Responses to, Stage Divas in Early Post-Unification Literary Culture," *Italian Studies,* 70 (2015), 330–46

La Moda Nel Tessuto Contemporaneo: Prima Rassegna Internazionale dell'Abbigliamento (Venice: Centro Internazionale delle Arti e del Costume, 1956)

Mora, Emanuela, "Collective Production of Creativity in the Italian Fashion System," *Poetics,* 34 (2006), 334–53

Morini, Enrica, *Storia della Moda: XVIII–XXI Secolo* (Milan: Skira, 2010)

Morini, Enrica and Nicoletta Bocca, "Stylism in Women's Fashion," in *Italian Fashion: From Anti-Fashion to Stylism,* ed. Grazietta Butazzi, 2 vols. (Milan: Electa, 1987), pp. 64–101

Morozzi, Cristina, ed., *Stile Italiano: Pier Paolo Pitacco, Twenty Years' Graphic Design in Italian Fashion* (Milan: Lupetti, 2000)

Mower, Sarah, *Gucci by Gucci: 85 Years of Gucci* (London: Thames & Hudson, 2006)

Munro, Simon et al., *Addressing the Century: 100 Years of Art & Fashion* (London: Hayward Gallery, 1998)

Muzzarelli, Maria Giuseppina, *Breve Storia della Moda in Italia* (Bologna: Il Mulino, 2014)

Nodolini, Alberto, Silvana Bernasconi, et al., *Brunetta: Moda Critica Storia* (Parma: Università di Parma, Centro studi e archivio della comunicazione, 1981)

O'Connor, Kaori, "The Other Half: The Material Culture of New Fibers," in *Clothing as Material Culture*, ed. Kuchler Susanne and Miller Daniel (Oxford: Berg, 2005)

Orsi Landini, Roberta, "The Sala Bianca," in *Bellissima: Italy and High Fashion, 1945–1968* (Milan: Electa, 2014), pp. 324–7

Pagani, Elisabetta and Rosanna Pavoni, "Clothing Manufacturing in the Sixties: Between Crisis and Innovation," in *Italian Fashion: From Anti-Fashion to Stylism*, ed. Grazietta Butazzi, 2 vols. (Milan: Electa, 1987), pp. 32–43

Palmer, Alexandra, "New Directions: Fashion History Studies and Research in North America and England," *Fashion Theory: The Journal of Dress, Body & Culture*, 1 (1997), 297–312

Palmer, Alexandra, *Couture and Commerce: The Transatlantic Fashion Trade in the 1950s* (Vancouver, BC: UBC Press, 2001)

Pansera, Anty, *L'Anima dell'Industria: Un Secolo di Disegno Industriale Nel Milanese* (Milan: Skira, 1996)

Paris, Ivan, *Oggetti Cuciti: L'Abbigliamento Pronto in Italia Dal Primo Dopoguerra Agli Anni Settanta* (Milan: Franco Angeli, 2006)

Paris, Ivan, "Associazione Italiana Industriali dell'Abbigliamento: L'Autonomia del Settore Industriale Da Quello Artigianale e i Primi Tentativi Per Un Controllo Istituzionale della Moda," *Università Degli Studi di Brescia: Dipartimento di Studi Sociali* (2005)

Paris, Ivan, "L'Archivio Storico della Camera Nazionale della Moda Italiana," *Imprese e Storia*, 35 (2007), 153–6

Paris, Ivan, "Fashion as a System: Changes in Demand as the Basis for the Establishment of the Italian Fashion System (1960–1970)," *Enterprise & Society*, 11 (2010), 524–59

Paulicelli, Eugenia, *Fashion Under Fascism: Beyond the Black Shirt* (Oxford: Berg, 2004)

Paulicelli, Eugenia, "Fashion Writing Under the Fascist Regime: An Italian Dictionary and Commentary of Fashion by Cesare Meano, and Short Stories by Gianna Manzini, and Alba De Cespedes," *Fashion Theory: The Journal of Dress, Body & Culture*, 8 (2004), 3–34

Paulicelli, Eugenia, "Cronaca di Un Amore: Fashion and Italian Cinema in Michelangelo Antonioni's Films (1949–1955)," in *New Perspectives in Italian Cultural Studies. Volume 2*, ed. Graziella Parati (Madison: Fairleigh Dickinson University Press, 2013), pp. 107–29

Paulicelli, Eugenia, "Fashion: The Cultural Economy of made in Italy," *Fashion Practice: The Journal of Design Creative Process and the Fashion Industry*, 6 (2014), 155–74

Paulicelli, Eugenia, "Italian Fashion: Yesterday, Today and Tomorrow," *Journal of Modern Italian Studies*, 20 (2015), 1–9

Pearce, Susan, *Interpreting Objects and Collections* (London: Routledge, 1994)

Piore, Michael J. and Charles F. Sabel, eds., *The Second Industrial Divide: Possibilities for Prosperity* (New York: Basic Books, 1984)

Prown, Jules D., "Style as Evidence," *Winterthur Portfolio*, 15 (1980), 197–210

Prown, Jules D., "Mind in Matter: An Introduction to Material Culture Theory and Method," *Winterthur Portfolio, 17* (1982), 1

Quinto, Enrico and Paolo Tinarelli, eds., *Italian Glamour: The Essence of Italian Fashion from the Postwar Years to the Present Day* (Milan: Skira, 2013)

Rasche, Adelheid, ed., *Coats! Max Mara, 60 Years of Italian Fashion* (Milan: Skira, 2011)

Rey, Guido, "Small Firms: Profile and Analysis 1981–85," in *Small Firms and Industrial Districts in Italy*, ed. Edward Goodman, Julia Bamford, and Peter Saynor (London: Routledge, 1989), pp. 69–93

Rinallo, D. and P, "Paper 3: National Mythmaking, Foreign and Domestic: A Historical Analysis of the Birth of Italian Fashion," *European Advances in Consumer Research, 10* (2013)

Rocamora, Agnès, *Fashioning the City: Paris, Fashion and the Media* (London: I.B. Tauris, 2009)

Rocamora, Agnès and Anneke Smelik, eds., *Thinking through Fashion: A Guide to Key Theorists* (London: I.B. Tauris, 2016)

Rogers, Meyric Reynold, *Italy at Work: Her Renaissance in Design Today* (Baltimore: Baltimore Museum of Art, 1950)

Romano, Alexis, "*Elle* and the Development of Stylisme in 1960s Paris," *Costume, 46* (2012), 75–91

Rosina, Margherita, "Como Printed Silk for Women's Wear: A Century of Tradition and Innovation," in *Silk: The 1900's in Como* (Cinisello Balsamo: Silvana Editoriale, 2001), pp. 70–81

Rosina, Margherita, "The Thousand-Carat Dresses," in *Italian Glamour*, ed. Enrico Quinto and Paolo Tinarelli (Milan: Skira, 2013), p. 195

Rosina, Margherita, "The Textile Industry and High Fashion," in *Bellissima: Italy and High Fashion, 1945–1968* (Milan: Electa, 2014), pp. 288–91

Rosina, Margherita, "Textiles: The Foundation of Italian Couture," in *The Glamour of Italian Fashion since 1945*, ed. Sonnet Stanfill (London: V&A Publications, 2014), pp. 76–93

Rosina, Margherita ed, *Taroni: The Fabric That Dreams are Made of* (Milan: Rizzoli, 2017)

Rosina, Margherita and Francina Chiara, eds., *Guido Ravasi: Il Signore Dell Seta* (Como: NodoLibri, 2008)

Rosina, Margherita and Francina Chiara, *L'Età dell'Eleganza: Le Filande e Tessiture Costa nella Como degli Anni Cinquanta* (Como: NodoLibri, 2010)

Rosina, Margherita and Francina Chiara, *Emilio Pucci e Como: 1950–1980* (Como: NodoLibri, 2014)

Rosina, Margherita and Lucia F., Savi, "Nattier: Textile Innovators," in *The Glamour of Italian Fashion since 1945*, ed. Sonnet Stanfill (London: V&A Publishing, 2014)

Rossi, Catharine, *Crafting Design in Italy: From Post-War to Postmodernism* (Manchester: Manchester University Press, 2015)

Rublack, Ulinka, "Renaissance Dress, Cultures of Making, and the Period Eye," *West 86th: A Journal of Decorative Arts, Design History, and Material Culture,* 23 (2016), 6–34

Sabel, Charles F., *Work and Politics: The Division of Labour in Industry* (Cambridge: Cambridge University Press, 1982)

Salvati, Michele, *Economia e Politica in Italia Dal Dopoguerra a Oggi* (Milan: Garzanti, 1984)

Sammarra, Alessia and Fiorenza Belussi, "Evolution and Relocation in Fashion-Led Italian Districts: Evidence from Two Case-Studies," *Entrepreneurship and Regional Development,* 18 (2006), 543–62

Sargenston, Carolyn, "The Manufacture and Marketing of Luxury Goods: The Marchands Merciers of Late 17th-and 18th-Century Paris," in *Luxury Trades and Consumerism in Ancien Régime Paris: Studies in the History,* ed. Robert Fox and Anthony Turner (Aldershot: Ashgate, 1998), pp. 99–137

Sargiacomo, M., "Institutional Pressures and Isomorphic Change in a High-Fashion Company: The Case of Brioni Roman Style, 1945–89," *Accounting, Business and Financial History,* 18 (2008), 215–41

Savi, Lucia F., "La Moda in Vogue," in *The Glamour of Italian Fashion since 1945,* ed. Sonnet Stanfill (London: V&A Publishing, 2014), pp. 248–53

Savi, Lucia F., "Italy's Autarky: Fashion and Textiles during the Fascist Regime," in *Dress and Politics. Proceedings of the 2014 Annual Meeting of the ICOM Costume Committee,* "Endymatologika" (Costume Studies), Nafplion and Athens, Greece, September 7–13, 2014, 5 vols. (Athens, KIKPE, 2015)

Scarpellini, Emanuela, *Material Nation: A Consumer's History of Modern Italy* (Oxford: Oxford University Press, 2011)

Scarpellini, Emanuela, "The Business of Fashion," in *The Glamour of Italian Fashion since 1945,* ed. Sonnet Stanfill (London: V&A Publishing, 2014), pp. 226–239

Scarpellini, Emanuela, *La Stoffa dell'Italia: Storia e Cultura della Moda Dal 1945 a Oggi* (Rome: Laterza, 2017)

Schneider, Jane, "In and Out of Polyester: Desire, Disdain and Global Fibre Competitions," *Anthropology Today,* 10 (1994), 2–10

Schoeser, Mary and Christine Boydell, eds., *Disentangling Textiles: Techniques for the Study of Designed Objecta* (London: Middlesex University Press, 2002)

Segre Reinach, Simona, "China and Italy: Fast Fashion versus Prêt-à-Porter. Towards a New Culture of Fashion," *Fashion Theory,* 9 (2005), 43–56

Segre Reinach, Simona, "The City of Prêt-à-Porter in the World of Fast Fashion," in *Fashion's World Cities,* ed. Christopher Breward and David Gilbert (Oxford: Berg, 2006), pp. 123–34

Segre Reinach, Simona, "*Fatto in Italia: La Cultura Made in Italy (1960–2000)* by Paola Colaiacomo (ed.)/*Oggetti Cuciti: L'Abbigliamento Pronto in Italia Dal Primo Dopoguerra Agli Anni Settanta* by Ivan Paris," *Fashion Theory,* 13 (2009), 121–26

Segre Reinach, Simona, "La Moda Nella Cultura Italiana dai Primi del Novecento a Oggi," in *La Cultura Italiana*, ed. Carlo Petrini and Ugo Volli, Vol. 4 (Turin: Utet, 2009), pp. 603–61

Segre Reinach, Simona, "Albini, Walter," in *The Berg Companion to Fashion*, ed. Valerie Steele (Oxford: Berg, 2010), pp. 19–20

Segre Reinach, Simona, "Milan as a Fashion City," in *Berg Encyclopedia of World Dress and Fashion*, ed. Joanne Eicher, 8 vols. (Oxford: Berg, 2010), pp. 259–63

Segre Reinach, Simona, "Fashion at the Time of Fascism: Italian Modern Lifestyle in the 1920s–1930s," *Fashion Theory: The Journal of Dress, Body and Culture,* 16 (2012), 117–21

Segre Reinach, Simona, "Italian Fashion: The Metamorphosis of a Cultural Industry," *in Made in Italy: Rethinking a Century of Italian Design*, ed. Grace Lees-Maffei and Kjetil Fallan (London: Bloomsbury Academic, 2014), pp. 239–51

Segre Reinach, Simona, "The Italian Fashion Revolution in Milan," in *The Glamour of Italian Fashion since 1945*, ed. Sonnet Stanfill (London: V&A Publishing, 2014), pp. 58–71

Segre Reinach, Simona, "Fashion Museums and Fashion Exhibitions in Italy: New Perspectives in Italian Fashion Studies," in *Fashion Curating: Critical Practice in the Museum and Beyond* (London: Bloomsbury Academic, 2017), pp. 170–82

Semmelhack, Elizabeth, "The Allure of Power," in *Shoes: Pleasure and Pain*, ed. Helen Persson (London: V&A Publishing, 2015)

Settembrini, Luigi, *Made in Italy? 1951–2001* (Milan: Skira Editore; London: Thames & Hudson, 2001)

Sparke, Penny, *Italian Design: 1870 to the Present* (London: Thames and Hudson, 1988)

Sparke, Penny, "Industrial Design or Industrial Aesthetics? American Influence on the Emergence of the Italian Modern Design Movement, 1948–58," in *Italy in the Cold War: Politics, Culture and Society, 1948–1958*, ed. Christopher Duggan and Christopher Wagstaff (Oxford and Washington DC: Berg, 1995), pp. 159–65

Sparke, Penny, "The Straw Donkey: Tourist Kitsch or Proto-Design? Craft and Design in Italy, 1945–1960," *Journal of Design History,* 11 (1998), 59–70

Stanfill, Sonnet, *The Glamour of Italian Fashion since 1945* (London: V&A Publishing, 2014)

Stanfill, Sonnet, "The Role of the *Sartoria* in Post-War Italy," *Journal of Modern Italian Studies,* 20 (2015), 83–91

Stanfill, Sonnet, "American Buyers and the Italian Fashion Industry, 1950–55," in *European Fashion: The Creation of a Global Industry*, ed. Lee Blaszczyk Regina and Pouillard Véronique (Manchester: Manchester University Press, 2018), pp. 146–69

Steele, Valerie, "A Museum of Fashion is More than a Clothes-Bag," *Fashion Theory,* 2 (November 1998), 327–35

Steele, Valerie, *Paris Fashion: A Cultural History* (Oxford: Berg, 1998)

Steele, Valerie, *Fashion, Italian Style* (New Haven and London: Yale University Press, 2003)

Steele, Valerie, ed., *The Berg Companion to Fashion* (Oxford: Berg, 2010)

Stephens, S., "Fashion Forward: An Italian Sense of Craft and Detail is Brought to New York City's Major Shopping Street by David Chipperfield's Design for Valentino," *Architectural Record,* 203 (2015), 90–95

Styles, John, "Response," in *Fashion and Modernity,* ed. Christopher Breward and Caroline Evans (Oxford: Berg, 2005), pp. 33–7

Taylor, Lou, "Paris Couture: 1940–1944," in *Chic Thrills: Fashion Reader,* ed. Juliet Ash and Elizabeth Wilson (London: Pandora, 1992), pp. 127–44

Taylor, Lou, "Doing the Laundry? A Reassessment of Object-Based Dress History," *Fashion Theory: The Journal of Dress, Body & Culture,* 2 (1998), 337–58

Taylor, Lou, "De-Coding the Hierarchy of Fashion Textiles," in *Disentangling Textiles: Techniques for the Study of Designed Objects,* ed. Mary Schoeser and Christine Boydell (London: Middlesex University Press, 2002), p. 68

Taylor, Lou, *The Study of Dress History* (Manchester: Manchester University Press, 2002)

Taylor, Lou, *Establishing Dress History* (Manchester: Manchester University Press, 2004)

Testa, Salvo, "La Specificità della Filiera Italiana della Moda," in *Storia d'Italia: La Moda,* 19 vols. (Turin: Giulio Einaudi, 2003), pp. 699–734

Tosi Brandi, Elisa, *Artisti del Quotidiano: Sarti e Sartorie Storiche in Emilia-Romagna* (Bologna: CLUEB, 2009)

Vänskä, Annamari and Hazel Clark, eds., *Fashion Curating: Critical Practice in the Museum and Beyond* (London: Bloomsbury Academic, 2017)

Veillon, Dominique, *Fashion Under the Occupation* (Oxford: Berg, 2002)

Vergani, Guido, *La Sala Bianca: Nascita della Moda Italiana* (Milan: Electa, 1992)

Vergani, Guido, *Dizionario della Moda* (New York: Baldini Castoldi, 2004)

Vergani, Guido, *The Fashion Dictionary* (New York: Baldini Castoldi, 2006)

Vergani, Guido and Maria Pezzi, *Maria Pezzi: Una Vita Dentro La Moda* (Milan: Skira, 1998)

White, Nicola, "Max Mara and the Origins of Ready-to-Wear," *Modern Italy,* 1 (1996), 63–88

White, Nicola, *Reconstructing Italian Fashion: America and the Development of the Italian Fashion Industry* (Oxford: Berg, 2000)

White, Nicola and Ian Griffiths, *The Fashion Business: Theory, Practice* (Oxford: Oxford: Berg, 2000, 2000)

Wickramasinghe, Nira, "The Sari – Mukulika Banerjee & Daniel Miller," *Journal of the Royal Anthropological Institute,* 12(3) (2006). 710–11

Wickson, Penelope, "Works of Art in an Age of Mechanical Reproduction: 'The Glamour of Italian Fashion 1945–2014' at the Victoria and Albert Museum, London (5 April–27 July 2014)," *Italian Studies,* 69 (2014), 434

Wilcox, Claire, *The Golden Age of Couture: Paris and London, 1947–57* (London: V&A Publications, 2007)

Wilcox, Claire, Valerie Mendes, and Chiara Buss, *The Art and Craft of Gianni Versace* (London: V&A Publications, 2002)

Wilson, Elizabeth, *Adorned in Dreams: Fashion and Modernity* (London: Virago, 1985; Berkeley: University of California, 1992)

Wilson, Elizabeth, "Fashion and Modernity," in *Fashion and Modernity*, ed. Christopher Breward and Caroline Evans (Oxford: Berg, 2005), pp. 9–14

Wolf, Allyson, "Fashion-ology: An Introduction to Fashion Studies, by Yuniya Kawamura (Berg, 2005)," *Fashion Theory: The Journal of Dress,* 10 (2006), 413–16

Yonan, Michael, "Toward a Fusion of Art History and Material Culture Studies," *West 86th: A Journal of Decorative Arts, Design History, and Material Culture,* 18 (2011), 232–48

Zeitlin, Jonathan, "Industrial Districts and Regional Clusters," in *The Oxford Handbook of Business History* (Oxford: Oxford University Press, 2008), pp. 219–243

Unpublished Secondary Sources

O'Connor, Kaori, "Lycra, Babyboomers and the Immaterial Culture of the New Midlife: A Study of Commerce and Culture" (unpublished PhD dissertation, University College London, 2004)

Palmer, Helen A., "The Myth and Reality of Haute Couture: Consumption. Social Function and Taste in Toronto 1945 – 1963" (unpublished PhD dissertation, Brighton University, 1994)

White, Nicola, "The Role of America in the Development of the Italian Fashion Industry 1945–1965" (unpublished MPhil dissertation, Kingston University, London, 1997)

Web Sources

"Appuntamento Con La Moda," *Settimana Incom,* 00972, 29/07/1953, https://patrimonio.archivioluce.com/luce-web/detail/IL5000027785/2/palazzo-pitti-sfilata-alta-moda-presentazione-modelli-della-stagione-autunno-inverno.html?startPage=0&jsonVal={%22jsonVal%22:{%22query%22:[%22Settimana%20Incom,%2000972,%2029/07/1953,%22],%22fieldDate%22:%22dataNormal%22,%22_perPage%22:20}} [accessed August 26, 2022]

"Costume Moda Immagine Palazzo Morando," http://www.costumemodaimmagine.mi.it/ [accessed September 4, 2018]

"Dagli Anni '50 a Oggi," https://www.pittimmagine.com/en/history [accessed September 21, 2022]

"Design della Moda," https://www.poliorientami.polimi.it/cosa-si-studia/corsi-di-laurea/elenco-completo/design-della-moda/ [accessed August 26, 2022]

Evening Dress, http://www.metmuseum.org/art/collection/search/98031 [accessed December 27, 2015]

Evening Ensemble, http://www.metmuseum.org/art/collection/search/87361?sortBy=Rel evance&ft=emilio+schuberth&offset=0&rpp=20&pos=3 [Accessed June 4, 2017]

Bowles, Hamish, "Inside the Wild World of Gucci's Alessandro Michele," *Vogue,* April 15, 2019, https://www.vogue.com/article/gucci-alessandro-michele-interview-may-2019-issue?verso=true [accessed July 6, 2019]

"Janet A. Sloane, 82, a Millinery Stylist," *New York Times,* May 6, 1996, http://www.nytimes.com/1996/05/06/nyregion/janet-a-sloane-82-a-millinery-stylist.html [accessed April 10, 2016]

"History," Dupont, https://www.dupont.com/about/our-history.html [accessed August 22, 2019]

"Laurea in Culture e Pratiche della Moda," https://corsi.unibo.it/laurea/CulturePratiche Moda [accessed August 26, 2022]

Linea Contro linea 1967/ 68: Le Sorelle Fontana: Rai Teche, https://www.youtube.com/watch?v=HfpZPWdLc7E [accessed November 24, 2018]

"Moda," https://www.csacparma.it/portfolio/moda/ [accessed September 2, 2018]

"Moda Italiana a Firenze," *Settimana Incom,* 00902, 06/02/1953, https://patrimonio.archivioluce.com/luce-web/detail/IL5000023833/2/v-mostra-alta-moda-italiana-palazzo-pitti-altri-sfilano-modelli-antonelli-emilio-luisa-spagnoli.html?startPage=0 &jsonVal={%22jsonVal%22:{%22query%22:[%22moda%20italiana%20a%20 firenze%201953%22],%22fieldDate%22:%22dataNormal%22,%22_perPage%22:20 [accessed August 23, 2022]

Mostra del Tessile dell'Avvenire, https://patrimonio.archivioluce.com/luce-web/detail/IL5000042219/2/mostra-del-tessile-avvenire.html?startPage=0&jsonVal={%22jsonV al%22:{%22query%22:[%22tessuti%20dell%27avvenire%22],%22fieldDate%22:%22d ataNormal%22,%22_perPage%22:20 [accessed August 23, 2022]

Storia della Bachicoltura Dalle Orgini Ai Giorni Nostri in Una Mostra a Venezia, https://patrimonio.archivioluce.com/luce-web/detail/IL5000042223/2/storia-della-bachicoltura-dalle-origini-ai-giorni-nostri-mostra-veneziana.html [accessed September 1, 2018]

Textiles that Changed the World, https://www.bloomsbury.com/uk/series/textiles-that-changed-the-world/ [accessed August 10, 2019]

Schnapp, Jeffrey T., "The Fabric of Modern Times," *Critical Inquiry,* 24 (1997), 191–245, JSTOR http://www.jstor.org/stable/1344164 [accessed January 6, 2019]

Simmel, Georg, "Fashion," *American Journal of Sociology,* 62 (1957), 541–58, JSTOR http://www.jstor.org/stable/2773129 [accessed January 6, 2019]

Specter, Michael, "High-Heel Heaven: A Visit to the Madcap World of Manolo Blahnik," *The New Yorker,* March 12, 2000, https://www.newyorker.com/magazine/2000/03/20/high-heel-heaven [accessed July 6, 2019]

Tosi Pamphili, Clara, *Moda e Militanza. Intervista a Maria Luisa Frisa,* https://www. artribune.com/progettazione/moda/2018/02/intervista-maria-luisa-frisa-mostra-palazzo-reale-milano/ [accessed August 26, 2022]

Vergani, Guido, "Anche 'l'Abito Fa Pensare' Se Lo Firma Il Grande Stilista," *la Repubblica,* April 14, 1989, https://ricerca.repubblica.it/repubblica/archivio/repubblica/1989/ 04/14/anche-abito-fa-pensare-se-lo.html?ref=search [accessed September 21, 2022] [accessed January 12, 2019]

Index